Communication in Education
A Rhetoric of Schooling and Learning

Communication in Education

A Rhetoric of Schooling and Learning

Gerald M. Phillips
David E. Butt
Nancy J. Metzger

Pennsylvania State University

With a foreword by
Donald J. Arnstine
University of California at Davis

HOLT, RINEHART AND WINSTON, INC.

*New York   Chicago   San Francisco   Atlanta
Dallas   Montreal   Toronto   London   Sydney*

Cartoons by Jim Wisnovsky

Copyright © 1974 by Holt, Rinehart and Winston, Inc.
Library of Congress Cataloging in Publication Data
Phillips, Gerald M.
Butt, David E.
Metzger, Nancy J.
Communication in Education: A Rhetoric of Schooling
and Learning
    1.   Interaction analysis in education.
2.   Teacher-student relationships.   3.   Classroom
management.   I.   Butt, David E., joint author.
II.   Metzger, Nancy J., joint author.   III.   Title.
LB1084.P48   371.1'02   73-15909

ISBN: 0-03-011006-8

4567 090 987654321

Preface

Communication in Education: A Rhetoric of Schooling and Learning is the product of several years of labor in the field. We talked with hundreds of teachers and students. We learned that the world was not nearly as bad as some polemicists would make it seem, but not good enough to permit teachers to rest on their laurels. We found that speech teachers who used oral communication to support their teaching were generally well respected by their students. They accomplished a good deal of teaching. We learned also that it is possible to teach the art of communicating effectively to teachers of all subjects and all grades, with surprisingly good effects on their daily teaching.

This book is the record of our experiences, and we acknowledge our debt to the teachers and students from whom we learned. There are far too many to name, more than six thousand at latest count. They came from all over the Commonwealth of Pennsylvania, from urban areas and rural. They were black and white, affluent and poor.

We owe much to the vision of two men. First, Frank Pilecki, former Title III Administrator of Area J of Pennsylvania, had faith in our efforts; his support when the going got rough enabled us to get started on this book. Second, it was Richard Swavely of the Pennsylvania State University Division of Continuing Education who had the imagination that enabled the experimental program to become a full-time operation devoted to the dissemination of the information in this book. To these two men particularly, we dedicate this work, hoping that in the future they will find other causes worthy of their stalwart support.

G.M.P.

D.E.B.

N.J.M.

Foreword

This is a different sort of book for teachers. It does not tell us what to teach, and it does not tell us how to teach what we ought to teach. Instead, it develops a set of proposals and methods that would create a climate for learning in school classrooms, regardless of grade level or subject matter taught.

Classrooms in America today are often arenas for the play of antagonistic competition among students and between teachers and students. *Communication in Education: A Rhetoric of Schooling and Learning* will help teachers to replace that antagonism with a spirit of cooperation born of a growing willingness and ability to express and share ideas. The focus of the book is communication, and the rhetorical view that is adopted proposes that the teacher reach his own educational goals by helping his students achieve *their* goals. Implicit on every page is the question "What is the point of bringing people together in a classroom if they are not able to communicate fully and freely with one another?" There *is* no sensible answer to this question, so the authors focus on the classroom conditions that would make such communication possible.

Since Professors Phillips,

Butt, and Metzger are concerned with the goals of children and the ways in which they can be helped to attain these goals more effectively, it would be tempting to classify this book as romantic, and place it in the tradition begun two centuries ago by Rousseau and carried into the present era by A. S. Neill at Summerhill. But this would be a mistake. The romantics focused on freedom for the child, and they assumed that the simple removal of adult constraints would result in a natural flowering of childhood into thoughtful and independent maturity. They assumed, in other words, that man is naturally good, and that he would grow to fulfill that endowment if only let alone.

But traditions have a way of distorting the views identified with their founders. Rousseau might not have recognized himself as a romantic, for he carefully planned an elaborate series of educational experiences for his idealized student, *Emile.* Thus the tutor described by Rousseau had no intention of simply freeing the child and letting nature take its course. The same can be said for the authors of *Communication in Education.* Nowhere is there a suggestion that children are "naturallly" good, and nowhere is it proposed that mere freedom—conceived as a release from constraints—will turn children into mature adults. Instead, the authors outline, even more deliberately than Rousseau, a set of planned interventions in order to achieve the conditions for growth toward maturity. These conditions include far more than freedom but much less than a prescribed set of studies for all students to master, and they go much further than high-sounding ideals, although not so far as to detail a long list of behavioral objectives. Thus if there is a tradition with which this book can be identified, it is probably the Deweyan variety of progressive education, with a strong leaning toward Herbert Thelen's conception of learning in small, communicating groups.

The authors of *Communication in Education* point out that, from the very beginning of their school careers, children are asked and expected to *use* oral communication, although they are seldom taught how. While a few children are lucky enough to learn effective communication skills outside school, many are not. Some of these latter children say too much, others say too little, and many more are simply unable to say what they mean. The ways in which they are tested and graded often lead to their being thought incompetent in various subject-matter areas, when in fact their problem is an inability to convey what they know. When such children experience repeated failure without getting any help in communication skills, they tend to protect themselves by a withdrawal from school activities which truncates both their intellectual and their social growth. In contrast, there are other children who have learned how to comply with teachers' expectations and who may mistakenly be thought competent in subject-matter areas. In both cases we misjudge our students and fail to teach them well.

For this reason, Professors Phillips, Butt, and Metzger propose not simply freedom, but a carefully articulated program of instruction. Yet this program is not another new course to be added to a curriculum already swollen by what has been called the "knowledge explosion." Nor is it one which calls for a new cadre of educational specialists. Instead, the authors claim that *all* schoolteachers can and should help their students to communicate more effectively, and that such help can and should be given in *every* course of study offered at every grade level in school.

The authors thus make it very clear that a person's communication patterns are not just another "subject" for isolated study. These patterns constitute his very identity as a person, for they embody the expectations and the responses of other people to him. To change a child's style of communication is to change his very personality. This is no task to be undertaken carelessly or left to chance (often called "freedom"), and it surely cannot be confined to any particular course of study or grade level. For this reason the authors would rightly claim that a teacher who said, "Communication is really not my line; I teach physics," did not understand his responsibility *as a teacher.* Nothing is effectively taught and learned in any course of study without effective communication on the part of teacher and students.

II

The authors' understanding of the educational process is a result of research on the phenomena of communication and communication theory, of their own teaching experience, and of a notably successful series of annual workshops they have organized for practicing public-school teachers. In the course of their work they came to reject the simplistic Shannon–Weaver model that reduced communication to the mere transmission and reception of messages, and instead saw human communication as the means by which people used gesture and symbols to influence others in order to achieve their own goals. Communication so understood is not commonly found in school classrooms where teachers all too often merely transmit, in the hope that some at least of their students will receive. Yet the strongest support for the rhetorical point of view developed in this book can be found in the work of America's most profound educational theorist, John Dewey, who cited the work of anthropologist Bronislaw Malinowski in writing that "language is primarily a mode of action used for the sake of influencing the conduct of others in connection with the speaker."

The significance of this conception of communication for school-classroom practices cannot be overestimated. For, while communication as a mode of mutual influence is a uniquely human enterprise, we continue to exercise our influence on students through the cruder instrumentalities of bribes, rewards, threats, and punishments. It may well be that at least a partial explanation of the pervasive cynicism of secondary-school and college students is their recognition of the inhumane character of their teachers' "motivating" devices: grades, recommendations for college, examinations, eligibility for athletic teams and after-school clubs, employment opportunities, and so on. In any event, these standard practices keep the students' attention focused on the reward or the punishment, not on the material that might be worth learning. In contrast to this, the emphasis of *Communication in Education* is on the *willingness* of the learner to participate in the changes sought by his teacher, and on the need for the teacher to understand how to *persuade* the learner in terms of the learner's own goals. Persuasion, in this light, is what communication is all about. In contrast, what educators call "motivation" is often little more than an appeal to power.

To conceive of communication as lying at the heart of education is to take seriously the impulses, desires, and goals of learners. But while we cannot communicate with our students if we ignore these desires and goals, we must also realize that these goals are only distantly related to the academic goals that we as teachers might like them to pursue. The task, of course, is to enable the student to make the teacher's goals his own. Phillips, Butt, and Metzger point out that one effective way of achieving this is to help the student see the relation between school activities and his life outside the school. Yet Dewey warned against the "standing danger that the material of formal instruction will be merely the subject matter of the schools, isolated from the subject matter of life-experience." The problem, said Dewey at the turn of the century,

> is just to get rid of the prejudicial notion that there is some gap in kind (as distinct from degree) between the child's experience and the various forms of subject matter that make up the course of study. From the side of the child, it is a question of seeing how his experience already contains within itself elements—facts and truths—of just the same sort as those entering into the formulated study; . . . from the side of the studies, it is a question of interpreting them as outgrowths of forces operating in the child's life, and of discovering the steps that intervene between the child's present experience and their richer maturity.

While teachers would be well advised to focus their instruction on the connections that can be found between the child's life and the more formal studies of school, the authors observe that those connections are easily forgotten and sometimes deliberately destroyed. Many teachers insist upon activities, manners, and patterns of speech altogether different from what is customary for children outside school. This is particularly apparent in urban ghetto schools, where children's colloquial speech is denigrated and the middle-class dialect of the teacher is thoughtlessly labeled correct. But the severing of the connection between school studies and life outside is just as apparent in any suburban school where, to take an instance, sexually maturing young men and women study frogs, flowers, and planaria in courses called "biology." For too many students, the classroom becomes a strange and hostile land, for no better reason than, as James Herndon put it, that's "the way it 'spozed to be."

Through their study of communication, the authors of *Communication in Education* throw new light on these rigidities and artificialities of schools. But they do not stop merely at exposing these shortcomings, for they also offer some down-to-earth assistance in overcoming them and establishing patterns of effective communication—and therefore effective education—in classrooms. The last three chapters of this book are directed toward a practical understanding of communication patterns and ways of enhancing them. The reader will find here explicit help in identifying successes and failures in communication, and he will find a broad variety of procedures that are likely to support and guide students as they use rhetoric in trying to deal with their world more effectively.

The concluding chapter presents a taxonomy of possible contents for an instructional program in oral communication. Newcomers to the field may find the extensive lists of goals a bit intimidating until they realize that, like the entries on a restaurant menu, they are not intended to be tried all at once. That these suggestions for goals in oral communication can profitably be sampled is demonstrated by the inclusion of two illustrative teaching units, one for a secondary school and another for an elementary-school class.

III

At the very end of this book, the authors write ". . . . involve yourself in the practice of rhetoric. Communicate with your students and encourage them to communicate with you." If I had a criticism, it would be that an additional chapter might have been written elaborating the implications of this advice. For there is no sense in pretending that we can have it both ways. We often cannot both create conditions for effective communication in our classrooms and transmit a curriculum in the form and in the amounts demanded by standardized curriculum guides, mass-market textbooks, and standardized examinations. This means that to take seriously and try to put into practice the sound advice in this book may not be easy. To communicate is to be willing to go where a discussion takes you, and that is a little like leaving your map—the curriculum—behind when you are exploring new territory. Innovations, though sometimes risky, are challenging.

The benefits to be gained are surely worth the risk, and it is even reasonable to think that teachers will give it a try if they can get a little help from their friends. Their friends, of course, can be found in their classrooms, for teachers and students must either learn something of value together or remain antagonists until the end of the semester or year mercifully separates them. Thus the first thing the teacher must do is try to communicate with the young people with whom he hopes to share a learning experience. In accordance with what this book is proposing, he must first try to get clear about some attainable goals for himself as a teacher. Then he must accept the reality and the legitimacy of the different goals that students have, and see what kinds of agreements can be found through honest and open discussion. This necessarily means that the teacher must come out from behind the protection of his institutional role, and expose a little of himself for his students to consider and communicate with.

In short, there is no need for the teacher to go it alone. How to teach and what to teach are serious questions, but it is the inadequate training given teachers that has encouraged them to try answering these questions all by themselves, writing out their lesson plans in spendid isolation, with only a textbook for a guide. But the world is full of wonders that will always elude the fattest, most pretentious text, and there is plenty of time for people in classrooms to determine together what is worth their study. When one person in the group—even the oldest and the wisest—*tells* the others what to study, then communication has broken down, and the need arises for all the devices of "motivation."

The choice is then a clear one, although its import is a little unsettling. Classrooms must either be places where communication takes place, or they will be organized by rewards and punishments distributed by authorities. With *Communication in Education* to serve as a guide, we cannot plead ignorance of the nature of communication or of how to promote it in schools.

Donald Arnstine
Department of Education
University of California
Davis, California

Contents

Preface   v

Foreword   vii

1. Examining Our Assumptions
about Speech   3
Reexamination of Some Old
Notions about Speech   6
Communication Defined   12
Research in the Classroom   18

2. Interpreting Communication
Behavior   25
Perspectives   29
Theories of Speech Develop-
ment   36
Learning Social Control—
Emergence of Rhetoric   51

3. Child Language Development   57
Stages of Development   61
The Abstract Communication
Perspective   64
Development of Message
Strategy   67
The Development of Conver-
sational Ability   78
Interrelationship of Language
Skills   80
Meaningful Use of Language   82

4. Understanding What Happens
When Humans Communicate
with One Another   89
Communication, Thought,
and the Teaching-Learning
Process   99
The Rhetoric of Schooling   108

5. Human Needs and the Responsibility of the School   117
Protection of Self and Society   120
Rhetoric as a Tool of Competition   124

Communication to Stimulate: Game Development   126
Communication to Understand: Maintaining Security   129
Communication for Territory: Status and Role   132

6. Winning and Losing: The Rhetoric of Goal Seeking   139
The Rhetorical Situation   140
How Goal Seeking Operates   143
Controlling Aggression through Social Rule   149
Goals in Relationships   151

7. The Clinical Responsibility of the Speech Teacher   163
The Personal Quality of Communication   163
What Happens When We Lose   169
Essentials of a Healthy Transaction   173
The Effects of Communication Failure   174
The Reticent Speaker   175

8. Building the Communication Atmosphere in the Classroom   187
Saving Face   193
Determining Success   197
Nonverbal Communication   199
Choosing Verbal Strategies   202

9. A Taxonomy of Possible Contents for an Instructional Program in Oral
Communication   211
Cognitive Goals   213
Affective Goals   220
Behavioral Goals   222
An Outline for a Syllabus in Rhetorical Communication   231
Self as Communicator (Teaching Plan)   236

Index   247

Communication in Education
A Rhetoric of Schooling and Learning

- To question some basic assumptions about teaching oral communication:

    1 Does training in public speaking help students in their daily lives?
    2 Does criticism in the classroom aid carry-over of skills into everyday life?
    3 Are there "basic principles" of speech?
    4 What is the student's stake in oral-communication instruction?
    5 Are communication models helpful in understanding the process and relationship of communication?

- To learn a basic definition of speech-communication as process plus relationship.

- To learn that symbols have varied meanings to people, and thus we need to understand the people with whom we communicate.

- To understand the role of rhetoric in the teaching–learning process: the teacher has goals to accomplish with students, and students have goals which may or may not be accomplished with the aid of the teacher.

- To learn three approaches to research which can be used by the teacher in his classroom:

    1 The work of the specialist (scientific perspective)
    2 The role of teacher intuition (naive perspective)
    3 Studying your own teaching (pedagogical perspective)

1

Examining Our Assumptions About Speech

OVERVIEW

The purpose of this chapter is to introduce some of the questions the speech profession is beginning to raise about its function in oral-communication instruction, and to offer some basic guidelines for this instruction in the classroom. The teacher is both researcher and practitioner in his work. He is constantly searching for ways of improving instruction to meet his own needs and the needs of his students more effectively. But, the teacher differs from the scientist in the laboratory, who also seeks improvements, since he is in close contact with humans daily, and people are more complicated and unpredictable than wheat seeds under a microscope or caged rats. Thus, the teacher needs human tools to carry out his teaching-research in the classroom. We will introduce in this chapter the teacher's primary tool of rhetoric in oral-communication instruction; students use rhetoric as well for their own purposes. How both teacher and student can use rhetoric most effectviely to meet their joint needs in the classroom is a main theme throughout this book.

FOR CENTURIES men have been attempting to study and understand human communication. They have made philosophy about it and written books; they have formulated rules of behavior and developed methods of instruction. More recently they have subjected human communication to micro-

3

scopic scrutiny through the most advanced tools of research. In spite of this, we are only beginning to realize how important communication is to our existence as human beings. As Ernest Becker said, "speech is everything specifically human."

Schools have a long and distinguished record of attempting to improve skill at oral communication. The original academics of ancient Greece were devoted to the teaching of rhetoric and oratory. Our present emphasis on the study of English literature, written composition, public address, philology, linguistics, and many other related disciplines can be traced in origin to these Greek schools.

Many of our efforts to teach oral communication have been quite successful. Some students have learned to speak well in public; others achieved skill as debaters. But there has been little discovered that can be applied to the communication needs of people in general. As we've heard so many times, for most students, "communication skills are caught, not taught."

Recently, however, the picture has begun to change. Recent investigations into the process of speech communication seem to indicate that we may be on the verge of some generalizations about human speech that might help us to discover effective methods of helping students to improve their oral-communication skills in ways that might be applicable to their life experience. The most helpful of these newer studies are characterized by their blend of "ancient wisdom" with empirical investigation.

To understand the literature of oral communication, it is not enough to rely solely on the wisdom of the philosophers, nor is it sensible to attempt to piece together a picture exclusively from empirical investigations. Many of the philosophical works have a moralistic or theological cast to them, and the newer empirical studies are still so fragmented that applicable generalizations cannot be developed. Some of the ideas offered by the philosophers are still viable today, but many of their notions, formerly heavily influential in directing the course of pedagogy, no longer seem to fit our needs. The philosophies on which speech training has been traditionally built had their origins in societies very different from our own. Consequently, it is necessary to sift through them with care in order to discover ideas that still seem to make sense in light of the needs of contemporary society.

Some of the great ideas of the ancient philosophers, however, still seem to fit. Isocrates, the Athenian, felt that a citizen of a democracy had the obligation to speak to influence the direction of his society. As we examine contemporary American society we find a society of change, "future shock." We discover that the services of every man are needed to come to grips with the perils of possible nuclear destruction, international xenophobia, population explosion, pollution, and many other problems. Aristotle's definition of rhetoric as ". . . the art of finding in any given case all the available means of persuasion" is still current. Aristotle felt that if all men were trained in oratory, rational ideas would prevail. The Aristotelian framework for understanding the influence of speech on man is still dominant in academic circles, and many of Aristotle's premises have been confirmed by empirical research. The ethical views of speech held by Plato, who felt that speech should seek "truth," and by Cicero, who felt that the "good speaker" should also be a "good man," are still valid when applied to today's uses of speech communication in propaganda.

We still owe a debt to Quintilian whose belief that people could be trained to speak well led to the organization of a formal school for that purpose. The original school of Quintilian has heavily influenced higher education in the Western World, for it was from his school, designed to produce orators, that we got our conception of the seven liberal arts, the basis of the instruction of the well-educated man.

Examination of the findings of research such as those contained in Berelson and Steiner and a glance at recent journals enable us to derive a long list of propositions about speech communication, which have been tested through experimentation. While most current studies have confined their conclusions carefully to the conditions of particular experiments, the budding social science of speech communication shows promise of more general discovery.

But classroom teachers are not "scholars." The problems they face are focused on how to apply "wisdom" in the classroom. Teachers want to know what is worth teaching, what is teachable, and how to teach it. The real question is if we teach speech communication as a cognitive subject will it help us improve speech-communication skills for students. We still do not know the relationship between learning about speech and the act of speaking itself. What seems most likely, however, is that learning about speech communication will help polish those who are already proficient at speaking, as well as help those who teach to understand more about their subject. However, the normal student needs to acquire skills and learn how to apply those skills to his daily life.

Although there is a great deal of literature devoted to public speaking, group discussion theory, oral interpretation of literature, debate, and so on, there is little that will help us understand our students' communication needs and how to help meet them through instruction. The teacher who seeks general improvement of communication skills in his students has little guidance. The assumption seems to be that learning speech specialties will somehow carry over to improve communication in the student's life experience. What is needed is knowledge about how speech develops in the child, what people in general need to be able to do to cope with the speech requirements of their lives, and how the classroom can play a role in imparting these skills.

It is exceedingly difficult to apply philosophical and experimental principles about speech to the act of teaching speech communication. It is clearly not possible to utilize some of the aristocratic ideas that came from the societies in which Aristotle and Cicero lived. Neither is it possible to exert rigid controls on the classroom in order to experiment and discover what systems of instruction work best. What this means is that the teacher of speech communication must generate his own philosophy, as best he can, and run his own limited experiments despite the unstable laboratory conditions that are found in the typical classroom. Because this book is designed for teachers who are willing and able to do this, we will attempt to combine material from the philosophers and the scientists with our own experience in teaching speech to young people.

From this information, it is hoped that you can generate your own ideas of what you can do in your classroom. We will not interrupt the text with footnotes, but at the conclusion of each chapter will suggest some sources that are readily available and that can help you in a further search for ideas. This chapter will orient you toward a practical view of communication, how it is defined, its importance, its uses. In the following chapters we will take a look at communication development in the child and explore general communication needs of humans: what happens when their needs are met and when they are not. Finally, we will suggest some possible communication goals for classroom instruction based on the information presented. We will offer some samples and models of instruction, but do not intend to provide you with a set of universal lesson plans. It is our feeling that your understanding of the principles of speech communication combined with understanding of your own students should make you a proper expert on what to teach and how to teach it.

REEXAMINATION OF SOME OLD NOTIONS ABOUT SPEECH

Is public speaking the core? Historically the teaching of speech communication has emphasized public speaking. While there are few empirical studies that confirm the point, most teachers of speech agree that it is possible to teach those students who want to learn how to speak well in public. It is questionable, however, whether public speaking can be taught *to everyone,* and, indeed, whether it is important that everyone learn it. There is some evidence of carry-over of learning from public speaking to everyday life, but for the most part, instruction in public speaking does not seem to relate to the kinds of speech experiences most people have. While the confidence that is gained from mastering the art of public speech may spill over and make one more competent in dealing with people in general, there may be more efficient ways of acquiring skill at meeting everyday speech requirements. There is a trend in our society away from formal speaking situations and toward interaction in small problem-solving groups. Today, the man who can work well with his associates to solve problems is very valuable to his employer and his society. Further, the possibilities of dehumanization inherent in our technological society make us more concerned about improvement of human relations. Emphasis on learning appropriate ways of speaking with spouses, children, and friends is becoming more important to contemporary men and women. Thus, public speaking can be a component of instruction in oral communication in the schools, but new ways of teaching people to perform effectively in small groups and in interpersonal situations are urgently needed.

Does criticism aid carry-over? It is not altogether certain that people can improve their speech skills by practicing technique and obtaining criticism. For instruction to be effective, it must be nested into the normal activities of the human. Throughout the history of speech education in the United States, the most (financially) successful teachers of speech based their instruction on the idea that a man's speaking skill could be improved by learning specific techniques of performance. By studying the methods of successful speakers, it was presumed that the student would be able to learn what to do in order to make himself more effective. A corollary to this was that once skills had been studied, they must be practiced in front of an audience under the eyes of a critic. It was further presumed that when the critic spotted a problem in speaking, the student would immediately be able to modify his behavior to fit the criticism. Eventually, it was assumed, after enough study, practice and criticism, that the student would be able to function in front of any audience. This type of instruction concentrated on techniques of using the voice, face, hands, and body. The result of such training was the production of a few stylized speakers, not necessarily able to function anywhere but in formal audience situations, usually in the classroom.

There is little evidence that such systems of instruction have been generally effective, although it is obvious that specific individuals have benefited greatly from them. The problem is that the systems become ends in themselves. The student's success is measured against requirements for success generated by the theory of the system. Fulfilling these requirements was considered good and sufficient evidence of competency. There was no reference to the needs of the student generated from his ordinary life, and thus any adaptation of principle that took place had to be made on the initiative of the student. While a few managed to translate the system to make it fit their needs, for the most part, formalized systems of instruction in communication produced graduates who all seemed to say the same things in the same way on similar occasions, but with no noticeable improvement in their ability to adapt to either their own needs or those of others.

Are there "basic principles"? Academic instruction in public speaking was based on the assumption that there were principles which, if mastered, would enable anyone to improve his speaking skills in a variety of situations. The necessary requirements were models to emulate (including written texts of great speeches), information about the nature of the speech act, instruction in technique, opportunities to practice, and the presence of a professional critic whose function it was to correct errors and suggest methods of improvement. Failure of the student to acquire skill in this system was generally ascribed to his willful resistance to the system. Very little formal measurement has been made of this approach to teaching speech skills, yet it is clear that under it, some students learn to speak well and others do not. What appears to be the case is that those students who come into instruction with considerable competency and commitment tend to improve, while those who lack skill to begin with tend to become even more inept.

Most people do not see the schools doing as well as they should in teaching communication of any kind. Despite all the formal training we give students in written compositions, professors and employers still complain about inadequacies these students show at writing. There seems to be a chain of blame through the academic system. Editors of journals allege that professors write poorly. The professors complain that their students cannot write clearly and blame it on the high schools. Secondary school teachers complain that they cannot do very much with the shabby product sent to them by the elementary language arts programs. The language arts teachers say they do their best, but considering the training the children receive at home. . . .

The picture in regard to oral communication may be even more dismal. Not only do we expect more oral output from our students, but we give less formal instruction in it. Indeed, in some academic circles it is fashionable to declare that it is pointless to try to improve students' oral skills. Speech is considered to be a frill discipline, not essential to the growth of a humane scholar. The assumption made by some people (without reference to their own often obvious speech inadequacies) is that skill at speech is built into the organism, and consequently, it cannot be taught. However, these same scholars have no qualms about awarding low grades to students under the assumption that inadequate oral performance is a sign of mental incompetence. The distinguished educator, Robert M. Hutchins, recently noted that competency at communication is the sole basis on which education in the future can be built. Since "knowledge" changes so rapidly, he says, only the skilled communicator will be able to keep pace.

While we may concede that instruction in public speaking alone is not sufficient to equip students with the oral skills they need to be competent in their social and professional life, we must assert that it is still a viable component of a speech program. In addition, however, students need instruction in oral communication skills such as talking to parents, children, spouses, friends, peers, work associates, subordinates, superiors; learning together with others and cooperating to solve problems. We need to talk in social groups, problem-solving groups, learning groups, clinical groups, and public meetings. It is questionable whether it is possible to learn to participate well in all of these merely by acquiring technique in public speaking. Generalizations about communication must be mastered and applied in various situations. The most appropriate learning about communication appears to be a blend of information and attitude which can be activated to meet imminent needs. A person needs to understand that he is competent to cope with whatever set of circumstances he finds himself in. He needs to know that he has alternatives of behavior at his disposal, and that he is able to do what he needs to do. Since oral communication pervades virtually every phase of human life, it would be foolhardy to attempt to teach for specific occasions. Rather, focus of instructional programs needs to be on the presentation of principles and modes of analysis designed to encourage skill in all phases of life.

Oral communication—an isolated skill? Students seem to understand instinctively that there is something at stake when they communicate with others. This knowledge seriously complicates the business of giving them instruction. Normally, students regard formal training in oral communication as threatening, regardless of their age or level of competency. Students know that when they speak in a classroom (and it makes no difference whether the class is "Speech" or "Show and Tell" or "Give a Science Report") in front of a teacher-critic, they are under the gun and they may be attacked through criticism. They put their personality on the line when they speak. Furthermore, recent evidence indicates that change in communication style will bring about change in personality, and the reverse. This places a huge responsibility on teachers whose job it is to change communication behavior. It is likely that some students resent and resist criticism of their talk because they sense that if they modified their oral communication style, they would not fit so well in their societies outside of the school.

Students who are aware of the potential threat that communication change poses to their self image will tend to resist becoming what their teachers want them to become. They will resist training by offering "AMC" or "absolute, minimum compliance." They will do the minimum that they can do in the classroom to get by, and they will make no effort at all to carry what they learn in school over into their lives. The question that needs to be answered about oral communication is: to what extent can oral and written skills learned in the classroom be made to support the communication behavior of the student in his life outside of school?

Sometimes students tell teachers about how they have changed—how communication training has helped them. Clearly, if there was no perceivable gain, the education system would have long since collapsed. Yet, we still tend to feel uneasy about the unrealistic settings in which we work as teachers. We know instinctively that much of what we offer has no direct relationship to matters that are important to the student. We are dismayed that students who get an "A" in English composition don't seem to be able to write sensible letters of application for jobs, and students who get an "A" in speech can't get through an employment interview. One of our most severe handicaps as teachers is that we are unable to predict the future. If we knew what demands society would be placing on students ten or twenty years from now, we might be able to do a more sensible job of setting realistic goals in the classroom. While we do not know the position of public speaking or group discussion in the world of the future, there is ample evidence that with the increase in leisure time and its expected epidemic of boredom, everyone will need to know how to communicate with friends and how to seek help from others. Our focus, then, needs to be on what can be taught about oral communication that will help students prepare themselves for what they will face and the needs they will have to meet.

Are models helpful? Another popular myth that affects the teaching of speech communication is the cause-effect conception that many people have of the communication process. One of the most widely accepted models offered to help understand the communication process is called the "Shannon-Weaver Model." It is adapted from a model designed for the telephone company by electrical engineers to help unsnarl interference of messages on wires. It presumes that communication consists simply of transmission and receipt of messages. Consequently, it does not take into account the problems of

Are models helpful?

interpretation and emotion that are characteristic of human communication. It makes the task too simple. The "Shannon-Weaver Model," for our purposes, is an oversimplification. If one speaker were to say, "zork," to another speaker, he might get a message; that is, he would hear what seems to be a word, but it would have no meaning to him except, perhaps, to impel him to ask for more information. He might decide that the source of the message is "not all there," and he might give up trying to communicate. In human communication, message is only one element, for when humans communicate, we have both a *process and a relationship.*

If neither speaker nor listener had a meaning for the word "zork" then all that has been communicated is some sort of signal. The electrical impulse analogy presumed that the person transmitting the signal is as much like the person receiving it as two telephone devices are alike. If this is the case, then any variation between what was transmitted and what was received could be ascribed to the mechanics of transmission, *outside* the speaker, and what was received, even if distorted, could not be ascribed to differences between sender and receiver.

The possibility for variation in meaning between people is very great. They can hear the same words and still get different messages. If we look at a simple phrase:

AARD FIMB KHULYAGES ZEVITCH

we discover that we can apply virtually every accepted mode of communication analysis to it. We can examine the elements as phonemes, or as linguistic units, or as grammatical systems. We might attempt to study the roots of the words, tracing them back to their Balto-Ugaritic or Circassian roots. We could even generate scholarly articles about the possible meaning of the phrase. The problem is, however, that it has no meaning whatsoever. It would be sensible only if it had roots in the symbol system of the culture, and even then, what would be important is not what the words mean, but what meanings were evoked in the mind of the person who received the message and how well these meanings corresponded to the meanings in the mind of the person who sent it at the time he sent it.

The minute we accept the premise that there might be differences in meanings of words between speakers and listeners, our whole conception of communication must change from the simplicity of causality to the complexity associated with the study of total human behavior. No longer can we assume that if we are lecturing to a class of students, it is sufficient for us to organize our remarks carefully and speak clearly and then assume that if the student doesn't get it, it is his failure, not ours. It is necessary, then, to reject mechanical and cybernetic analogies that are made about communication. While they may be simple to memorize for quizzes, they do not adequately explain what happens when people communicate with one another. We will discuss a model which explains communication in Chapter 4.

Potential variation in images and symbols can lead to considerable confusion; consequently our dictionary, a historical record of semantic snarls, is often of little help to us. Suppose, for example, you heard one man say to another, "she was fast." Would he be talking about an Olympic racing champion, his typist, his mistress, a race horse? When you discovered that he was talking about his boat, it would surely mean that the boat won some kind of race. How surprising to discover that he really meant that his boat was tied up tightly at the dock. It is an interesting language that gives us a word, "fast," that means to "run rapidly," when we know that if the colors on our sweater don't run at all, they are also "fast." Most of our English words have this capacity for multiple meaning, which seriously complicates the communication process.

COMMUNICATION DEFINED

Perhaps now is the time to attempt to define the communication process-relationship.

HUMAN SPEECH—Communication is a process in which two or more human beings become related through the exchange of symbols that evoke meanings, and through which meanings they may become further engaged in relationship.

Communication is a process because it is dynamic and in motion, connecting the behavior of one person with that of another. It is a relationship because engaging in that process connects in a variety of ways the minds and emotions of the people involved. Process and relationship are related functionally. This means that one doesn't cause the other. A person becomes related to another through engaging in the process, and engaging in the process is based on the nature of the relationship and thus changes it as the process proceeds. Change in relationship alters process; change in process alters relationship. Thus, it should be clear that simple attempts to explain human communication should be avoided. It is helpful to contemplate the utter complexity and desperate fragility of the act of human communication. Understanding how complex, fragile, and important it is helps us to avoid making overly simple assumptions about what happens when people engage in it.

To return to our discussion of the possible variation in meanings, we can clear up some of the confusion by asserting that meanings do not reside in words but in the people who use the words. Though electrical engineers can identify and describe the impulses, which they consider communication, with great precision, the exchange of symbols between people defies simplification. Humans have no clear compendia of meanings. The dictionary, which represents our main source of possibilities, is a frail instrument, for what it offers us is a historical record of the meanings a word has had, without giving specific information about the meaning it might have in a given case. With any word that has more than one possible meaning, only the context in which it is used can give us any idea of what the speaker has in mind. For example, take the common word "tough," which traditionally meant having strong resistance or ability to withstand shock. Few dictionaries are sufficiently up to date to tell us that for a large segment of our population (but not for the whole population), the word "tough" might mean, "too bad," and for an even more avant-garde segment, the word might mean, "attractive, pretty."

Because symbols have variable meanings, it was necessary to modify the simple models of communication to include some information about translation of meaning. Some theorists equipped their models with "black boxes," mysterious entities in which coding and decoding went on. Allowing for data processing in the mind, however, did not explain to us precisely what went on. Thus, attempts at precise study of the human communication process have not been too sucessful. There is still no way we can draw diagrams of what goes on when people communicate. We can, however, offer this proposition: *the impact that communication has on the people who engage in it is best understood when we understand the people who engage in it.* A behavioristic approach to communication study may be fruitful in a laboratory, but in the classroom it tends to break down since the generalizations that may help us explain events in a controlled setting somehow do not seem to have high predictive value when applied to a particular child in a specific situation. Thus the teacher is left with the admonition that *understanding the child is more important than understanding generalizations about the child.*

The Role of Physiology. An approach to understanding the process of communication has been made through the study of the role played by human physiology. Here also, study provides some information about process in general, but little information about particular reactions. Even though we may be able to graph neurophysiological processing in the brain, we do not know what the graphs mean in terms of feeling, commitment, emotional involvement of the people engaged in communicating. Research recently has been heavily preoccupied with the study of physiological variables in communication. There may be potential in this kind of study for understanding some of the reasons for disturbed communication, but there is little in it to explain how communication between normal people can be improved.

Physiology is involved in the act of communication. There seems to be reasonable evidence to indicate that interaction between people brings about measurable and influential changes in the physiology of the body, and that defective interaction may thus result in both physical and mental illness. We do not know, however, the nature of the relationship between the variables, i.e., do changes in the body bring about changes in behavior, or do changes in behavior bring about changes in the body? This kind of information may leave the teacher with considerable concern for the importance of communication in the life of the child, without offering useful tools for the classroom to bring it about. Perhaps, as a generalization about generalizations regarding communication, we might declare that *most studies of the communication process to date gives us considerable information about how vital communication is in the life of the human, without giving us ways and means to aid its development in people.* Physiological variables in communication will be explored more completely in Chapter 2.

Motivation and perception, for example, are concepts that recur in books written for teachers. But they are loose concepts; it is not clear that the terms themselves offer the teacher anything specific to do. It is rarely clear to the teacher whether the threat of punishment through poor grades is an efficient motivation, or whether good grades, when everyone gets them, are really seen as a valid reward. While studies seem to show us that people learn best when they are rewarded for progress, we have no way of ascertaining what might constitute a reward in any given case.

Generalized rewards in schools seem to support the proposition that most activities carried on by teachers tend to enforce compliance behavior, while genuine learning remains an individually motivated act. If this is so, then we might have to agree with Christopher Jencks that success is largely accidental and cannot be ascribed to any known variable in school. It might be more rational to assume that both structure and freedom are necessary in order to provide a maximum opportunity to persuade students to involve themselves in learning. If we accept this proposition, we can begin to discover a connection between the study of communication and the motivation process in the classroom.

Certainly students give considerable evidence that something happens inside their heads that either turns them on or off about school. But all teachers see is behavior. They have to interpret that behavior to derive conclusions about its meaning. A given behavior may be interpreted as willful reisistance to the system or as an exciting contribution by an original mind. We can always deceive ourselves into believing that what is supposed to happen is happening. But more and more each day, we discover that the communications that students beam at us seem to mean that school is not a relevant force in their lives, and that individual success is a random occurrence. We could be fatalists and just let it happen, but our training as professionals declares to us that we must believe that *school can be a positive force*, provided that we, as teachers, can take a hand and make the work have meaning to our students.

The study of communication, approached holistically and applied to students, can help us discover what happens in the mind of a student that either gets him committed or defeated in school. To do this we must examine rhetoric. We must inquire what the student is trying to persuade us of when he communicates with us, and we must inquire into the quality of our attempts to persuade the student to do what he must. Clearly students use a rhetoric in their dealings with the world. They choose goals and they attempt to influence their society, including teachers and school officials, to participate in helping them achieve those goals. It is necessary to examine the student rhetoric, the way students attempt to influence others, in order to discover what teachers might be able to do to bring students into involvement in the act of learning.

Both teachers and students use rhetoric. They are persuaders. The student seeks to generate a life for himself that is satisfying and pleasing. The teacher seeks both control and achievement of objectives. One of the hazards in the encounter between teacher and student is that their perceptions are often so vastly different that the student cannot distinguish what the teacher might offer that would be useful to him, and the teacher cannot discover what the student is seeking that he might be helpful with. Understanding the student rhetoric and what it seeks may help the teacher adjust his own rhetoric so that he may adjust the kinds of perception that students make of the situations they find themselves in. The teacher might, in short, influence the student to choose methods that might lead to a more effective pattern of learning behavior.

A rhetorical view of teaching implies that a teacher has goals he seeks to accomplish with his students. He has defined ways to evaluate results. If he is a careful rhetorician, he understands his student audiences and beams his appeals at their needs. He is aware of Aristotle's dictum, "the fool tells me his reasons, the wise man persuades me with my own." He serves as a model to his students, helping them to learn mature rhetorical strategies.

A rhetorical view regards humans as thinking creatures able to exercise will and control of themselves. They are something more than laboratory animals to be conditioned into "correct" behavior, or machines to be programmed. One of the more popular analogies in the literature today is the comparison between human and computer. The thought of machines being able to carry on what we perceive as thought is frightening, even though it is clear that what goes on in a computer is something like what goes on in a human head, even though on a very rudimentary level. A computer receives data, stores it, processes it on command, and reports it out. A computer can be trained to write poetry and music, though it cannot be trained to judge the quality of what it produces. In some ways, the computer can be regarded as analogous to the logical component of the human extended to maximum efficiency. The computer can solve mathematical problems beyond the scope of human effort simply because it can move more rapidly and remember more detail. It can do this because it is not complicated by the necessity to make evaluations, express emotions, or respond to extraneous stimuli. It can move consistently because it is programmed to be consistent and nothing else. It is distressing to think of human minds being forced to submit to the kind of control that is necessary to get a computer to work properly. Often, however, in some of our new techniques of teaching, we seem to regard students as small computers and treat them as though they were only logic-makers and not emotion-makers as well.

We know that the human mind is partly programmed by external influences, and that it is partly programmed through will. We also know that part of what goes on in mind is purely random. Data processing in the brain is only partly logical. We may assume that "creativity," for example, is within the grasp of every human, but we cannot explain what makes some people produce exciting communications while others seem to remain on a mundane level. As we will point out in detail later, communication is the result of thought. It is the only way that we have to get an idea of what is going on in someone else's mind. Perhaps it is possible for everyone to think all the thoughts there are to think, but only a few have the capacity of deciding which of these thoughts are worth reporting to the world. The capacity for processing data inside the mind is almost limitless for everyone, but some people seem to lack the criteria by which they can judge the worth of their own thinking. The problem may lie in the mind and the decision-making that goes on there, or it may lie in the capacity that some people have to report (communicate). We simply do not know how many important contributions have been denied to human society simply because people lacked skill at influencing others or could not bring their ideas to the attention of people who should hear them.

It is for these reasons that a rhetorical view of the speech-education process is so important. Skill at speech is based on the ability to make decisions about goals and ideas and to have opportunity and skill to express them. Teachers may not be able to influence the internal decision making of their students, but they do have the capability to provide regular opportunities for students to report, if they want to, and furthermore, they may help students acquire skills to make their reports more accurate, cogent, and interesting to listeners. The study of communication technique helps the individual student who wants to communicate to improve what he does express. It may even help stimulate him to a greater willingness to communicate his ideas, and through this, expose more people to varied and exciting information. Quality communications from students give the teacher an opportunity to give rewards which, theoretically, should encourage students to continue to produce well. Thus, to focus on theory of communication is not so helpful as concentrating on how to help the student to use rhetoric in order to exert his influence on events around him.

What needs to be discovered is how to persuade the quiet people to take a try at it also. A recent work by a distinguished psychiatrist makes the point that human emotional states are largely volitional and that even mental illness is usually an elective act. If we are to understand why humans communicate as they do, we must understand how they go about making the choices they make and for what purpose. Communication is the only tool humans have to meet their needs. This will be discussed in detail later on in this book, but one noted scholar declared that communication is the only act that humans have at their disposal that distinguishes them from other animals. Man is the only animal that can use symbols to accomplish his goals. Our concern as teachers must be with the use of symbolic rhetoric by our students as they struggle to maturity.

Virtually every endeavor carried on by man can be regarded as a rhetorical effort. Humans influence others through the clothing they wear, their hair styles, the way they stand, smile, or move. They influence through facial expressions, body movements and hand gestures. On a more sophisticated level, they persuade or motivate through the use of oral and written symbols. The communicative artifacts produced by humans represent the history of their attempts to influence the world around them. To understand a person's behavior, we must understand human rhetoric, the goals he seeks to achieve through communication, how and why he selects the strategies of communication he uses, and how he can be persuaded to alter his behavior. Rhetoric provides us with a means of activating our understanding of oral communication.

In this book we intend to examine communication behavior from a rhetorical perspective, especially the communication of the developing child. We will examine the needs which all humans have and how they communicate to achieve them. Our goal is to help the teacher to develop a rhetorical approach in the classroom, through a synthesis of theory and practice.

RESEARCH IN THE CLASSROOM

Broadly conceived, the term "researcher" can be applied to any individual who consciously attempts to understand the nature of his experience. His intention may be to understand the movement of various species of fish in the world's oceans, to understand the characteristics of bodies falling in space, or the transformation of water into ice or steam, or the behavior of children at play.

Virtually any aspect of our experience which we can identify and define can be the target of research: the weather, automobiles, learning. Within the study of communicative behavior and development of children, the following have been defined and studied systematically: the child's development of vocabulary, of grammar, his use of verbal concepts and communicative strategy. Research activity has produced a body of information pertaining to the child's communication which can assist us in understanding and anticipating the normal and regular aspects of development. It can lead us to make more efficient use of time and talent. The teacher who understands the norms can assess the development of the child systematically. He also can adapt materials and opportunities to the needs and capabilities of exceptional students.

Research activity does not operate in a vacuum. Individuals who do research are a product of their intellectual and emotional experiences. They are influenced by the dominant ideas, myths, and beliefs of their time; the world is flat, the world is round; children are miniature, immature adults, children are emerging potentials; language is style and syntax, language is communicative behavior. They are motivated by the unique features of their human curiosity which impels man to go beyond his immediate experience in an attempt to search out abstract causes and connections among events, as well as by the social pressures for status, success and identity in the community.

The popular image of the scientist in a laboratory, hovering over a microscope, or isolated from the world doomed forever to observe the behavior of flatworms, rats, and monkeys, has obscured similarities shared by all humans as they attempt to understand the universe;

1. Man seeks pattern in experience. He searches the unknown from the perspective of the known to find similarity in diversity and uniqueness in the familiar.

2. Man, through the use of verbal patterns, attempts to anticipate more accurately, and more effectively control, his experience. Man-as-researcher seeks to act upon experience rather than merely respond to it.

The history of science is paralleled in the intellectual development of the child. For example, the noted Swiss psychologist, Jean Piaget, has reported fascinating insights concerning the child as a researcher and theory builder. Admittedly, the content of science and the mind of the child are not similar. Piaget suggests, however, that in the child's ability to make patterns, to observe, to differentiate, to analyze, and ultimately interpret experience mentally, one may observe the rudimentary and essential structures and processes characteristic of science as we know it. His work has been helpful in assisting teachers to understand their students.

Research activity follows as a natural consequence of living in a world where ideas are possible and useful in mastering experience: Problems are encountered, curiousity is aroused, needs are stimulated. Thinking man formulates questions, designs means to answer them, collects data, interprets and acts on his interpretations. The scientist in the laboratory and the teacher in the classroom have at their disposal various orientations to research.

The work of the specialist (Scientific Perspective). The scientific community is continually engaged in the production of knowledge which influences our daily living. Most of us are consumers of what full-time scientists produce. The recall of potentially defective automobiles, the use of nonphosphate detergents, the attempt to provide early innoculation against rubella, and literally thousands of other large and small "dos and don'ts," "shoulds and oughts," "ifs and thens," have emerged from the activities of the scientific few for the consumption and betterment of the many in our society. Decades of intelligence testing, diagnostic grouping, programming of materials, etc. have influenced and continue to influence the way we, as teachers, relate to and provide for the teaching of our students. Research in one form or another has influenced almost every formal aspect of our teaching day: the texts we use in teaching, the norms we use in evaluation, the arrangement of our curricula, and so on. Most of us, as teachers, have neither the time nor the specialized knowledge to engage in this kind of formal research. We are consumers of what the experts tell us. Our responsibility is to examine and decide what we can use.

This should not imply that the scientific community has produced a utopia in the classroom. Far from it! One needs only to digest the penetrating critique of American public education offered by Charles Silberman in *Crisis in the Classroom* to understand where research has failed or where we, as teachers, have failed to use research productively. We are specialists on our own classrooms, and our research is often based on our own intuition.

The role of teacher intuition (Naive Perspective). This research activity is based on intuition and may take the form of personal journals, diaries, progress reports, or "notes to myself." A teacher may attempt a private experiment such as rearranging seating patterns or restructuring groupings in language arts to "see what happens." Results rarely become part of public knowledge. Interpretations tend to be unsystematic and are rarely tied to an abstract or objective scientific theory.

The value of private research is that it often can be used as rhetoric, to dramatize a point. A number of private researches have become useful in a manner similar to Herbert Kohl's *36 Children*, Herndon's *The Way It 'Spozed to Be,* or Sylvia Ashton-Warner's *Teacher.*

Studying your own teaching (Pedagogical Perspective). Teaching often suffers because it lacks clarity or it is second hand. Many of us are often asked to teach from a syllabus prepared by someone else, using methods that do not suit us. Also, we often slip into teaching styles without attempting to discover whether other approaches might be more effective. A rhetorical approach to research in our own classroom would consist of examining the ideas of others, responding to our intuitions and experimenting to find the kind of teaching style that seems to get more of what we want from our students.

For example, we may look at various scientific theories to see what they might suggest about our own behavior. Learning theory might indicate we ought to give more rewards. Sociocultural theory might suggest greater acceptance of individual deviations. Furthermore, we might feel a discussion is in order even when our syllabus does not specify it. We might try out the discussion to see if test scores improve a little. All of this we do to offer a more successful persuasion to the student to participate in the learning process.

Research may proceed in two directions. We can study a behavior in a great many students to draw a general conclusion or we can study one student thoroughly in all aspects of behavior to understand the student better. As a classroom teacher you will be called upon often to do both. Like any researcher, the teacher starts with a goal and a set of hypotheses about a method or a behavior. Both teacher and researcher manipulate environment, holding some things constant and changing others, and then interpret outcomes. A teacher cannot rely, however, on abstract scientific theory. The teacher's commitment is to the individual child, and the children in his classroom. No theory alone can explain the nature of human development sufficiently to provide all the answers. Absolute generalization cannot be made from even the best research studies. Theory building, as it relates to understanding human communication, is a continuous process which includes speculation, definition, observation, testing, analysis, and pure insight. Scientific theory can provide insights or frames of reference for comparing and contrasting points of view. Ultimately, however, it is important for the teacher to blend his understanding of his own students with a solid understanding of what is known or believed for good reasons in order to make his performance more effective, to discover ways in which he can act systematically to encourage communication growth in his students. In the next chapter we will examine various theories of communication behavior in the child to provide you with a theoretical basis on which your own investigations may rest.

SUMMARY

Our goal in oral-communication instruction in the classroom is to cope with students' everyday life requirements placed on communication.

Whether public-speaking instruction combined with criticism can accomplish this goal is questionable, though most speech programs in the schools are still focused on public performance activities such as public speaking, debate, oral interpretation, and so on. What needs to be developed is a program in which communication, as process and relationship in which varied meanings of symbols are exchanged, is examined and taught in relation to human activities that take place daily: conversation with strangers, friends, parents; talk in school with teachers, classmates, counselors; talk during a job interview, talk on the job or talk in school (making presentations), etc.

To decide what approaches to oral-communication instruction will work most effectively, the teacher needs to function as researcher, and he does this by drawing on three basic research areas: knowledge supplied by specialists, his own intuition about his students and the material he teaches, and by studying his own teaching in a systematic way. Finally, both teacher and student operate from a rhetorical perspective in their dealings in the classroom: both have needs to accomplish and both seek the most effective ways of fulfilling them. How the teacher can utilize rhetoric in motivating students to acquire oral-communication skills to meet their needs is our primary focus in this book, and one on which we will elaborate in the following chapters.

WORKS CITED:

Ashton-Warner, Sylvia. *Teacher.* New York: Simon & Schuster, 1963.

Becker, Ernest. *Birth and Death of Meaning.* 2d ed., New York: The Free Press, 1971.

Berelson, Bernard and Steiner, Gary. *Human Behavior.* New York: Harcourt Brace Jovanovich, 1964.

Cooper, Lane, Ed. *The Rhetoric of Aristotle.* New York: Appleton-Century-Crofts, 1933.

Flavell, John H. *The Development Psychology of Jean Piaget.* Princeton, N.J.: Van Nostrand Reinhold, 1963.

Herndon, James. *The Way It 'Spozed to Be.* New York: Simon & Schuster, 1968.

Jencks, Christopher. *Inequality.* New York: Basic Books, 1972.

Kohl, Herbert. *36 Children.* New York: New American Library, 1967.

Rabkin, Richard. *Inner and Outer Space.* New York: W.W. Norton, 1970.

Silberman, Charles. *Crisis in the Classroom.* New York: Random House, 1970.

WORKS RECOMMENDED:

For information on classical uses of rhetoric see Section 1 of Lester Thonnsen and A. Craig Baird. *Speech Criticism*. New York: The Ronald Press, 1948.

For a solid view of public speaking training see John Wilson and Carroll Arnold. *Public Speaking as a Liberal Art*. Boston: Allyn & Bacon, 1972.

For information on group problem solving see Gerald Phillips and Eugene Erickson. *Interpersonal Dynamics in the Small Groups*. New York: Random House, 1970.

For a good brief introduction to communication theory see Don Fabun. *Communication: The Transfer of Meaning*. New York: Glencoe Press, 1968. See also Chapter 3 of Elwood Murray, et al. *Speech: Science-Art*. Indianapolis: Bobbs-Merrill, 1968.

For a concise explanation of the use of evidence in research see Bernard Huppe and Jack Kaminski. *Logic and Language*. New York: Alfred A. Knopf, 1957.

- To recognize that the teacher cannot assume that the child has developed sufficient oral communication skills in the home.

- To note that because of this, the teacher must understand the natural development of communication capabilities in the child to know what level of skills is appropriate for a given child in classroom instruction.

- To understand that the process-relationship function of communication affects the identity and goals of the child.

- To realize the need to develop alternate strategies for instruction to allow students to meet their needs in the most effective ways.

- To remember that without adapting communication instruction to student needs, students view instruction as separate from their real lives and resist learning.

- To note that the rhetorical view of instruction involves assisting students in setting of goals in communication important to them and designed to help them solve problems.

- To learn how linguistic, conceptual, and sociocultural theories of speech development can aid in observing and understanding communication behavior of the child.

2

Interpreting Communication Behavior

OVERVIEW

Explanations of the process of developing a rhetorical approach to classroom instruction start in this chapter. It is crucial that the teacher not assume too much about the communication abilities of the child entering school (or of students in higher grades). As we will elaborate in the last half of the chapter, children have phases of development during which communication skills are most readily learned. Linguistic capacities are biologically based, and, despite consistent exposure to communication activities, if a child has not attained the biological equipment necessary for skill acquisition instruction does little good. Conceptual development concerns the child's learning about abstract features of his language, and sociocultural influences revolve around what the child learns from his role associations with others.

Throughout the chapter, our aim is to point to the need to adapt and alter instructional strategies to meet the needs of students in the classroom. Without this rhetorical view, the teacher often finds himself engaged in instruction which is met with indifference or "absolute minimum compliance" by the students, since they see it apart from "real" communication situations.

THERE IS NO WAY that a teacher can avoid dealing with communication. If he is formally designated a teacher of communication, it is his responsibility to do as

25

good a job as possible of training his students to express ideas, ask and answer questions, make reports, participate in oral group activities, express points of view, talk with others, make requests, and ask for help. His mission is to deal with the great number of communication urgencies that characterize the life of every human. Primarily, it must be assumed that oral communication is an art to be learned. The teacher cannot rely either on the home or the previous education of the child in any way, shape, or form, for the best evidence is that instruction in oral communication is spotty at best. Walwick, in his survey of elementary school speech programs, discovered that most elementary curricula contain no instruction at all in oral communication, though most require performance in the form of show and tell, creative dramatics, or the giving of reports. It is, in his words, somewhat like asking students to write compositions before they have learned calligraphy.

The Dunham studies indicate that a similar vista is presented by the secondary schools. There is almost no instruction in oral communication given on the junior high level, while such instruction as there is on the senior high level is confined to speech specializations like debate, formal discussion, contest activities, play production, and so on. Even on the junior college level, a recent study by Berko shows this same kind of specialization. There is almost no information or practice given to the student anywhere in his curriculum about how to do what the school requires him to do. Those students who acquired skill somehow, either because of a rare learning experience, home influence, or emulation, have a decided advantage over those students who have received no formal instruction or practice.

There is a strong message in this for every teacher, for many of the demands placed on students are for oral output. Teachers customarily evaluate this output as evidence of mastery of subject matter. They ascribe problems in speaking to incompetence with subject matter. Thus, there is the strong possibility that many students go unrewarded or are actually punished simply because of a gap in the educational system occasioned by the assumption that somehow we all learn how to speak at our mother's knee.

This results in handicapped people. As pointed out in later chapters, inability to express personal goal seeking through oral communication can disable a person as a human being. Without learning fundamental skills of oral communication, it is not possible for a person to exert his share of influence on events around him. This, in turn, creates a person turned inward, not contributing to the society, not contributing even to his own growth and progress.

Rather than attempt to argue on behalf of the usually ineffective and interminable "educational revolutions," and "oral-communication revolution," it is the "message" of this book that if teachers understand the principles of communication, contained herein, they might be able to provide instructional opportunities for their students that would make them more able to participate orally in their school learning process, not to speak of enhancing their performance at home, in the community, at work and at play. This would include an understanding of the natural progression of development of communication capability in the child, the communication process per se, some insight into the possible problems students who cannot communicate well might have, and some methods for training all students to some acceptable level of oral-communication skill as well as means for dealing with those students who are orally deficient and for whom there are no special education opportunities. If it is possible to generate a full-blown curriculum, so much the better.

The teaching of oral communication is not yet, and probably never will be, a science. There is no firm agreement on principles of development, and there is considerable controversy about the techniques and strategies to use. What seems to be a central proposition, however, is that every person acquires his identity through response to communication, reflects his identity through communication, and uses communication as the main method by which he seeks to attain his human goals. Thus, we might conclude that every human makes rhetoric most of the time he talks. We are concerned here not only with the formalities of language development but with the alternative uses of language by teachers and students alike. Thus, we will frame our discussions in rhetorical terms; we will argue a case for a rhetorical view of the speech education process. In this chapter we will examine various ideas of how speech develops in children. In the subsequent chapters we will look at theories that explain how communication is used by adults and children and, throughout, we will concern ourselves with how all of this influences teacher behavior in the classroom. Now we need to understand some ways by which the teacher can systematically examine his pedagogy.

It is difficult for someone to be teacher and researcher at the same time. Over the past few decades, there has been a heavy emphasis on the formalities of research. Investigators have borrowed liberally from the techniques used by the "hard sciences." They have applied to humans the same type of experimentation that has been applied to bacteria and electrons. When humans could not be studied, rats, dogs, or pigeons were used. While some generalizations useful to teachers have resulted from this kind of research, the usual case has been an increasing separation between those doing the research and those interested in applying it. The pure researcher seeks to fill out a theory of human behavior and he is willing to wait patiently for it to evolve out of many experiments by many different people.

The classroom teacher, however, cannot wait. He is on his own. He needs to have information to apply immediately to the students in his charge, and no one can provide it for him but himself. The classroom teacher is responsible for research into the effects of his own behavior. He must make decisions about how to manage his actions in the classroom, and hopefully these decisions will be based on orderly investigation. The following material can serve as a basis for examining both content and method of an oral communication program. The study of oral communication includes the inferences we make about the way people use words to express ideas and to control their own behavior and the behavior of others. The control the child has over these processes helps him plan and coordinate what he has to say to other people. Understanding them will help the teacher devise a set of learning experiences that will help the student learn communication through communicating.

Learning to communicate orally as part of the whole learning process offers a challenging alternative to traditional approaches to communication which require a child to learn reading, writing, speaking, and listening as ends in themselves, not as means to obtain information, pleasure and ideas. Walwick's survey of elementary schools demonstrated that most teachers were vague in their definitions of "speech" and "oral communication." Furthermore, they were generally unsystematic in teaching what they called "speech." Most instruction focused either on remediation of voice and articulation problems or on preparation for performance in drama, debate, and public speaking. There was little attention paid to understanding the communication process or to skills which could be carried over into life experience either in or out of school. Teachers who responded to the survey seemed to feel that instruction in speaking and listening was sufficient if they provided regular "Show and Tell" periods, and allowed some kinds of dramatic performances in their classrooms.

The authors conducted their own interviews with more than five hundred teachers about what they taught under the label "oral-communication skills." Most admitted to being unprepared to offer systematic instruction in oral-communication concepts and skills and most of their teaching covered oral communication interpreted as oral reading, reciting, and reporting. When asked to state their goals for instruction in oral communication, most teachers discussed their desire to remedy what they saw as particular deficiencies. They wanted to get a particular child to speak louder, to be quiet, to be less frightened when reciting, or to speak more clearly and use better grammar.

Many of the teachers felt unprepared to diagnose and develop systematically the various oral-communication skills which a child needs in order to become a successful communicator. Taking courses in the teaching of the language arts did not appear to help prepare teachers in oral-communication instruction. Their actual teaching experience apparently did not provide the understanding they needed, either. It is for this reason that we are offering a start toward establishment of a perspective for teaching oral communication skills.

To develop skills in the teaching of oral communication means acquiring a variety of ways to interpret and respond to the communicative behavior of children. We can assume that the younger the child, the more the adult must anticipate, interpret, organize, and search for the reasons and motivations which underlie the child's talk. If a teacher desires to change a child's communicative behavior, he must try to determine the possible reasons why the child is not behaving in desired ways. It is then necessary to discover what changes in the use of oral communication the child must make.

We will now take a look at concepts and techniques to use in developing an understanding of the child as a communicator. It will be necessary for us to draw from such diverse fields as linguistics, developmental psychology, speech science, sociology, rhetoric, and education theory. Each of these fields has contributed to our understanding of the child as communicator. Each has drawn our attention more strongly to the significance of oral-communication skills in the child's development of personality, ability to think clearly, effectiveness in social interaction, and general impact on his life-world.

PERSPECTIVES

As noted in Chapter 1, we can examine the communicative development of the child from three perspectives: *naive, scientific* and *pedagogical.* From a naive position we simply act, react, and interact with the child without considering how his behavior relates to past or future. Playing house, talking on the telephone, arguing, informing and telling stories are activities most of us engage in with the child on the naive level. Our actions toward the child are based on our prior contact with him, our vested interest in him, and our experiences with other children similar to him. The way we view the child's actions and the inferences we make about his communication skills are clouded by how we *expect* him to behave. These expectations make a difference in how satisfied we are in relating to the child, and they influence how we interpret the child's action toward us. Our naive expectations often lead to biases which make it difficult to make systematic decisions about development of oral-communication skills.

A second persepctive on the child's communicative development is the scientific. We take this view when our main concern is with generalizations about behavior. We might attempt to "fit" the specific features of the child's talk into a more general framework so that we can understand its abstract qualities. The important point is that we attempt to go beyond the level of our individual wisdom in interpreting the behavior of the child. This approach is characteristic of the scientist. For example, the developmental psychologist is interested in the stages of communicative development; the cognitive theorist is interested in the relationship between the child's thought and his communicative behavior; the linguist inquires about how language used by the child differs from language used by adults; and the sociologist asks about the influences of the child's groups on his ability to think and communicate. These specialists offer valuable information against which to compare our naive perceptions of students we encounter in the classroom.

The third perspective combines the first two in a pedagogical perspective. By combining the naive and scientific views an estimation of the best program of instruction within constraints posed by grading, grouping, curriculum, and so on can be developed. This prognosis is central to the pedagogical perspective. To function pedagogically, the teacher needs to assume rhetorical responsibility. He should be aware of his naive responses; he should attempt to identify and control his underlying biases and attitudes toward the child; he should be capable of interpreting the theoretical significance of some of the child's behaviors; and he should be committed to the task of developing the child's communicative potentials. He needs to do this in order to generate the rhetorical goals his classroom strategy seeks to attain.

The importance of teacher commitment and expectation in the development of skills has already been discussed. In addition, it is helpful to know that most young children are ready to learn almost anything they see as relevant, useful, fun, or in some way interesting. They are naturally curious, and when left alone to determine their own pace, they can quickly master many complicated tasks. This is important, because readiness to learn implies a readiness to communicate. Additionally, readiness to learn means that the child can begin to see himself now and compare that to what he might be later as a result of participation. Because communication is closely involved with the child's view of himself, the systematic development of communication skills touches the child where he is most vulnerable. Any approach to the development of new skills must be initiated from the child's own desire and willingness to risk change in himself. This really means that much of teaching centers on *persuading* the child to be ready to change. The teacher's persuasion can be made more effective if he is able to understand what the child is trying to persuade the teacher to feel or do and to provide a variety of appropriate opportunities for the child to experiment with the desired communication alternatives. Training older students is somewhat more difficult. A junior or senior high student has firm notions about what his behavior ought to be, and he will resist instruction if he sees that it may interfere with what he sees as a peer-approved style.

In any case, it is impossible for a teacher to alter communicative behavior by ordering a student to change in line with criticism. It is not a simple matter of changing a word or syntactic form, or of increasing the child's vocabulary. Communication change, regardless of the age of the student, involves a reorganizing of the student's thinking about what works in a given situation. The student must be motivated to restructure the relationship which he sees between himself, his messages, the situation, and the others to whom the messages are directed. Obviously, the younger the child, the more the adult must be prepared to interpret what he means and the greater the necessity for providing a wide range of opportunities for the child to respond to the teacher's direction. The teacher must be prepared to demonstrate alternatives (observable for the child) in a variety of concrete ways: through role playing, deliberately making mistakes, dramatizing stories, or simply suggesting, "here's another way to do it, let's try it out and see what happens."

There are two reasons why traditional school experiences work against learning of oral skills. The first is that children are normally forced to participate in groups that are larger than they can conveniently manage. They are mostly displayed as performers, not participants. Older students are normally graded on their performance in the classroom. In a graded situation, students often do not know what their grade measures. Interviews conducted by the authors with students on both secondary and college level indicate that it is as likely for them to feel that the grade represents an evaluation of personality as it does evaluation of knowledge of subject matter. That is, a student receiving an "A" on a history report is likely to regard the grade as a measurement of his knowledge of history, while the student who receives "C" or below is likely to feel the grade is a negative evaluation of his personality.

Second, students find it quite difficult to articulate what they experience inside and outside the classroom. With their parents and peers they do not give formal reports, nor do they engage in artistic performance or small group discussions with fixed agendas. Outside the classroom, the focus of the student is on making friends and surviving in the peer group. Thus, the atmosphere of instruction in oral techniques tends to keep the student from talking, for it is most likely that he will comply routinely with requests for oral output and see those experiences as isolated from experience, containing little or no value for application outside the school.

It is for these reasons that it is necessary for the teacher, operating from a rhetorical perspective, to have alternate strategies at his disposal. By alternate strategies, we simply mean a way to analyze the speech needs of a student so that the teacher can respond to cues by offering both experiences and rationale for experiences that might apply outside the classroom. We cannot expect the student to bring the natural fluency of his interpersonal communication into the classroom unless he is motivated to do so. Furthermore, only rarely will he discuss school subject matter with his peers, though often he will discuss school politics, the unfairness of the system, and the vagaries and peccadillos of his fellow students. While we are not suggesting that gossip become part of the curriculum, we are suggesting that means of motivating greater fluency and involvement in the school and carrying over techniques learned in school to outside experience should be part of the teacher's repertoire. For the person who teaches speech per se, teaching for carry-over could very likely mean discussing problems with peers inside the classroom, and devising experiences which the student can take with him into his community.

It is, therefore, a good idea for the teacher to discover how students view others, what kinds of talk they make with their friends, and how they use talk in their normal interactions. An incisive audience analysis done on the students in the classroom enables the teacher to devise more alternatives for experience. Outside the classroom, the student is not aware that he is "acquiring speech skills." Until he understands that he cultivates his communication style in both places, he will not be able to make the connection between school and life.

While the question of teaching for carry-over plagues most school subjects, it is particularly important in oral communication, for without a conception of carry-over, the student will regard his oral assignments as "pledge duties" to be survived. Because changing communication habits strike at the heart of personality, people in general resist alteration. Most adults experience difficulty when they consciously try to alter their communication. Normally, communication skills are developed indirectly by learning how to take appropriate social roles, or as a consequence of close involvement with a few significant others, or as a function of the natural inclination to play and imitate. When the student encounters speaking, listening, reading, and writing as subjects, this creates an artificial barrier to learning, and he finds it difficult to associate what he does naturally with what is now a formal operation of the classroom. For example, some students may appear to be nonreaders but show considerable skill with shop manuals outside the classroom. To guarantee survival outside the classroom, the child may have to block his learning inside the classroom. Inner-city students will resist alteration in grammar and diction if such alteration would subject them to ridicule in their peer group.

Communication normally functions as a unified whole. Through oral communication a person initiates, responds to, and maintains relationships or destroys and prevents them. Communication is directed toward a goal set by an individual and it involves the use of verbal and nonverbal patterns chosen as appropriate to a particular set of circumstances involving other people who matter. If the classroom does not offer training in communication skills with this kind of process in mind the student may make a rigid distinction between normal communication which he carries on all the time to maintain his identity, relationships, and socializations and what he sees as communication drills in the classroom. Students can learn a great deal of communication outside the classroom and yet resist learning it inside the classroom. Since all other learning rests on the ability to speak, write, listen and read, the teaching of communication must be alive, relate to the student's existence, and involve the sense of socialization which characterizes communication in life.

This can mean that the teacher may have to pause and get more information before evaluating a communication behavior. For example, many teachers react immediately and punishingly to the child's use of profanity. Physical punishment, threat, isolation from the group are but a few of the numerous responses to the child's use of "damn it" or "mother-fucker." These responses may stop the behavior momentarily, but rarely do they encourage the reorientation toward desirable language uses. One possibility is to ask the child to explain or clarify *what he means* when he uses the undersirable terms. Frequently, the child does not know. The teacher discovers this and is in a position to assist the child in discovering his meaning and using more acceptable language in which to express it. "Does it mean you're mad at me, mad at your partner, upset with yourself?" "Draw me a picture of what you mean." "See if you can show me what your message wants me (us) to do." Thus, the teacher is in a position to assist the child in rebuilding his communication potentials from within. When he feels that it can be understood by the child, the same teacher might well respond with a sense of personal hurt or anger or whatever reaction seems appropriate to show that the undesired word achieves a response, although it might not be the response needed or desired on the child's part. Pedagogy, thus, becomes a matter of rhetorical strategy derived from inferences about what might be going on in the child's head in relation to the situation in which he must survive. Sometimes you ignore, sometimes you teach directly, other times you teach indirectly through play.

The rhetorical view of pedagogy assists students to set goals or to discover them as they encounter and seek to resolve communication conflict. It necessitates that teacher response encourage the student toward communicating as a "way to get things done; a means for solving problems." The theory and research discussed in subsequent portions of this text can assist the teacher in making more rational and precise decisions about the approach most appropriate for his students.

As we've already suggested, smaller children may not be ready to generate the specific alternatives, although the teacher may be able to persuade them to see a need for change in their communication behavior. They may need concrete examples and specific opportunities to participate in alternate modes. Materials strategically arranged to facilitate acting out of new communication strategies may be introduced to younger children during playlike lessons. For example, the teacher may involve children in role playing in which they learn a new behavior as appropriate and discover that they are able to do it. Evaluation can be elicited by asking "How do you feel?" "What happened?" "What did you want to happen?" etc. This will assist the child to understand behavior alternatives.

The essence of rhetorical communication is the understanding that there are alternatives in meanings of spoken ideas. Teachers and students alike can and must exercise choices to determine what is potentially the most effective way of influencing others. Rhetorical communication, because it adapts to personal needs, audience and situation, recognizes that people are not only physically separate from one another, but also symbolically separated. It is necessary, then, to incorporate the unique needs and experiences of other people involved in analysis of a situation when attempting to talk to them.

In devising an instructional program for oral-communication skills in the classroom, it is necessary to make a careful distinction between what we observe the child doing and what we know of his underlying linguistic, conceptual, and rhetorical control. We can examine communication behavior in three ways: 1) development and use of language (linguistic), 2) development and application of verbal concepts in organizing and elaborating language (conceptual), and 3) capacity to use alternative strategies to motivate behavior of others (rhetorical). It is recognized as a basic principle of human communication that neither children nor adults speak in linguistics, in concepts, or in rhetoric. They speak as total human beings in response to their

Teacher locked into a naive perspective.

needs. Often they are not even consciously aware of why they speak, but they are urged on by their desire to exert their human influence. The individual is basically concerned for his self-maintenance when he communicates with others. Therefore, when we want to change the way a child normally communicates, we are dealing with change in his *unique methods of survival*. The teaching of communication skills affects the whole person. It is more than the study of linguistics, concept formation, or rhetoric. We must be aware of the whole person in response to our teaching; both his verbal and nonverbal messages to us must be taken into account. Without consideration of the human who speaks and the needs he seeks to meet by speaking, we cannot bring about meaningful change.

The value of theory as a teaching guide or framework for establishing instructional goals has often been questioned by those who teach communication skills to children. It is understandable to object to artificial manipulation of talk in laboratory research. It is easy to become frustrated in the attempt to "boil down" volumes of study on communicative development to derive a set of propositions to use in the classroom. Yet, without some theory and research, how could we attempt to understand and develop systematically oral-communication skills in children? Where would we begin? How would we direct skill development? How would we measure progress? Without theory or a conceptual model, the teacher is locked into his private and biased experience. He is trapped and cannot go beyond his naive perspective. This book will conclude with a list of possible goals for communication training. They will be based on the soundest available theory and, hopefully, will be sufficiently practical to activate them in the classroom.

We do not wish to imply that theory ought to replace practice, particularly that of teachers with many years of practical experience with children. Rather, a theory should be viewed as an alternative perspective against which the teacher can check his own experience and expectations. We are suggesting the pedagogical perspective, the blending of naive and scientific approaches, from which to look at the oral behavior of students.

A number of conceptual and theoretical models have been devised to help in the systematic observation and understanding of communication behavior. Some deal with general development from birth to death; others are more specific and focus on selected aspects of communicative behavior. Some models look at the child's over-all potential and its relationship to the communicative demands of his social environment; others interpret selected features of the child's communication in specific tasks or situations.

THEORIES OF SPEECH DEVELOPMENT

Theoretical models and concepts may be classified under three headings: 1) linguistic, 2) cognitive—developmental or conceptual, 3) sociocultural or rhetorical.

Linguistic Theory: Biologically Based. Major features of language development occur systematically and regularly in children. This development proceeds according to a genetically determined timetable. One researcher suggests that from birth to two years of age is the *period of speech-readiness.* Reflex-crying, babbling, lalling, and imitative utterances are changes that occur in the infant's prelinguistic vocalization during this time. These are viewed as biologically paced phases within the general period of speech readiness. The period extending from age two through adolescence is considered a critical period for the acquisition of language. The potential which is inherent in the genetic make-up of the child is realized and developed as the child produces speech sounds, words, phrases, and sentences. Finally, as adolescence is approached, the child refines and elaborates semantic and syntactic forms. The critical period of language development refers to phases when biological processes make the child most sensitive and responsive to certain kinds of stimulation and learning. During the critical period, the child is capable of rapid growth with relatively little direct teaching from others around him. The significance of all this is that *it is not reasonable to expect linguistic performance from a child who is not biologically ready.* While good teaching may help the young child learn to his biological limits, teaching cannot take the child beyond those limits.

A biological model can assist the teacher in understanding the contributions of neurological and chemical factors to the concept of language readiness. For instance, manipulative experience stressing the use of materials that emphasize the interplay of sensory perception and action are important to the developing child's readiness to learn. The Montessori approach to teaching has been so successful because the pedagogy is based on a sensitivity to neurological and physical-growth processes operating within the child and is strategically designed to permit the child a natural and spontaneous opportunity to move, to sense, and to interact symbolically.

Linguistic Theory. This kind of theory is based on the assumption that the child has a language acquisition device or set of potentials for discovery of the rules underlying verbal communication in his native tongue. These potentials apparently enable the child, when he is biologically ready, to generate a large number of correct phrases and sentences based on his use of a limited number of rules for constructing them. These rules are developed as the language input of the child is processed by the child's potentials of "linguistic universals."

This process can be seen by noting the verbalizations of children who have had no previous exposure to certain phrases and sentences. The following are behaviors that the child demonstrates without specific teaching from an adult prior to his entrace in school. The child learns to perfect his language with continued exposure to it.

1. The child can approximate the relationship and position of the subject-predicate and the verb-object as used by adults ("I is").

2. The child can produce phrases and sentences that correspond to word orders used by adults ("There truck" for "There is a truck"; "I going?" for "Am I going?").

3. The child can distinguish between obvious syntactic meaning of a verbalization and the deeper psychological meaning implied. For example, he is able to distinguish the subtle differences of meaning implied in the following sentences of similar syntax. ("Susan is nice to be with" and "Susan is nice to others.")

4. The child can produce a variety of sentence forms based on tranformation of a limited number of sentence patterns. ("The dog is brown." "Is the dog brown?")

5. The child can distinguish between the rules applying to sound changes, construction, and meaning. ("He runs," "He runnded," "He gonna run.")

It is assumed that any infant is initially capable of learning any language. People in the infant's social environment provide specific language input in the form of words, phrases, and sentences. Those surrounding the infant also provide the impetus for talk, and as the infant matures biologically, he undertakes the task of "breaking the code" or learning the system of rules which underlies the talk of other people. In a sense, from this standpoint, the young child is an hypothesis tester who moves into the adult language community with the help of his language acquisition device.

At least three processes are involved in the child's development of language skills: 1) the adult must imitate and expand the incomplete phrases and sentences initially produced by the child. 2) The child, through a process of induction, must discover the structure inherent in the talk of adults before he can distinguish between the use of different word forms. 3) The child must gradually reduce his use of irregular word forms and adopt regular forms used by adults.

One study, for example, clearly demonstrates that even the youngest children spend a lot of time in trial-and-error linguistic practice. Furthermore, linguistic theory has encouraged people to notice children's use of irregular word forms and to probe beyond the superficial features of children's talk; it has provided a tool for estimating the linguistic quality and power of the child when he enters school. Reference to linguistic theory will help the teacher understand what it is reasonable to expect from his students. It also provides a basis for understanding conceptualization processes which provide a bridge from oral language used imitatively and language used to adjust and control environment in a rhetorical mode.

Development of Concepts. Cognitive-Developmental Theory. Cognitive-developmental theory focuses on the child and his changing

Child entering the adult language community with his language acquisition device.

mental capacity to organize, interpret, and respond to experience. Much has been written on the mental development in children as they gain capacity for self regulation and self control in problem-solving and communication.

The cognitive-developmental model explains the operation of the child's thoughts, memory, anticipations, and insights which affect the way he organizes and produces talk in different communication situations. We can look at this communicative development in a series of stages. Each stage is characterized by a dominant behavioral tendency regulated by mental abilities. For instance, the infant from six months to a year initiates communicative activity only with those familiar to him by visual and auditory cues.

The preschooler's production of sentences is assumed to be based on knowledge of the underlying rules of sentence formation. The middle school child's use of communicative strategies with individuals of varying age, sex, physical appearance, background, and language style is apparently based on awareness of abstract qualities of people such as feelings and potentials for action.

Continuity between developmental stages may be explained by the tendency in the child's biosocial makeup toward differentiation, specialization, integration, and hierarchical organization of mental processes. In order to account for observed changes in behavior of children toward objects, individuals, and events, it is necessary to hypothesize some scheme of organization of mental processes. This organization also helps explain the infant's growth from a helpless, dependent organism to an individual of relatively independent symbolic status who is able to control both self and others.

Development of concepts is a continuous process through which the child's capacity for production, unification, elaboration, and adaptation of talk is accomplished. We can view this communicative development in a series of stages. First, the child must be biologically ready to think and to speak. Through experiences and practice, the child then begins to differentiate roles; he makes an agreement to learn communication behavior. Once this agreement has been made, the child can learn specific skills and store them in his memory associated with particular people and situations. Finally, the child learns to use memory as a source of direction. He cannot only apply strategies, he can select them.

The first stage is considered a period of readiness when the child is biologically capable of responding to stimulation from people around him. It appears, however, that this latent readiness can be activated with stimulation through language spoken by adults surrounding the child. Their talk releases the developmental process of the child's language.

The actualization of language readiness potential in the second stage occurs at different rates in all phases of communicative development. Syntactic structures develop most rapidly during childhood. Abstract terms and use of verbal concepts manifest themselves during the middle school years and develop fully during adolescence.

In the third stage the teacher can have his greatest impact, for specific and unique choices made by those teaching the child will result in rapid mastery of social situations. Basic language patterns seem to be acquired similarly by all children in some way, regardless of differences in social class. The child's subsequent use of language in thought and communication is directly related to the linguistic norms of influential people like his family, his peers, and his school.

The final stage of conceptual development is activated as the child becomes capable of performing in the absence of those who have taught him the uses of language. The impact of the previous stage can be noted in the child's tendency to use specific modes of communicating learned in his family and modified by important social groupings.

The stages of conceptual development and their association with communication behavior are shown in the following chart. By relating conceptual development and linguistic development, the child's communication in a social milieu can be better interpreted. We are primarily concerned with the use of oral language in a social milieu, for the focus of most speech training is on social behavior. We now turn to

Outline of Conceptual Development

Stage of Development	Characteristics of Communicative Behavior	Underlying Influences
Prelinguistic Birth—two years	Crying, noncrying vocalizations, gestures, pointing, reaching, visual following, smiling as social release, imitation of adult sounds.	Behavior organized according to sensorymotor patterns reflecting (1) affective sensitivity, (2) capacity to differentiate and respond to patterns of reinforcement; behavior modified by infant's physiological coping pattern.
Childhood Two—six years	First words, primitive sentences; production of sentences, nonverbal manipulation; crying, whining, repetition, abstract language to project and anticipate role playing and imitation; use of social routines appropriate to situation; preverbal concepts used as organizing schemes.	Formation of role systems underlying sentences, complex perception processes underlying utterances; differentiated role experiences in family serves as cue to social responses.
Early elementary Four—nine years	Use of stylized social routines; communication adjusted to overt demands of others and apparent demands of situations; linguistic self-references; socialized participation in games.	Symbolic awareness of others as potentially capable of responses; abstract awareness of situational demands; symbolic awareness of self precipitated through feelings of shame and guilt.
Middle school Eight—fourteen	Symbolic, conceptual use of language; abstract vocabulary; calculated use of stylized routines.	Cognitive capacity to de-center and maintain dual perspective (see page 51).
Adolescent to adulthood	Symbolic perception of self; communication consciously adapted to the view of others, and done for a purpose.	

an examination of how the child learns to influence events through talk
directed at shaping the behavior of others around him.

The Development of Rhetorical Capability. A Sociocultural View.
The sociocultural theory of communication development deals with
the impact of group experiences on the development of the child's
communication potentials. The model underlying this theory is that of
a problem-solving, task-oriented small group. Role, or the system of
behaviors used by people as they engage in various tasks confronting
the group, is the basic focus of this theory.

Basically, the group is viewed as a social system in which
individuals are aware of and respond to each other as they
communicate about problems of the group. It is necessary, at this point,
to outline some general propositions which are characteristic of groups
as social systems.

The group is sensitive to pressures exerted by individuals within the
group. People actively seek recognition and security within a group.
People also frequently resist group pressures and violate norms of the
group, and this behavior results in tension and conflict. Thus, what one
member of the group does affects the actions of other members.
Individual roles are interdependent. A change in one individual's
status, demands, expectations, or actions necessitates adjustments from
other members of the group. If our goal is to encourage significant
behavior changes in the people in a group, we must consider the
importance of this role interdependence. Related to the classroom,
what is implied is that a deliberate and calculated change in the
behavior of one individual in the group (teacher) is capable of
encouraging adjustment of the other members of the group (students).

The teacher can help students change their communication style by
altering his own. For example, as he shifts from an authoritarian style,
where he questions and students answer, to a posture of democratic
group leader, students must necessarily assume more responsibility for
talk. If a child is not seen as influential by his peers, the teacher may
slide him into a leadership role, so that his associates must respond to
his new role by changing response to him. The assumption is that any
change on the part of a member of a social system will evoke responsive
changes by other members.

Another way of looking at the dynamics underlying performance of
group members is to think in terms of four essential features that are
characteristic of any group system: structure, process, norms, and
goals. Group structure refers to the way individuals are organized in
the group as leaders and followers, parents and children, managers and
workers, and so on. The position of one individual in the group defines
the position of the others in relation to him. The position each
individual assumes in the group has both formal and informal

characteristics. Formal characteristics are legislated and enforced by those who take responsibility by law or tradition for the group. For example, parents are required by law to fulfill certain responsibilities toward their children, such as financial support. Family tradition also requires certain behaviors, like the periodic trip to the zoo.

Informal characteristics emerge as individuals seek to incorporate individual differences into their group roles. This means that formal requirements of a position or role are modified to fit the particular individual who fills the position. For example, a teacher finds that he doesn't have to conform exactly to policy the way it is stated, for to do so would make life uncomfortable for his students. Or, at home, a child discovers that there are times when he can have influence over the decisions his parents make, although this is not often the case. The informal features of group structure enable each person to put a personal stamp on the role he plays in relation to others in the group. This concept of structure is of particular significance in our study of communicative development, since children spend most of their early group experiences playing roles or following scripts prepared by others. What the child learns in this phase is very valuable to him later on, for it forms the background substance out of which he may develop rhetorical skill.

Group process refers to the ongoing action and reaction of members toward each other and of the group as a whole toward external pressures. Process can be seen in the various verbal and nonverbal signals and symbols used in organizing member behavior to solve group problems. The effects of this behavior can be supportive or destructive to other members of the group; they can contribute or detract from the group's solution of problems. Teachers often set group process norms in the classroom without realizing it or without paying much attention to possible positive or negative results. In a later chapter, we will note how classroom climate can be constructed to help facilitate positive group process.

Norms emerge when members show consistent behavior according to the expectations of other members. Often, people who seek to change the behavior of other members in the group overlook the strength of group norms. Without careful consideration and planning, it is exceedingly difficult to inhibit or deflect the influence of group norms on a group's members. The teacher, therefore, should give careful thought to the planning and directing of norms in the classroom for oral-communication-skill development. He must take into account, particularly, the kinds of norm behaviors that are essential to the child in order for him to survive in the groups to which he belongs, and be careful that what he is asked to do in the classroom does not jeopardize important roles he may play elsewhere. Often, for example, to single out a child for praise or criticism may subject him to ridicule from peers.

Structure, process, and norms all relate to group goals. Group goals can be identified in the consequences of actions taken by individuals in the group toward one another and by the group toward external forces. Work groups, social groups, learning groups, and therapy groups differ in function. Depending on the purpose of a particular group, the outcome of behavior will be altered. Furthermore, the demands made on individuals in the group will vary along with expectations of individuals toward each other and toward the group as a whole. In the classroom, for instance, children could discuss what happens when a new child moves into the neighborhood and how he begins to make new friends. How does it feel to be new? How would you want to be treated by others? How does a group of friends who play together welcome a new person? Questions like these can help stimulate understanding of norms, rules, and roles.

In our look at group goals in the sociocultural model, it is important to understand the importance of role. Role consists of those actions performed by people toward one another and toward their work. If we look at the requirements of a certain group of people, we will see that roles may be adjusted to meet the needs and talents of the individual, or the individual may find it necessary to adjust himself to the roles available to him. Role includes behaviors necessary to maintain both the formal and informal requirements of a position in a group.

The role one person takes affects the roles taken by others in the group. Roles are acted out with an awareness of and an expectation toward others in the group. When role expectations are thwarted, the whole structure and function of a group can be jeopardized. Thus, when teacher changes his role and "becomes one of the boys," or changes from permissive to authoritarian, each of his students must make some kind of adjustment in his role in response.

We can summarize the major features of role behavior as follows:

1. People take roles that are expected of them by other members in a group.

2. Taking of roles implies an obligation and responsibility of individuals toward one another in a group.

3. Role taking provides a basic source of identity of individuals in a group.

4. Role performance is a basis from which communication skills are developed by the individuals in a group.

In the sociocultural model, our concern is with the important influences of primary group experiences on the communicative development of the child. These primary group contacts teach the child how to communicate; at the same time, they encourage the child to develop specific ways of thinking about himself and others in the group. Roles also serve as goals. Much use of talk is directed toward persuading others to view us in a particular role. In most cases, the skills acquired by the child in the family are useful to him in group contacts outside the family. In some instances, however, the child's family may deviate from group norms, and the child experiences difficulty in fitting himself into roles outside the family.

Role experience with family, perhaps, has the most profound impact on the child's communicative development. As a social system, the family has essentially two tasks to resolve. The first is survival as a unit and as a social system. Structure, pattern, role systems, and linguistic codes help to assist each family in maintaining itself. But self-maintenance doesn't necessarily imply movement toward comfort, security, stability, or health. Frequently family roles operate at the expense of individuals in the family or at the expense of the family as a system. Despite these problems, members of a family generally think that "their way is best."

When a family experiences economic, political, or social pressures from the outside, or when there are psychological pressures from within, adjustments need to be made. These adjustments are focused on the division of labor and management of interpersonal relations in the family. Interpersonal relationships are negotiated to provide a reference point for family members which determine where they stand in relation to other family members. Relationships enable the members to determine position in the family "pecking order" and to justify and even encourage feelings of "in-ness" and "out-ness." They also function to establish and maintain channels for giving and receiving affection, intimacy, and trust.

The second task facing the family is not often felt until someone in the family encounters conflict with someone outside the group. When this type of situation occurs, it is necessary for the family to prepare for effective role performance in the social, political, and economic realms of the larger group, society. Effective role performance must be learned by the children in particular.

In the sociocultural model, communication skills, including the child's learning of language, are developed as a natural result of his fitting into various roles in the family system. As the child gains experience and becomes sensitive to the potentials available in his family, he may also enhance his communicative development by experimenting with assigned roles. He may test limits he feels others have put on his role and actually role play the positions of the others.

The child's capacity for imitation, symbolic play, and fantasy assist him in developing a repertoire of roles appropriate for performance in the family. At least five years of the child's life are spent exclusively negotiating roles that have been structured by the expectations of other family members, both deliberately and unconsciously. Older siblings, parents, relatives, children and adults in the immediate neighborhood, as well as substitute caretakers (babysitters, teachers) project role possibilities to the child. Potentials of these roles significantly affect the communication skills the child develops, for he will communicate as his role dictates. Thus, altering role will necessarily result in altering communication. For the teacher, this proposition has great importance, for it means that improvement in communication must come about within the child as a result of role change, rather than change directed externally by the teacher. Alteration of role offers a child potential for sharing of information and exchange of personal points of view, for participating in decision-making processes of the group, for trying on and earning the consequences of taking new roles in the group, and for creative involvement including recreation and close relationship building with others in the group.

These potentials are inherent in most social systems. The extent to which they are realized and applied in the maintenance of a particular family system varies in relation to the number of individuals in the system. The regularity with which individuals interact in the system and the length of time individuals spend with each other in interaction are important influences. The flexibility of the underlying role system, including sensitivity to individual differences, and the nature of the controls, including rewards, punishments, and sanctions operating in the family system, are also influential in shaping the family system.

It has been suggested that the child's socialization is almost exclusively directed toward the resolution of immediate problems and conflicts within the family. Pressures are imposed upon the child by parents and older siblings for increased mastery of assigned roles and norms in the family unit. According to this theory, the child emerges in the family as posing a series of tasks to be resolved so that the system will be maintained.

The relationship between infant and mother is the first instance of role performance of the child. Much has been written about the mother's contribution to the personality development of the infant. The most significant determinant of the infant's adjustment seems to be the attitude that the mother takes toward her role and its effect on the child. One specialist notes that the infant is not humanized by being fed, changed, or picked up when he feels need. He is humanized by finding out that his crying brings relief from others in accordance with his timing: that his smile evokes a parallel or otherwise appropriate response from his mother. It is the socialization process that humanizes the infant more than any particular actions toward him.

For the infant, the consequences of interacting with the mother result in the development of a coping style; patterns emerge from the mutual influence of mother and infant. In early infancy, patterns are dominated by the child's own constitutional tendencies. Environment then begins to exert an influence. The child must now cope with the roles of others as well as with his body needs. Eventually the child learns to cope with winning and losing in relationships. This process is described in detail in Chapter 5.

It is suggested that a major shift in the child's position in the family occurs as he moves from his exclusive relationship with his mother to relationships with other family members. It is in this transition that the child becomes aware of role functions. The nuclear family is differentiated according to task assignments and status positions in the family. Parents are viewed as superior in status. Their concerns are with tasks and interpersonal relations essential for the maintenance of the family as a unit. Siblings, to a greater or lesser degree, participate in the fulfillment of roles related to those assumed by the parents.

The child's success in performing his assigned roles within the family is derived from his mastery of the communication skills essential to those roles. Part of this mastery includes performing roles from the perspective of other family members, roles which the child learns to internalize. When the child learns appropriate communication skills and role performance, he receives symbolic rewards from other family members. These rewards are incorporated into his emerging identity and enhance his self esteem, for he knows where he fits. The child's ability to form linguistic identity and to use it as a link between himself and society is seen as an important potential source of autonomy. The child, as he learns language, learns the importance of the spoken word to his survival. Language identifies the child as an individual; it defines him as a person responded to by other people. It is the medium through which the child receives positive or negative responses that affect his identity. The child learns to take on responsibility for what he says as he realizes the importance of language to his identity. He becomes more involved in relationships with others and develops a clearer perception of certain aspects of the world around him.

Basically, the identity the child develops within the family is his basis for negotiating interpersonal relationships in groups outside the family, particularly in school. We can summarize the contributions of the family to the child's potential for the development of a communication orientation as follows: *To the extent that the family's linguistic orientation encourages the child's experimentation with alternatives in his performance of assigned roles, he will learn to search for and select from alternative means of influence.* As a consequence, he will be encouraged to view the communication situation from an abstract rather than an immediate perspective. This means that the child can learn to deal with verbal meanings in a variety of situations and contexts when he is encouraged to experiment with role performance, *but he is restricted in verbal learning when role performance is restricted.*

Patterns of decision-making within the family influence the child's ability to exercise choice in determining how he participates. In one method of family decision-making, there is a clear separation of roles determined by status of family members. Because of this delineation of roles, communication among family members is rigid and restricted. In another method of decision-making, there is no clear separation of roles within the family. The child, for instance, can choose his preferred mode of participation, for status is of minimal concern in role performance. Because of role flexibility, the communication among family members is more open, not subject to constraint by assigned roles.

In the family with role choice, the child is encouraged to seek alternative roles when he fails. If he has attempted a coercive role, he is not locked into it by defeat, but is encouraged to select a more cooperative, contributive role. When the roles are restricted and assigned, the child who fails has little recourse other than to project frustration toward the parents who have higher status. The operation of role performance and role adaptations due to failure and success takes place through language, for the most part. In a family where the child is not encouraged to experiment with role, he is also not encouraged to experiment with language. Thus, he does not develop the range of alternative behaviors needed in his relationships outside the family unit. This is of very great importance for the classroom teacher who will need to maintain the possibility of alternatives open at all times, so that inevitable occasional failure does not lead to a feeling of generalized failure. Given that each child will fail at something, sometime, it is useful and productive to maintain the possibility for the child to take other roles that are potentially more rewarding to him.

Communication within a family can be examined through the method of control used in it to direct actions and talk of members. One way of examining control is to note differences in handling discipline and directives for role performance. One approach is the imperative form of control that reduces the child's role options and limits the possibilities to rebellion and withdrawal. This approach is carried out through a restricted language code, for example, "shut up," "don't," or "stop it!" A second approach is the appeal form of control which regulates the child's behavior according to varying degrees of discretion. Appeals show the child that his unique feelings are understood, for example, "I know it is hard for you, but reading this will help you learn about your pet fish." By using the system of appeals, the child is provided an alternative to resistance, since role restrictions are lessened. It is not so necessary that the child fight back. On the other hand, the child influenced by imperative forms of control is offered little opportunity to learn to exercise choice or to search for linguistic alternatives in dealing with others. The classroom teacher can build a more effective program for himself and his students by providing a maximum of possible linguistic alternatives through maintaining the widest possible choice of roles in his classroom.

Such efforts might center on formal training in styles of seeking control. The teacher must understand that attempts by the child to influence others are based on what he has learned previously. However, his natural style may be counter to the norms of the group and thus render him ineffective in his efforts to influence others. As we see communication as goal seeking and purposive, excessive interpersonal defeat can teach a child that he is unworthy, injure his self-esteem, and either impel him to activity potentially injurious to others or cause him to withdraw.

We can summarize the sociocultural view of communicative development in the following propositions.

1. Socializing agents teach the child potentially effective means for communicating with particular social units. The language of the adult contains the raw materials from which the child can develop his linguistic pattern and his store of verbal concepts. As the adult interacts with, toward, and before the child, and as the child observes how others are directed in the solution of problems, he learns the rituals and routines appropriate for communication within the family and in the classroom.

2. The methods employed to direct the child and those the child observes to direct others eventually become the means the child uses for communication, self-stimulation, and self-control. In other words, the way adults conceptualize and use language encourages a similar conceptualization and use by the child when he is independent of the family. If the child is exposed to rigidity, he will tend to become rigid in his own behavior. In a rigidly run classroom, the only alternatives for a frustrated child are opposition or withdrawal. The other children will suffer dissonance. They may comply with the teacher's will out of fear, but they will not necessarily internalize the important material the teacher presents to them.

3. Symbolic interaction with adults enables the child to develop a socialized (dual) perspective and sense of identity. The child has opportunities to experiment with the roles required of him to a greater or lesser extent. Through this experimentation, he develops a greater

awareness of his uniqueness and self-worth and constructs linguistic references, thus offering him the potential for influencing others. As the child's symbolic self-awareness grows, he attempts a corresponding symbolic adjustment to those with whom he communicates. It is through this process that abstract communicative perspectives appear. If the child is to learn productive communication, he must have experiences which tell him he is capable of using oral language to attain his objectives. This he does by learning skills in group relations from which may come skills of rhetorical communication. Among the basic skills the child needs are awareness of reinforcement and stimulation as it operates within the family, so that he can engage in the same type of learning in the classroom. Further, he must acquire the ability to use language in thinking and communicating. If he does not acquire this skill at home, then the classroom must remedy the deficiency. It cannot be assumed that any given child will be able to use language in a learning paradigm. Additionally, he needs to know the differentiated use of language in the performance of both assigned and optional social roles. In the classroom, he must know what is absolutely ruled out, and what his options are about what is ruled in. Finally, the child needs to master the use of verbal concepts to elaborate and organize thinking and communicating. In the classroom he must not get the idea that his communication is a skill separate from his other activities. He must learn to speak, listen, read, and write to implement learning rather than as skills to be learned for their own sake.

These skills underlie thinking and communicating required of all humans. The classroom, therefore, cannot afford to convey the idea that any aspect of communication is an isolated skill. We learn to speak and listen, read and write, in order to partake in communication with the past, influence the future, and cope with our daily lives. Thus, all instruction in communication must focus on purpose: What the student can accomplish with it. It is this kind of approach that affords maximum carry-over. Through learning communication to a purpose, the child may see himself as capable of influencing what happens around him. He acquires a sense of competency. Without this sense of competency, the developing human cannot participate with and negotiate well with others and thus faces the possibility of emotional disturbances.

We have devoted considerable space to our discussion of the sociocultural approach to the problem of communication learning, largely because it is the most pertinent to the activity of the classroom teacher. While it is useful to know how the child develops biologically, there is little the teacher can do about it. Even though he can do little to modify the effects of biology and previous growth, he can manipulate the environment in which the child learns, so that the most positive sociocultural influences possible pervade the child's environment, as he confronts learning to use communication as a means of social control.

LEARNING SOCIAL CONTROL—EMERGENCE OF RHETORIC

The most distinctive characteristic of rhetorical communication derives from the student's ability to establish and maintain an *abstract dual perspective*. (See the chart on page 41.) This perspective represents his ability to behave symbolically toward others. It allows him to conceptualize himself as a potential source of influence and to select and adapt alternative communications to people and situations.

Developmentally, the acquisition of rhetorical perspective represents the child's shift from egocentrism to a socialized perception of himself and those with whom he communicates. This dual perspective allows him to compensate for some of his biases and weaknesses and to understand that other people have feelings and thoughts similar to his. It is the ability not only to think and act, but to judge the thought and action and to monitor choices, that aids the child's growth as a communicator. This dual perspective also enables the child to place himself symbolically in the position and state of mind of other people and to be able to judge the world from different perspectives. Once he is able to do this, he is able to exert rhetoric, that is, he can employ language to organize people and events to behave in somewhat similar fashion to the way he would like them to behave. He is able to function as a relevant adult, exerting his share of influence on his own destiny.

In this chapter, we have noted that changes in language development occur as the child is provided with opportunities to experiment with social roles, as he receives symbolic evaluations of his performance of roles, and as he develops a capacity for imitation, play, and role taking. We have also suggested that while biology influences the capacity to grow, the child will not grow according to expectations unless he is provided with proper stimuli and opportunities to experiment with change.

Cognitive developments which enable the child to imitate, play, and participate in games and socializations also contribute to the development of an abstract communicative perspective. One expert suggests that play and imitation in infancy provide the rudiments of a similar symbolic functioning in later life. Thus, we can expect the growing child, as well as the adult, to continue to model behavior around the relevant people he finds in life.

In play, the child is able to create experience on his own terms; he can experiment with various roles in a judgement-free context.

Imitation, initially seen in action gradually becomes internalized so that the child can take the role of another person in thought. Eventually, the child will be able to select what he wants from various people, and thus will become an independent maker of symbols able to use language as he needs to, to exert the influence he desires. Eventually, in thought, the child will become capable of distinguishing between his own views and the views of others. Many scholars have noted that organized play, games, and appropriate learning experiences are as significant a means for encouraging the child to become more sensitive to social situations and the perspectives of people in them as is training in the family. The child's goal, of course, is to be able to assume the roles necessary for him.

Throughout experience, the child continues to learn that the game of communication is won and its integrity preserved to the extent that he can anticipate and perform according to the expectations of others. He learns, in short, that *he must give something to the other in order to gain what he wants.* He becomes, in that sense, a functioning persuader, using rhetoric to influence and responding to a rhetoric designed to influence him. It is in the exchange of rhetorics that communication reaches full maturity for him.

The classroom provides the basic milieu in which the student learns to use rhetoric. The teacher, by exerting his own rhetoric, provides a model to emulate, exactly as the student learned what he knew before entering school through the exchange of rhetoric in his family. It is for this reason that the behavior of the teacher influences communication behavior of the student in all contexts. If we are particularly interested in learning, then it must be regarded as a real situation and not separated from the natural learning of communication behavior in other aspects of the student's life.

SUMMARY

Communication affects the identity and goals of the child. When linguistically and conceptually ready to handle social contacts with others, the child learns that his communication experiences with others have an influence on him. From this, he learns something about what he needs from others and some ways to attain these needs through talk.

When the child enters school, however, he may not have experienced full conceptual development or exposure to enough communication roles to understand how communication can function for and against him. In some instructional settings, he may not have developed linguistic capacities to understand much at all. For these reasons, the teacher cannot assume too much about the communication skill development of his students. He needs to assess their communication behaviors in line with explanation of linguistic, conceptual, and sociocultural theories in order to understand the needs and goals of his students. Subsequent instruction needs to be carried out in conjunction with student needs, for without this rhetorical approach, students see little connection between the classroom and the outside world.

WORKS CITED:

Axline, Virginia. *Play Therapy*. Boston: Houghton Mifflin, Co., 1047.

Berko, Roy. *Speech Programs at Coeducational Community Colleges*. 1971. Unpublished Ph.D. Dissertation, Pennsylvania State University. Department of Speech.

Brown, Roger, and Bellugi, Ursula. "Three Processes in the Child's Acquisition of Syntax," in *New Directions in the Study of Language*, Lenneberg, ed. Cambridge, Mass.; The MIT Press, 1964.

Church, Joseph. *Language and the Discovery of Reality*. New York.: Random House, 1961.

Dunham, Robert, "Speech Education in Pennsylvania High Schools." *Penna Speech Annual*, 22 (September 1965) pp. 56–69.

Hess, Robert D., and Shipman, Virginia. "Early Experience and the Socialization of Cognitive Modes in Children." *Child Development*, 36 (1965) pp. 869–886.

Lenneberg, Eric. *The Biological Foundations of Language*. New York.: John Wiley & Sons, 1967.

McNeill, David. *The Acquisition of Language*. New York.: Harper & Row, 1970.

Murphy, Lois. *The Widening World of Childhood*. New York: Basic Books, 1962.

Sarbin, Theodore, "Role Theory" in *Handbook of Social Psychology*, G. Lindzay, ed. Reading, Mass.: Addison-Wesley, 1954.

Walwick, Paul A. "The Status of Speech Instruction in the Elementary School." Ed. D. dissertation, the Pennsylvania State University, Department of Speech, 1967.

Weir, Ruth. *Language in the Crib*. The Hague: Mouton and Co., 1962.

WORKS RECOMMENDED:

For a contemporary view of the role of speech in general education see Gerald Phillips, et. al., *The Development of Oral Communication in the Classroom*. New York: Bobbs-Merrill, 1970.

For a comprehensive discussion of the role of the student in contemporary school setting see Carl Nordstrom and Edgar Friedenberg. *Society's Children.* New York: Random House, 1967.

For a description of and procedure for studying the various dimensions of language and communicative behavior in children see Dan Slobin, ed. *A Field Manual for Cross Cultural Study of the Acquisition of Communicative Competence.* Language-Behavior Research Laboratory, University of California, Berkeley, California, 94720.

●To learn that there are five basic competencies which comprise maturity in rhetorical skill.

●To note that a child's ability to produce and discriminate speech sounds doesn't necessarily equip him for mature communication.

●To outline the stages of language development of the child and note propositions derived from them.

●To note that the most important aspect of elementary school is the socialization process which takes place (helping the child learn to take the perspective of another person).

●To look at the development of message strategy in the child.

●To present the stages of role taking ability in the child.

●To introduce interrelatedness of communication forms.

3
CHILD LANGUAGE DEVELOPMENT

Overview

In this chapter you are introduced to a new view of communication development. The concern here is with the growing child and how he uses language to accomplish his purposes, and what this means to the classroom teacher. Perhaps you are going to teach in a secondary language arts program and so believe you do not need this information. Don't be so sure! In order to diagnose speech needs of students on any level, you will have to understand how humans develop. Thus, the material in this chapter will provide the basic diagnostics you will need to perform an appropriate evaluation of student performance.

In addition to all this, your understanding of rhetoric and how it grows should be increased by reading these pages. Instead of focusing on development of sounds and sentences, we are concerned with development of strategy and use. This represents still another criterion against which you can judge speakers. We offer the concept of communication maturity as a guide to what is possible on any level, elementary, secondary, or college. The attributes of the mature communicator can serve as a set of goals for your own communication growth, as well as for your teaching.

PRIMARILY, this book is concerned with the development of rhetorical skills in mature communicators. Understanding the concept of a mature communicator is helpful both to elementary and secondary teachers. The elementary teacher must be concerned, for frequently, his students are not fully mature and are, therefore, limited in some of the possibilities of instruction. For the secondary teacher, the concept of maturity provides a diagnostic around which the teacher can work. Holding a normal expectation in view, a curriculum can be designed. Those students who seem unable to achieve the goals specified in the curriculum might be candidates for additional training. They may, however, also be candidates for remedial work so that they can be helped to develop to maturity. As we seek, in this chapter, to discover how language develops in the child, we need the concept of mature communicator to define the end point of our study.

As the child progresses from infancy to adulthood, he develops five basic competencies which, together, might add up to mature rhetorical ability.

1. Role-taking ability

2. Situational awareness

3. Message flexibility

4. Sensitivity to response

5. Symbolic, conceptual, and linguistic resources

Role Taking. The mature communicator is able to put himself in the position of the other person and conceptualize a communication situation with himself acting as other. He is able to think through or fantasize how the other person would behave and thus be able to devise units of talk designed to appeal to that other. Even though, on occasion, an individual may lack experience with a particular person or type of person, he can use information gathered from experience to assist in planning subsequent engagements. Without the ability to take the role of the other, development of rhetorical skill is impossible.

Situational Awareness. The mature communicator understands the limitations that situational norms place on his behavior. He understands the difference between public and private communications, is aware of the concept of "intimacy," and can judge what is appropriate in a given case with a particular person. He is also able to respond critically to communications directed at him and make judgments about their propriety. Rhetorical skill is heavily dependent on the ability to assess the requirements and limitations of social situations.

Message Flexibility. The mature communicator can identify message purposes. He is able to establish hypotheses about the possible effects of a method and select a mode in which to offer it; to make a request, to explain, to argue. If he does not receive the desired response, he is able to use the information to prepare and correct subsequent messages.

Sensitivity to Response. The mature communicator is aware that communication is not a linear process and that his message must adapt to the responses he receives. He is aware that the person to whom he speaks is also seeking to accomplish goals with his talk, and is therefore willing and able to "negotiate" topics, purposes, and effects. Mature communication is characterized by responsiveness. Anticipation of response and ability to adapt to it is imperative in developing rhetorical skill.

Symbolic, Conceptual, and Linguistic Resources. The mature communicator has an adequate vocabulary to serve as a supply of words applicable to particular audiences and occasions. He is able to put images and symbols together to form thought units, and he is able to connect symbols together in acceptable order so that they are intelligible to others. The substance of rhetoric is a thought unit, constructed linguistically and phrased adequately in symbols.

The mature communicator, therefore, is a person who has social sensitivity, the ability to use memory, and tools with which to proceed. As we observe the child develop language skills, we need to examine how he adapts to others in various social situations, how he utilizes information he receives from experience, and what sort of equipment he has with which to put together messages.

Traditionally, the study of speech development has emphasized the production of sounds by the child, from the birth cry to the emergence of the ability to manage double and triple consonant blends around the age of eight. While this is interesting in its own right, and of particular importance to parents and speech therapists, the ability to produce and discriminate speech sounds does not necessarily enable the child to function as a mature communicator. It is when the child is able to utilize the sounds to put together influential remarks in interpersonal situations that speech becomes an act that has some consequence.

For the most part, elementary language-arts teachers receive a great deal of information and curricular materials devoted to the appropriate development of the sounds so that correctives can be administered where necessary. There is little information available on how to guide the small child through experiences which might help him extend his social awareness and test his skill at altering the behavior of others through the use of the spoken word. Even public recitations like "show and tell," are sufficiently ritualized so that the child may focus on the correct production of sounds rather than on the communication of a message that has some impact on the listeners. Our main concern in this chapter is with making the translation from the focus on phonetic skill to the use of the mastered phonemes in purposive speech.

For the past fifty years, the literature on speech development was confined to the study of speech-sound production. The description of how the child spoke his language, together with nonlanguage modes of influence, was ignored, overshadowed by concentration on precise descriptions of the *form* of the language used; how the child pronounced his words, and how he fitted them together to form sentences. Speech as action used to influence others, to achieve goals, to satisfy basic needs received no systematic attention.

The need for such description was understood, however. In 1930, one authority wrote:

> For what purpose does the child talk? What does he satisfy by the use of verbal responses? In what situations are verbal responses brought forth, what kinds of responses are used in these various situations and what changes do these responses show as the child grows older?

Thirty years later another authority chose to respond to similar questions for studies "of the manner in which children learn to control situations by language." Today, there is a glimmering of concern about the rhetorical development of the child, what he says and for what purpose.

Even so, with a budding interest in "rhetorical communication," the bulk of the studies done today on child language pertain to form, not content. Most studies deal with phonology, syntax, semantics, and the relationship between speech and thought. A small body of literature has been produced on what is known as "pragmatics" of communication. This new literature offers some insight into how the child employs speech as goal-directed action. Some of the main examples will be discussed later in this chapter. To date, however, what is known about rhetorical development is quite scanty.

Research interests tend to run in waves. In the more recent past linguistic theory represented the basis for most studies. Scholars attempted to discover how linguistic competence developed. A reconceptualization of linguistic competence into "competence for use" provides the impetus for new kinds of inquiries into the communicative development of the child. Dell Hymes has suggested that theorists "have to account for the fact that a normal child acquires knowledge of sentences not only as grammatical but also as appropriate. . . . There are rules of use without which the rules of grammar would be useless." In 1968, the New Orleans Conference of the Speech Association of America set as a research priority the understanding of the rules of communication competence; "that part of his understanding of the rules of communication which enables him to tell when and in what manner he can apply linguistic rules to communication strategies."

The substance of this chapter is an effort made by the authors to approach language development in a new way. We have based our effort on our contact with classroom teachers. It is our view that research about learning and schooling ought to be useful to teachers, and that teachers ought to know enough about research in order to investigate their own classroom problems. While precise descriptions of the development of phonemes and syntax are interesting in our understanding of children, it is the verbal behavior of the child that is most pertinent to the typical classroom teacher. We will try, in this chapter, to summarize language development as rhetorical behavior in mature communicators. Because of the limited amount of research available, each teacher will have to rely on his own research efforts to apply some of the material we offer. What is most important to know is how the child learns to understand situations, limitations, the roles of others, and himself so that he can integrate all of them into communicative action for a purpose. Once this is known the teacher can apply his understanding to his own rhetorical behavior.

STAGES OF DEVELOPMENT

Language development is commonly approached through stages. Stages are a convenient way to study developing language, since there are appearances of important abilities at relatively precise times of life. We have already noted in the previous chapter that it is difficult to deal with development of rhetorical control until the basic development of language has taken place. Teachers need to take care that their expectations for behavior in a child do not exceed his developmental level.

The traditional stages offered by most of the literature are infancy, early childhood, preschool, elementary-primary, elementary-intermediate, middle school, adolescence, and adulthood. In each case, the acquisition of skill relates to the ability to take on some new challenge or perform some new life task. What we expect from the child concords with his level of development. We do not expect the child to make conversation until he has grammar. We do not expect grammatical sentences until he has words, and so on.

Infancy is considered a prelinguistic period. From the beginning, however, the child is sensitive to human signals around him. He is interested in the "noises" produced by others; he can apprehend highs and lows, louds and softs, and thus he can, at some point, develop a conception of rhythm and intonation. In his own behavior he develops an extensive repertoire of sounds. While many theorists regard these sounds as manifestations of physiological states rather than a practice period getting ready for articulate speech, there seems to be a relationship between the sounds produced by the infant and the sounds produced by adults around him, so that during the first six months he is able to localize sounds, to distinguish between voice and other sounds, to respond to the vocal qualities of familiar and unfamiliar voices, and to respond to the intonation and affective cues in human sounds directed toward him. Thus, while the infant's sounds may be "accidental" in that they are associated with various stages of physiological development, at some point they become associated with other sounds around him so that he begins to understand some basic linguistic relationships.

For example, in addition to crying and noncrying vocalizations, infants have been observed to communicate through movement and gesture patterns, reaching, touching, grasping, visual following, and the use of the smile as a releaser of attention. We could hypothesize a parallel development sometime during the prelinguistic period. The child somehow learns that movements on his part have the capacity to influence movements on the part of others. We might conjecture that crying begins as an undefined behavior but then becomes defined after time, so that when appropriate responses are made, food given, clothing changed, and so forth, the cry takes on a specific character as a request for a specific service.

We must remember, however, that the child does not have a sense of self. We are confronted with a "chicken-egg" problem, for we hypothesize that self does not emerge until the child can use symbols, but the child cannot use symbols unless there is some sense of self. Without attempting to reconcile this problem, there is no question but what most infants learn that there is a relationship between sounds emitted from the mouth and behaviors in the environment. Infants also learn that there are characteristic sounds, as well as sights, associated with most objects in the environment. Out of these learnings emerges the capacity to become linguistic.

Infancy can be looked on as a time of readiness. The infant develops the muscles needed for walking, climbing, using fingers. He learns to focus his eyes, to respond to smells and tastes. His auditory and vocal developments are part of a developmental package which gets him ready for learning experiences.

As a toddler, a creature who can move rapidly up and down, around, and frequently into objects, the child can explore and seek experiences. He does not have to wait for some accident to put him into contact with something that interests him; he may move about and seek that contact. He begins to learn that he has some control, that there are willed decisions that he can make. He can "go it alone," and scare the daylights out of the adults around him, for he does not know the consequences of touching most of the objects he seeks to contact. Adult humans take care to protect him. They take elaborate precautions to see that his bumps will not be too severe, that he will not burn his fingers or cut his hands. To enforce the prohibitions, strong vocal support is needed. There are the "don't's" and the "no's!" associated often with physical movement that help to shape the child's orientation to the spoken word. Communication as legislation is introduced. The child gets "information" from the various shouts from the adults around him and he is helped to respond, often with tugs, pushes, shoves, and a variety of daring rescues.

What is most important is that the legislation is not one-sided. Most parents are concerned that their toddler have experience and learn about his world, and so they make reciprocal adjustments in their behavior in response to the cues the child gives them. The ways and means of reciprocal adjustment vary from culture to culture, from family to family, and even from child to child in the same family. In each case, there is some sort of timetable organized around the child based on who takes care of certain needs, in certain ways. The infant-toddler signals his state of being and is, in turn, responsive to the irritability and pleasure states communicated by the people who care for him. As the toddler becomes more mobile, he gets more messages. As he becomes more concerned with exploring his environment and begins to develop wants, it is necessary for him to give off more messages. The child-in-motion is a threat to the territory of the others around him, and therefore, he must learn to understand a "people game," which has a great deal to do with what is mine and what is yours and what is permissible and what is not.

With all of this development in locomotor power and increased independence comes a new word-making skill. This skill, observed in presleep and early morning self-talk of toddlers in the crib, is of very great importance to the child. It is a tool for commanding attention and producing responses. Well used, it gets the toddler at least some of what he seeks from his environment. It may deny him the attractive bottle, but it may award him some cuddling affection; the use of words makes him a linguistic being, though still preconceptual. For example, a child of two may have a vocabulary of twenty words, including some combinations, but his language is not yet symbolic, for he is not able to deal with abstractions.

Nevertheless, his language serves some uses for him. He can direct some behaviors in others, he can point to things that interest him and make simple requests. During the period from eighteen months to his third birthday, he will add about 400 words. During this time, he begins to make patterns out of his words. At one year he uses single words, often as imperatives. By fourteen months he can make two-word phrases, and many children use three-word phrases by the time of the second birthday. By the age of three, the child can make four-word sentences, conforming to some extent with the grammar we expect.

What is most important in this stage is that the child is becoming a linguistic being, both by acquiring rules of language use and by seeking out communication contact. He wants to know how words and things go together.

The preschool child extends his language contact to familiar and unfamiliar people, and tries out new situations. Between two and three, the child begins to learn to adapt. "She's never this way at home," says mother, indicating that her daughter has learned that proprieties observed in the home may be avoided elsewhere. Specific kinds of responses to mother and father, the siblings, the relatives, strangers, begin to develop. The child begins to learn situational behavior. As the child sheds diapers and adopts the rigid bowel mores of the adult world, he begins to learn that the way he handles his conversation makes a difference also. Much of what the child does is imitative. During this stage, he may reveal inadequacies in early training.

From age three to five, communication is still preconceptual, although the capacity to visualize situations is beginning to develop. For the most part, language and meaning are bound to the immediate situation. Adults watching and listening to a child at this stage will probably not be able to understand much of his talk, for the child acts as though adults are completely familiar with his environment. But along with this, the child is learning to question, to obtain information, and to take turns in conversation. The preschooler can imitate; he can handle house talk, telephone talk, doctor talk, *if he has been exposed to it.* In becoming a mature communicator, the child may often be handicapped by lack of experience with talk at this early stage. Many adults respond to new situations in childlike fashion, as will be noted later on when we discuss some of the disabilities in communication that affect adults.

The imitative process also helps inculcate the glimmerings of a strategic awareness in the child. He is able to call names, to pretend to engage in verbal conflict, though he may not understand rule following behavior and negotiation. His growth in vocabulary is amazing. His 400 words at age two become approximately 1500 by age four and a half. He is able to articulate more than 80 percent of the sounds in his language correctly, and put together sentences of five and six words observing rules of grammer as he has been exposed to them. Sometimes, he will show his preconceptual state by using such constructions as "I comed," "he goed," and "my footses."

THE ABSTRACT COMMUNICATION PERSPECTIVE

This is the child who will enter kindergarten. He will be regarded at the moment of his entry into school as having sufficient abilities to take orders, ask questions, perform tasks, recite, participate in group activity, etc. The purpose of the school is to teach him how to do these things, and it assumed that his language is adequate to the task. Although there are many allowances that can be made for language deficiencies in the elementary grades, it is presumed that the child will be able to take an abstract communication perspective with his talk, for without this, the child is unable to meet the requirements of school.

The acquisition of abstract communication perspective can be seen as the child shifts from self-centered involvement in his own point of view, to the exclusion of others, to a socialized perception of himself and those with whom he communicates. Presumably, to have an abstract communication perspective means to have an "I" and to be able to conceptualize about the behavior of that "I" at future times and in other situations.

The process of socialization together with acquisition of symbols useful in the socialization process represents the foundation of the capacity to make rhetoric. In development, conceptual, linguistic and strategic potentials come together. The child becomes autonomous, able to conceptualize options, to defer action, to plan and to anticipate the consequences of his communications. It is the difference between the child who demands a birthday party, and the child who maneuvers his parents into making a surprise party.

The attainment of the abstract communication perspective is the end point of elementary school training. While school purports to offer knowledge in common to all students, the most important aspect of elementary school is the acculturation agent of society. In school, the child learns what he needs to do to in order to get along. Some learn early, some late. There are many adults who are unable to take an abstract communication perspective, who incessantly make demands and who respond narcissistically. In Chapter 8 we will discuss the results of this kind of immaturity.

Ernest Becker characterizes the abstract communication perspective as symbolic maturity, a state in which the child is no longer dependent on others for the meaning of his symbols. He is able to decide between desirables and undesirables on his own, using his memory of experience as a guide. Erik Erikson notes development as the point where the child assumes full responsibility for his communication choices. Joseph Church describes it as a "dual perspective," where the child is aware of his own behavior and has control over it, understanding at the same time that others, too, have their viewpoints. At this point, it is possible to persuade, to bargain, to exchange. The child is socialized, mature, and ready to stylize his rhetorical operations.

Various socializing opportunities help build the abstract perspective that is vital in a mature communicator. Play during the preschool period enables the child to experiment with various identities and roles. Assuming roles in the family, big brother to one sibling and little brother to another, helps inculcate the notion of rankings and hierarchies. Observation of parental behavior, as well as that of firemen, policemen, mailmen, and others conveys an idea of diversity of role potential. The school assists development of the child's communication maturity by offering him opportunities to share his viewpoints with others, and to learn to listen to what others are saying. The arts, painting, creative dramatics, music, and so on help him to become expressive and to respond to the expressions of others. Even second-graders can take the role of another, if they are provided with a context and focus in which this is possible.

Vicarious experiences are also useful. Encouraging children to live through the communication circumstances of others as reflected in film, literature, and drama assists in extending their sense of alternatives. Identification with characters in a film or story helps the child experiment with various identities until, eventually, he finds a set of roles that become his own. But once elementary school is over, the problem of re-identifying comes in junior high. Boys and girls discover each other. New relationships need to be made. A similar process continues throughout life, and thus, what the child needs most is the ability to sense new situations and new needs of the people in them. Once he has attained this kind of maturity, he is not so easily thrown when he encounters new circumstances.

One word of caution; a number of commercial programs have been marketed designed to "enhance the child's self-concept and to sensitize him to the feelings of others." When and if these programs work for the child, it is not because of the material or the packaging, but because of the special relationship between teacher and child. A child does not need training in sensitivity to extend his human capabilities; rather he needs an informed and concerned "other," you, the teacher, in whatever capacity you can honestly provide for him. As we will discuss in the following chapters, communication development can best be managed by an individual who is committed to doing something about communication skills in the classroom with an eye toward the outside, and who is conceptually aware of the variety of options and limitations offered in a classroom setting.

There are five major propositions about language development in the child, similar to the five basic competencies that add up to mature rhetorical skill:

1. The child cannot learn language until he is biologically ready. The infant will communicate without language, however, for communication is imperative to human survival.

2. The child cannot converse with adults until his verbal concepts are in line with the verbal concepts used in his language community.

3. The child needs to have mastery over code, symbols, and syntax before he becomes a credible communicator.

4. The child cannot be effective at communication until he understands that he is able to exert personal influence by understanding the role and perspective of others.

5. Even after he reaches communication maturity, the child must be cognizant of the ethical questions raised by communications. Indeed, one sign of maturity and mental health is the understanding that others are also seeking to achieve goals through communication and that it is both unethical and unprofitable to attempt to achieve one's goals at the expense of others.

The concepts are abstract, indeed. Perhaps one reason why so many adults never attain communication maturity is that we do not make a real effort to teach communication as social control, nor do we help the child understand the practical and ethical questions nested in the study of rhetoric. Perhaps we are frightened by the necessity to deal with "strategy." In the following pages we will consider message strategy as a formal operation. We do not consider "strategy" to be an unpleasant word. Learning strategy is a process of learning options within the framework of situation, including limitations, the needs of others, and the personal goals for which one communicates.

DEVELOPMENT OF MESSAGE STRATEGY

A major feature of mature communication performance is strategic formulation of messages considering the perspective of others for whom the communication is intended. The small child communicates egocentrically. He does not concern himself with the inconvenience of his demands. He presumes that his needs are felt as strongly by those to whom he addresses his wants. In the early stages of his development, his assumptions are often borne out, for parents are inclined to provide service on demand for very young children. As the child grows physically, and as his needs become more complicated, he learns that demands no longer work and that requests and exchanges are more likely to get him the action he seeks.

During early childhood, the other person needs to make the effort to make sense out of the child's messages. "Dinky wawa" may sound like a college cheer, but the parent learns to decode it as "drink of water." The alert parent will attempt to correct the phonemes, but in any event, the water is provided. In preschool days, when the child plays with others of his own age, there is much pointing and talking referring to objects immediately present; communication is situation-bound. It is not possible to talk intelligently about communication strategy until the third or fourth grade. Up to that point, the child uses strategies that have been inculcated and encouraged. He tends to communicate in ways that have rewarded him in the home, apparently under the tacit assumption that everyone will assume the role of parent. A recent study of communication strategies in early elementary school children indicates that the younger the child, the more limited are his alternatives for influencing others. If sufficiently frustrated, children of this age will cry and indulge in tantrums or other egocentric means of response.

About the middle elementary years, however, the child will begin to test a range of communication alternatives on others. There is much probing for persuasive language, much testing of roles during play. The child of this age will experiment with profanity and persuasions and will start to offer exchanges; "you be the bad guy this time and I'll be the bad guy next time." Much of the play of middle elementary children is characterized by rule following and turn taking.

In addition, the child will experiment with different kinds of statement to achieve a purpose; "give it to me," "please give it to me," "wouldn't you like to give it to me?" He will use restatement; "you mean you want me to go to the store," "you mean I should put my toys away." Pretending is also characteristic of this time period; "I'm superman and he can't go to the store," "Roy Rogers doesn't eat salad," "a movie star doesn't have to help her mother." Through this kind of activity, the child begins to develop an interpersonal repertoire of behaviors from which to choose subsequent strategies. It is at this point where the transformation to communication autonomy that Ernest Becker talks about begins to happen. Experimentation with language indicates that the child is beginning to see the possibilities of other viewpoints and particularly that others will respond from their own frames of reference. The understanding that there are different points of view means the necessity to develop some means of reconciliation. Particularly important at this age is the development of rule-following behavior with others. A study of fourth-grade children indicated, for example, that children of this age are very careful about formulating the rules of exchange. "I do his homework and he lets me swim in his pool." As the child learns more and more about the possible positions others can take, he begins to acquire role-taking skill, so that he can present himself in ways that are compatible with the needs of the other. In public-speaking classes, we would refer to this process as the learning of "audience analysis." It represents one of the most significant communication achievements, for its application spells the difference between the trial and error moves of the young child and the strategies of the mature communicator.

Numerous studies indicate that the ability to take the role of the other person emerges developmentally in the perspectives of some children, though the child has to be taught how to take advantage of this perspective and to translate it into action. Researchers have found that as the child grows older (though no specific age can be stipulated), he is better able to empathize with others. Popularity with peers helps to develop a social insight. Children aged six to thirteen were tested on their ability to take different roles and to identify thinking patterns different from those they normally used. Those aged ten to thirteen had more skill than younger children. The difference in skill level between the younger and older children was attributed to differences in developed ability to conceptualize abstractly. Thus we have a combination of biological and cognitive maturity, which tells us that a child must develop his language biologically until he can perform certain psycholinguistic actions, like the formation of abstract concepts. Somewhere in the process of growth, the child is also socialized. He may, as a result, develop the capacity to empathize, which is crucial in exerting a rhetoric. But his ability to do so is more a function of his socialization than a function of either biological or intellectual growth. There are many children and adults who are unable to empathize and therefore unable to exert rhetoric. We note this, for it is the most significant aspect of communication that can be dealt with in the classroom. The ability to exert rhetorical control is a learning function more than a developmental function.

A series of studies was conducted on the communication performance of pairs of nursery school children on a block-stacking task where senders, who knew the correct order of the blocks, could not observe the performance of their receivers who had no knowledge of the correct order. The children ranged in age from two to four years, and adults were also included in the pairings. It was found that significant differences existed in the descriptive terms used by adults and those by children. Children tended to use phrases of two or three words and often dealt in private descriptions and meanings in directing receivers about block placement. The most successful placement of blocks occurred when the persons giving directions spoke in terms that were already used and understood by those receiving the messages (taking the others' perspective). This most often occurred when an adult gave directions to a child, rather than when two children were paired.

Another series of studies observed differences in verbalizations of kindergarten, first, third, and fifth-grade children in response to specific directions given by adults. The authors of these studies were interested in the growth of socially accepted communication behavior, that which takes into account the goals of both people involved in the communication situation. Differences in growth of communicative perspective were noted in the responses of children of different ages. Adults communicated to children a variety of cues designed to encourage their message modification, i.e., "I don't understand what you mean," or "tell me more about it." The older children (grades three to five) were able to modify their communication and relate new descriptions to the adults, while the younger children could not adapt their conversation. *We presume that adults who are unable to adapt their talk to suit people and circumstances have never had sufficient congitive ability or have never learned adaptive strategies or both.*

From these studies of verbal behavior of young children, the conclusion can be drawn that the capacity for socially appropriate behavior increases with age. This means that the child, through socialization, gains the ability to appeal to the feelings and goals of others in order to satisfy himself, and also understands that his appeals to others must provide some gratification for them as well as for himself. The ability to understand the viewpoints of others is the groundwork that needs to be laid in gaining control over communication. It is the beginning of rhetoric.

Flavell described a number of tasks to test children's ability to assume the roles of others and points of view that were different from their own. Generally, children in the lower grades (second through fourth) had more difficulty adopting a new perspective in their communication than those in higher grades (fifth through eighth). Flavell also experimented with the ability of children to employ game strategies which involved outguessing the moves of another person. Children under fourth grade utilized what Flavell termed "simple strategy," which involved following the simple directions given by the experimenter with minimal display of thinking about probable actions of the other. Those children in fourth grade and beyond employed "complex strategy," which involved consideration of the probable actions of another person. Two fifth-graders and two eleventh-graders engaged in a strategy which was quite complicated, thus indicating that after a certain point, the ability to consider the other is subject to influence from socialization and instruction. Flavell also found that some children were even unable to adapt their communication when asked to explain something to a blindfolded adult. They persisted in talking in terms of picking up "this" and putting it "over there," while pointing.

Flavell suggests that, whenever it begins, the child's development of role-taking ability progresses through five major stages, beginning with his recognition of alternative points of view, and culminating in his ability to apply his discriminations in the choice of ways of adapting to the points of view of others. He suggests that it is not until the age of twelve to fourteen that most children become capable of manipulating all the aspects of role taking successfully. Some never learn it at all, and most need assistance from home and school. The five stages of role-taking development according to Flavell, are as follows:

1. *Existence.* This is the point where it is understood that there is such a concept as "perspective," that is, people's perceptions, thoughts, and feelings in a given situation do not necessarily coincide.

2. *Relevance.* This is the realization that it is useful to discover the perspective of the other person in a situation in order to attain one's own goals with more success.

3. *Ability.* This involves the planning methods to analyse or discover the perspective of the other person.

4. *Performance.* Here the person is faced with the problem of holding the point of view of the other in mind long enough to be able to use it in directing subsequent behavior.

5. *Application.* The person is now challenged with using the results of behavior engaged in through the previous stages as the means to some behavioral end or desired action.

Thus skill in role taking occurs developmentally as a result of specific changes in cognitive capability, as well as a consequence of various socialization experiences and pressures. Adults and older children encourage performance according to assigned roles (son, daughter, toddler, and so on). In addition, the child's capacity for play and imitation and eventually for participation in social games also provides impetus toward role taking.

In play the child is able to experiment with various roles that may be encountered in future circumstances. This imitation, initially seen in action, gradually becomes internalized so that the child is able to take the role of another in thought. He becomes socialized by others: *he is socialized as he imitates.* The variable which most influences the success at socialization by any given child is the model he is presented with in home, neighborhood, and school. This variable accounts for wide differences in socialization patterns observed in children at school.

What is most hazardous here, however, is that play can come out any way the child wants it to. In his fantasy world, he can always win. The child needs to be helped by careful teaching to understand that the other person also has goals and dreams, and the best mode of accomplishment is one which helps both parties accomplish their goals. The teacher needs to listen carefully and observe the children as they socialize, and use what he sees to offer instruction that will help the child to understand that his best interests lie in considering the best interests of others. The child, furthermore, needs to understand that not everyone is empathetic, and he needs to be properly suspicious of what is offered him by others. Careful selection of associates and friends is a function of understanding the perspective of others, yet recent research tends to show that children select their associates more on propinquity than any other variable. The college students referred to earlier when asked "if you were in a defeating relationship, would you exchange loneliness for the relationship," almost universally responded that even a poor relationship was better than none at all. Thus, we have an urgency for socialization, including the cultivation of deep intimacy, on the part of people who are ill equipped to take care of their own needs, let alone those of others. Discussion of the meaning of human relationships needs to be a part of every classroom to help cognitively mature children achieve social and rhetorical maturity.

Even organized play and games in childhood are felt to be significant as means for encouraging the child to become more sensitive to the rules of games, of social situations, and the roles of those playing the game. But, once again, the analogy is dangerous, for games are played to win and the child who has learned to win will probably carry this urgency with him into his social relations. Effective operation in games necessitates that children be able to take the attitude of everyone else involved and understand that these attitudes, rules, and roles have a definite relationship to and affect on each of the players. The child who is prevented from losing or the child who is never sanctioned for violating the rules never learns what losing means, and is poorly prepared to respond to it. Furthermore, the child who learns that winning is legitimate even when done at serious cost to other participants may show sociopathic tendencies in adulthood when he does not consider the feelings of others as he seeks his own ends. Robert Ardrey notes that if children have too easy a time of it when young, they are unable to cope with the challenges presented by adulthood. Jordan Scher notes that children need some kind of innoculation, i.e., putting them into situations where they fail and take the consequences of failure so that they learn in a controlled atmosphere what it means to fail and how to succeed without doing injury to others. Teachers need to organize their instruction so that children can fail when the stakes are not too high in order to gain empathy with others who have failed and courage from failure.

Thus, we can see that the developing child continues to learn that the game of communication is won to the extent that he can anticipate and perform according to the expectations of other people. This is a rhetorical position and subject to the strictures and moral codes of the rhetorical mode. The child, at least the one who succeeds, realizes that his own success and control comes only when he strives for an understanding of others. His cognitive ability, expanding experience in role taking, and willingness to participate in new situations should demonstrate to him that other people have feelings and ideas that make a difference in how they behave. His own desire to control can be best realized when he understands what moves others. It is sufficient here to say that children must be carefully taught to exchange rhetorics; we cannot assume that the capability will emerge on its own. It is this aspect of communication skill that needs careful attention by the teacher, and later on in this book we will explore alternatives for instruction in rhetorical control. Of course, the child cannot be taught until he is ready. Therefore, we offer three features of rhetorical readiness that will indicate that the child is able to receive instruction in communication interaction on a rhetorical level:

1. Since the essence of rhetorical control is understanding the other, the child must demonstrate that he understands that others are seeking goals, have feelings, and can help him as well as hurt him.

2. Once the child discovers what will please others, he is able to use his discoveries to exert control over them for the purpose of getting what he wants.

3. The child's use of language for the purpose of control improves as he gains more understanding of the other, is able to synthesize and interpret this information, and improves his use of verbal strategies in applying this information. Only through careful speaking and listening with the child, will the teacher be able to recognize the existence of these qualities. This means that his classroom must provide a variety of situations in which children can talk and interact in ways that will give him clues.

Developmentally speaking, communication presents the elementary teacher with a fascinating blend of contrasts. The students are so different each year. Even if an elementary teacher started with Grade 1 and followed his students through Grade 6, he would encounter a brand new group each year. The first-graders who couldn't make "r" sounds or substituted "w" for "l" speak like veterans by the time they reach third grade. All his concern was in vain. But the third-grade teacher may now have some problems, for those children who have not made the full articulation development may need some special help at this time. They may yet "grow out of it," but if they are permitted to get into fifth grade and still have difficulties in pronunciation, then their communication will, most likely, develop awkwardly.

The question is how do you provide special assistance without stigmatizing the child? Often you can't just let him be. Excessive sound distortions *might* be symptoms of some serious neurological problem. The teacher needs to be very subtle in testing for accuracy in sound production. An informal diagnostic kit is helpful, word cards, pictures, objects, some sort of game format will help you tune into problem communicators. This is the time when the classroom teacher needs a close link to the speech clinician. And it doesn't hurt to be informed on your own. Some readings in speech correction listed at the end of the chapter are very helpful in guiding you to a satisfactory diagnosis of whether or not a child needs remedial treatment.

By the time the typical child is four he is able to produce most of the sentence patterns he will ever need. Between kindergarten and grade three most of the irregularities will work themselves out. "Comed," becomes "came," "foots and feets, " will be "foot and feet," and so forth. It is interesting to note that there is not very much that formal, corrective schooling can do to change grammatical patterns, particularly those features that are part of the child's home and neighborhood dialect. The child will speak his own language and ingest his own rules. He will need to succeed in his home and neighborhood and success will not be so vital in the school. Consequently, many children will resist alteration of grammatical patterns. They understand that what they have is good enough for their own people, and they will wonder why the teacher doesn't take the trouble to understand what they see to be perfectly good English.

If the classroom teacher is terribly concerned about grammar, it may be possible to cue the child into "school talk," let him learn that there is a special "dialect" for school. He can learn his new grammar as he would a part in a play. It is much less fuss than a drill and pattern-practice session. It will not threaten the child very much, and as he develops an ability to learn an abstract perspective, he can be taught why it is important to use a grammar that is suitable for a particular situation.

There has been considerable ado about the impact of teacher diction and dialect on the child in the elementary classroom. Most elementary teachers go through some kind of articulation screening process to make sure their pronunciation is "standard." However, there is absolutely no evidence that children really change their native patterns because of a teacher. They may pick up some of the teacher's talk if they care very much about him, but when they go home, they will talk as they have to.

One of the authors, in his work with black children in Philadelphia, experienced an interesting situation. He was discussing language styles with a group of fifth graders and the discussion worked its way around to "that's my talk," "that's your talk." The situation was sufficiently loose so that the adult as well as the children played each other's parts. The classroom teacher who had been trying to change some very basic black pronunciation with very little success was amazed to hear perfectly standard white English coming from many of

When you're messin' with my words, you're messin' with me.

his black students. The indication is that the child can do it, if he wants to, and if there is some reason to model after the teacher, he will do so. But to force oneself on the child and attempt to make him change ways that are productive to him at home is dangerous. As one fourth-grader put it, "teacher, when you mess with my words, you're messin' with me, and I might not like it."

The most significant of all changes to occur in communication capability during the elementary years has to do with the child's consciousness of himself in relation to others; who he is, who they are, what they stand for, who he wants to be like. It is the developing of the sense that enables the child to play the "people game," and begin to use his language for goal attainment. These changes can be observed not only in the topics children talk about and the quality of information they reveal, but in the appeals they employ to influence, as well. The preschooler or kindergartner argues from an obligatory base such as "You're my mommy and you are supposed to." One of the writers, in an attempt to discover what supporting proofs a child of kindergarten age would offer to convince him to climb a tree and retrieve a kite, asked the child why an adult should climb the tree. The child replied, ". . . cause I want it, besides, you're the teacher and teachers are supposed to help children get kites" (or anything else the child desires). Another child standing nearby added "teachers are nice people and they're supposed to help kids." Needless to say, the writer climbed the tree.

The same writer, in observing the speech development of his own children, has noted that toward later kindergarten, the approach changes to "my teacher said . . ." Obligation remains, but now the child has testimony of authority to add. This is followed by the emergence of a situationally based strategy emerging some time during second grade. "Everybody else has one!!" "I need it because I'm supposed to have it." To this is added, "I want it because it's the good thing, the right thing." It is interesting that some of these appeals are precisely what contemporary advertisers consider.

By the end of third grade, we can see the beginnings of an appeal system which eventually will transcend specific individuals and situations. This does not mean that the child's strategies reflect less self-interest. On the contrary, no matter what he says throughout the elementary age range, he's talking and thinking from his own viewpoint. It is questionable whether this ever changes. All that happens is that we acquire skill in understanding others so that we can take their welfare into account in addition to our own.

A description of a typical summer playground situation may be helpful in understanding how young children use verbal appeals. Four children, three of them third-graders and one a fifth-grader, were playing "hit the stick" with a basketball. While the fifth-grader was involved, the game went smoothly. But as soon as the three younger children were left to play the game alone, disagreements, tears, threats, and name-calling followed. The children began yelling, "It's not the rule!" "You don't play fair!" "You cheat!" It was obvious to the teacher that every child was operating from a different set of rules, in each case, a set of rules that would help the child win, and no one could consider all the viewpoints to formulate one set of rules that all could follow.

The teacher asked each child to come back into the school to explain his version of how to play the game. He recorded each of these statements. When this was completed, all three children were asked to listen to the tapes. The result: laughter, a look of surprise, and hopefully a beginning realization that finding out about common rules before you start might help to avoid tears and make the game more fun.

Of course, fights did not stop that summer. However, this year the children are older and conflict over rules is less frequent. When a problem occurs now, it's over an infraction or interpretation of a rule that is understood in advance. "Playing fair," according to the rules becomes a part of the fourth-grade appeals system, not only on the playground but in the classroom as well. The talk changes. Children appeal on a basis of, "she punished us all, just because of one kid!" "That's not fair." "Eddie got gum and I didn't." What is just, right, and fair becomes a matter of major concern.

At this point, the child can understand persuasion. He can understand that he uses it, and others use it on him, and he can even begin to understand something of the formalities of the strategy of persuasion. He knows how to make an appeal, and he even uses rudimentary evidence. By the end of sixth grade, the "blackmail" and "bribery" characteristic of the young child have been replaced with a contractual understanding reciprocity, "you do this for me, and I'll do that for you."

Another development in rhetorical control that can be observed around the fourth grade is the child's sudden sensing of verbal concepts, that words themselves don't make meaning, people do. The child begins to get a sense of metacommunication, he begins to attend to meanings. Some of the arguments seem to be based on Humpty Dumpty reasoning:

> Humpty has just defined the word *glory* to be "a nice knock-down argument."
> "But 'glory' doesn't mean a 'nice knock-down argument," Alice objected.
> "When I use a word," Humpty Dumpty said, in rather a scornful tone, "it means just what I choose it to mean—neither more nor less."
> "The question is," said Alice, "whether you *can* make words mean different things."
> "The question is," said Humpty Dumpty, "which is to be master—that's all."

The children appeal to what they had meant. "You didn't understand me. What I meant was. . . ." They seem to find the fine print, the hidden clauses, the "Catch 22s."

Beyond the sixth grade, teachers need to worry about the rhetoric-producing child. Most of the children that come out of elementary school are ready to make rhetoric of one sort or another. Their social acculturation will determine their ethical stance, their level of exposure will determine the skill with which they use supports, and which supports they use. But they should be ready to understand exchange. They can be expected to analyse situations and have some repertoire of behaviors from which to choose appropriate responses. They will be able to take the place of other people in planning their remarks. They will be working toward goals, although, as we will later note, they may not be consciously aware of what their goals are. They are young people using their language purposively. They are rhetorical, fully mature communicators and ready for training. Those children who do not reach maturity will suffer the penalties. They will be ineffective in their goal seeking. They may be very effective but at the cost of alienation of the people around them. They will need some sort of special treatment if they are to be become fully functioning members of society.

THE DEVELOPMENT OF CONVERSATIONAL ABILITY

We now turn to some special considerations of importance for teachers. We have discussed the growth of rhetorical capability in the mature communicator. We need to look at how this operates in the development of conversational skill.

Very little is known about the progression of events that leads to conversational skill. Many adults are deficient in that area. There are really very few people who move beyond socially prescribed small talk and become skilled conversationalists. Small children don't make much conversation. Their words are service directed, designed to accomplish some immediate event. In adult life, however, it is necessary to survive a myriad conversational encounters in the course of a typical day; social greetings, asking for and giving information, providing assistance, gossiping, killing time, and much more.

The writers conducted a study of the ability of preschool children to talk in a conversational situation. It became clear that even three-year-olds understood "conversational pattern," although they were unable to manage the sustained referential activity required to make conversation. It was clear that even at this early age, the children knew some of the basic rules of conversation: (1) One person speaks at a time. (2) Questions asked are answered before new topics are introduced.

The three- and four-year-olds observed were able to employ a variety of strategies for initiating talk with others: "Is that your pumpkin," led to sustained talk about the pumpkin. Exclamatory phrases: "Hey, look at that doggie over there," engaged the attention of others as well as provided a focus for continued talk about the dog. Direct summons by name, "Carl, Carl," commanded the attention of the other, typically resulting in a "what" response which then provided a basis for continued exchange. Interrogative phrases: "We don't go to my house today, right?" committed the respondent to at least one additional response. Nonverbal visual presentation was observed as the young child literally presented his comment nose to nose with the potential respondent.

Conversations were either informational or relational. The children employed talk for the purpose of sharing information. More significantly, however, the bulk of their conversation served some relationship function, significant not so much for the content of what was said but for how it affected the participants. Through conversation, the children displayed their choices and preferences. They selected individuals for conflict, friendship, play and fantasy, as well as for practicing verbal routines learned in the nursery school (ABC's, counting, songs, and rhymes).

Analysis of conversations produced by older children suggests that age and experience permit more extensive referencing, more directed purpose seeking, as well as acquisition of adult strategies for controlling conversation flow. Schools have done very little with conversation. Most of the speech routines done in the schools are formal, requiring some sort of advance preparation, rehearsal, or planning. It would be interesting to discover what distance could be gained from conversational training. Preschoolers seem to have a glimmering of rhetorical strategy in their casual talk; it may be that conversation is the place to build training for effective communication.

The mature, adult communicator understands the difference between communicating in public and communicating in private; between the demands of a formal presentation and the latitude operating in a relatively casual encounter. The mature adult is also able to manage his behavior to make situational constraints work in his favor rather than against him. Recent studies indicate that children vary greatly in their ability to adapt to various situations.

One major study in this area conceptualizes the communication situation in the following terms: topics talked about, tasks that accompany talk, listeners with whom the child talks, settings in which conversation is observed. The conclusion was that situational factors constrain the child's language activity. Briefly, children will talk more and use more diversified language if they are encouraged to talk about topics familiar to them and in which they are interested. They will be more focused and will be more precise in referents if they are permitted to talk about objects and events presented in the immediate situation. Furthermore, statements will be longer in conversations with familiar listeners, particularly familiar adults. Finally, in any case, the child will choose to talk more about his activities than those of others, and his talk will be more elaborate and diversified to the extent that he is comfortable in the situation in which he is functioning and is equal in status to those with whom he is conversing. Another authority suggests that the optimum conversational setting is obtained by positioning a familiar adult, informally dressed, on the floor next to the child and a friend of the child, and passing a bag of potato chips during the interview.

This information about children is not particularly startling, since it is clear that for most adults the same constraints apply. Most adults do better in conversation when they can talk about familiar matters with people they know reasonably well. Most adults are intimidated by strange situations, unfamiliar people, and those of higher status. If this is the case, then it would appear to make sense to begin to offer formal interpersonal training to children. By familiarizing them with the circumstances where talk takes place, it may be possible to help expand their maturity by enabling them to function in situations that might otherwise intimidate them.

These observations about children's responses to conversational situations are particularly important since most of the information about the child's language development has been obtained in relatively structured interview situations which tap only a small portion of the child's repertoire. Furthermore, it suggests that the classroom teacher who is informally concerned with diagnosing the communication needs of students can conduct "field observations" of his children in natural settings in order to choose the kind of situation that might be most natural for the child to seek information. Observation of talk during free play with peers, with familiar adults, with strangers; attendance to situations such as requesting and providing information will provide a basis for understanding the capabilities of conversation in the individual child. Indeed, careful observation could well be a substitute for formal interviewing. Whatever is learned through observation could be augmented through creative dramatics, imitation, and role playing.

The understanding of this similarity between children and adults is very important. In no case can we ever assume that any of our students is totally at ease in situations. In any case, we must take care to teach understanding of the situation and the limitations it imposes before requiring the student to perform in it.

INTERRELATIONSHIP OF LANGUAGE SKILLS

While the focus of this book is on speaking and listening, we cannot ignore the central thrust of most curricula, reading and writing. Language skills can be conceptualized as competency in speaking, listening, reading and writing. Each of these skill areas can be divided into subdivisions of interrelated skills. Speaking can be conceived of in terms of articulation, phrasing, syntax, diction, completeness, organization, message appropriateness and originality. In each case, specific diagnostic procedures or criteria can be used to assess the capabilities of an individual or to compare different individuals of similar age. References will be made in the bibliography to this chapter to some major studies in interrelatedness.

One major report noted that characteristic changes came about in children as they progressed through kindergarten to sixth grade. In this study, children representing all socioeconomic levels and ethnic origins were observed in interviews once a year for seven years. In addition, teacher ratings of oral and written proficiency were compiled. Oral language skills were assessed in terms of vocabulary, syntactic complexity, information content, and organization. The following conclusions were drawn:

1. Children initially judged as high in language ability in kindergarten remained high in this ability through the seven years.

2. Children in the high group communicated more information with greater fluency than children in other groups.

3. Scores in reading and writing correlated significantly with oral language proficiency.

4. Social class differences were related to proficiency in language skill.

These results square with the results of other studies. Taken collectively, they seem to add up to the conclusion that competency in oral language is positively related to success in reading and writing and achievement in school in general. What is not clear is whether training in oral language administered before the child learns to read and write enhances his capability to read and write. Various reports have noted recently that there is at least a possibility of hereditary factors playing a prominent role in accounting for differences between children in school achievement. While oral language was not considered in these studies, the hypothesis that heredity and language skill are closely related cannot be rejected.

There is, furthermore, a possibility that situational factors account for differential performance. A sizable body of literature tends to support the contention that children will differ on tests because of unfamiliarity with the testing procedure, complexity of test materials, interviewer or tester status, degree of formality in the testing situation. One study, for example, shows a tendency for middle-class children to converse more extensively, in any case, than lower-class children.

The implication of these studies for the classroom teacher, among other possibilities, is that it is very likely that in any case, the teacher will encounter a broad range of oral capabilities among his students, regardless of level. It is unwise, given the data, to impose arbitrary standards to which all children must conform. By the same token, it is nonproductive to permit children to avoid achieving a reasonable level of intelligibility. In developing curricula for oral communication training, the diversity of the students must be taken into account. Throughout this book we will advocate the use of options for activities and experiences. Given what we have discovered so far in this chapter, we could assume that the most productive curricula provide experiences individual children can relate to their life outside the classroom and which will then allow them the maximum opportunity for oral expressiveness.

MEANINGFUL USE OF LANGUAGE

Before leaving the study of the young child for a look at communication in general, it would be wise to take a look at a map of the language used by young children. So often adults we encounter seem to be awkward or dysrhythmic in their speech. Consideration of the childlike qualities of speech indicate that these adults may have "frozen" their language very young, and never made the transition to mature communicator.

The language used by children reflects a delightful blend of social competence, syntactic sophistication and conceptual primitivism. Socially, most children are able to engage in the conversational forms of their immediate language communities. They are able to initiate and sustain some routines, make their needs known, and respond to the demands of others. They can also engage in routinized and rule-bound play as well as conflict. As to grammatical skill, most of what the child needs is developed by the time he enters school. Thus, concentration on vocabulary and grammar, so characteristic of language arts instruction, may not be as productive as we might think. Our thrust in this book is toward rhetoric, the purposive and productive use of speech. Concentration on content becomes a key to successful rhetoric. Most school instruction focuses on form.

For example, examination of a child's conceptual use of language as a tool for making and sharing references presents an image that is very different from development of grammar and learning of social forms. Language use reflects mental development. Until the middle school, conceptualization is limited in scope to the familiar, the concrete, the obvious, and the primacy of personal needs and desires. It is interesting that a great deal of adult language seems to reflect this same primitive conceptual level.

The thinking of the young child has been characterized as "egocentric," reflecting his, and only his, view of a situation. While he may be able to take the role of the other in order to develop a request in a way that will get it granted, there is little concern shown for reciprocation, that is, fulfilling the needs of the other. Child thinking also is centered, focused on isolated aspects of situation to the exclusion of others. Child language is characterized by selective perception, tunnel vision, and so on. The child may see that he has been wronged in a situation. "I wasn't doing anything. I was just talking to Judy." "But if everyone talked, no one could hear." "But everybody wasn't talking, it was just me." Child language is also highly "distractable," that is, subject to quick change when external stimuli impinge. It is hard for a child to stay focused, to stick to the subject—another problem that many adults seem to have. Finally, a child's thinking is dominated by "private imagery," which reflects his unique, pleasurable and unpleasant experiences as if they were common to all. These features come through in the following explanation of relationship terms given by a four-year-old.

QUESTION:	ANSWER:
What's a brother?	A brother? Don't know. We could make one out of clay.
Do you have a brother?	Yes, Mikie. (A neighbor boy)
Are you a brother?	Yes, Mikie's brother.
How come?	Cause, I care about him.
Is every boy a brother?	Yes.
How come?	Just because.

We might extend this analysis to some adult conversation.

Do you think you wrote a passing paper?	Yes, I need a good grade in this course.
But is your paper good?	My grades aren't so good in my other subjects. I need this grade.
How did your paper meet the standards set?	I tried very hard.

And so on. Indicating, of course, that many of us never get beyond the level of the four-year-old in our conceptualizations, even though our language may become more complicated, our vocabulary more extensive, and the amount of aplomb with which we make utterances greater.

One authority suggests that the young child's words represent a fusion of sense impressions and idiosyncratic impressions that extend beyond the adult's system of meanings. "Doggie" may refer to every four-legged animal a child encounters, while at the same time, a house pet might be "Tini," and "she no doggie." (In the adult world "Polack" might refer to everyone of Polish ancestry except for a friend, Mike Dombrowski, who is "my friend, Michael," with no further questions asked.

Our conclusion is that word meaning, including the specific words in a child's vocabulary, evolves through a series of stages which reflect (1) biological maturation, (2) mental development, and (3) social experience including the use of language in the home environment. This particular authority feels that the major responsibility for making sense resides with adults and older children who are models for conceptualization. (In the case of adults, the immediate language community would control conceptualization.) It is interesting now to speculate whether most of us ever reach communication maturity, if conceptual maturity is indeed part of it.

A simple study which could be conducted in any classroom can be used to discover how children of various ages use and interpret double-function terms. Double-function terms are words which have both physical and abstract referents. Words such as hot, cold, crooked, bright, deep, soft, hard, were presented to children aged three through adolescence. Findings revealed that younger children understood the terms as they could be applied to concrete, physical attributes like hard rocks. Seven- and eight-year-olds used the terms to label psychological characteristics as well as physical properties: sweet candy, a sweet person is nice, but did not understand how the same term could be used in the two instances. Children beyond ten were able to handle the terms and give reasons for the use of the words in both contexts.

What is evident in the above study is a gradual ability to abstract and conceptualize which occurs as words come to represent categories of relationships and potentials rather than specific events or objects. A similar conceptual use of language is observed in the following responses to the question, "tell me about trees," asked of three children aged three, six, and fourteen. The children were in a situation where trees were not visible. The three-year-old was unable to reply until presented with a picture stimulus. The six-year-old responded: "When you chop them down a seed comes out and it grows again."

QUESTION: Anything else?
SIX-YEAR-OLD: On the bark are little bugs.
QUESTION: Anything else?
SIX-YEAR-OLD: Trees are pretty tall, taller than you, taller than a leaf.
QUESTION: Anything else?
SIX-YEAR-OLD: After that comes winter. Leaves fall off. Spring comes and it's growing again. Then August comes, then January.
QUESTION: Anything else?
SIX-YEAR-OLD: No.

The fourteen-year-old replied, "Let's see, what can I tell you? There are different kinds. They look different at different times of the year. They produce different kinds of wood and have different leaves and seeds. All have circulation systems. What do you want me to talk about?"

In each instance, the private image of the six-year-old dominated the word picture painted in his response. The fourteen-year-old evidenced an abstract-conceptual use of language reflecting a variety of conceptual potentials for organizing responses. She might have discussed different types of woods (a classification), how trees grow (a time sequence), what a typical tree looks like (a spatial layout), how evergreens and deciduous trees are similar and different (comparison and contrast), the influence trees have on the economy (cause–effect), how tree blight can be treated (problem–solution). In short, the mature communicator is capable of abstracting qualities and finding several varieties for response in any given case. When adults are unable to utilize this kind of variety they are immature both in their conceptualizing and in their uses of language to attain their objectives. If we accept the premise that the immediate society has the greatest impact on conceptualization, then we must assume that school needs to make some effort to train students to elaborate their conceptualizations so that they can become more adult in their use of language.

The private imagery of children is illustrated in the following conversations with preschoolers:

FELECIA on cookies: You can eat cookies, and you can play a game with them, put your cookies in the cookie can. You can dip them in milk. You can decorate your house with them. Tape them on the windows, tape them on the furniture, any place. (Felecia then proceeded to discourse on Christmas, decorating, and fun in winter.)

FELECIA on water: You can drink water. Doggies drink water. Bunnies drink milk and eat carrots. You can clean your house with Windex.

DANNY on water: Ducks and alligators live in the water (looking around the room). They're not lights in the water. Lights go at home.

BOBBY on water: I like waterfalls. Fishes goes in water. We go in water. I go at Whipples (a park nearby). I swim at Whipples. Milk comes from cows.

SUSIE on trees: They need snow, they need dirt. God has to make them grow.

MICHAEL on trees: There were berries on it and I ate and I got poisoned. A little girl was riding her bicycle and she hit it. My mommy smashed into a tree and the gas got on her.

SAM on trees: Trees are for chopping wood when you want to make a fire. When the school bus comes you get on with your lunch. There is wood on the school bus.

LESLIE on trees: There's leaves on them. There's stuff that itches. They're on Christmas trees too. The trees are bare. Some look dead.

LESLIE on snow: Santa Claus comes, I like snow. It's freezing. My mommy and I were playing. My mommy and I were throwing snow at each other. We laughed.

In each instance the words used reflect underlying patterns of private images. The researcher who collected these examples also noted that children tended to talk about a particular topic until something mentioned in the discussion triggered a related association. Furthermore, changes in topics were observed as the children incorporated objects of the interview setting into the talk, and finally, children would frequently announce a change of topic and proceed to another topic without troubling themselves with a relationship to anything that had gone before.

Oddly enough, there is little here that would be unfamiliar to one who listens to adult conversation. The implications for the classroom teacher seem quite clear. While very young children may not be amenable to any sort of conceptual training, as early as possible the teacher must attempt to bring about a higher ability to abstract in the use of language. Time and patience are the imperatives in this sort of training. Gentle questioning by the teacher and offering more complicated alternatives from which the child can pick are helpful. Many teachers have found that introducing children to any understanding of structure is very useful. The bibliography of this chapter refers to a set of available materials for the use of this method.

Throughout the growth from childhood to maturity, there is a struggle to be able to do more and more with talk. Content and application to situation are the crucial variables. Instruction pointed to this end provides the readiness to encounter the real world of communication which we will detail in the following chapters.

WORKS CITED:

Asch, Solomon, and Nerlove, Harriett. "The Development of Double Function Terms in Children, An Exploratory Investigation," in B. Kaplan and S. Wagner, *Perspective in Psychological Theory*, New York: International Universities Press, 1960.

Becker, Ernest. *The Birth and Death of Meaning*. New York: The Free Press, 1962.

Church, Joseph. *Language and the Discovery of Reality*. New York: Random House, 1961.

Erikson, Erik. *Childhood and Society*. New York: W.W. Norton, 1963.

Flavell, John. "Role Taking and Communication Skills," in *The Young Child: Reviews of Research*. Hartup and Smothergill, eds. Washington, D.C. National Association for the Education of Young Children, 1967.

Hymes, Del. in Cazden. "The neglected situation in child language research and education," in *Language and Poverty*, Williams, ed. Chicago: Markham, 1970.

Krauss, Robert. et al. "Communication Abilities of Children as a Function of Status and Age," *Merrill-Palmer Quarterly*, 14 (1968) pp. 161–173.

Loban, Walter. *The Language of Elementary School Children*, Champaign, Ill.: NCTE, 1963.

McCarthy, Dorothea. "A comparison of children's language in different situations and its relation to personality traits," *Journal of Genetic Psychology*, 36 (1929) pp. 583–591.

Templin, Mildred. *Certain Language Skills in Children,* Minneapolis: University of Minnesota Press, 1957.

Travis, L.E. *Handbook of Speech Pathology.* New York: Appleton-Century-Crofts, 1958.

Van Riper, Charles, and Butler, Katherine. *Speech in the Elementary Classroom.* New York: Harper & Row, 1955.

WORKS RECOMMENDED:

For a pessimistic view of schooling see Jules Henry, *On Education.* New York: Vintage Books, 1972.

For a discussion of the significance of adult influences on children's communication, see Haim Ginott, *Between Parent and Child.* New York: Macmillan, 1965.

For a discussion of a methodology recently devised for the study of young children's conversations, see Daniel Fogel, "A Methodology for the Study of Children's Conversations in Natural Settings," Unpublished Masters Thesis, Pennsylvania State University, Department of Speech, 1973.

- To present a model that explains the process-relationship of communication.

- To realize that our ways of perceiving, analysing, and communicating seem to follow rules, and what we do is reasonable to us at the time.

- To realize that we cannot always assume that others will see our behavior the same way we see it, for their rules of communication may differ from ours.

- To note that every communication behavior affects the person who perceives it, thus influencing his response to it.

- To understand that as teachers, we cannot assume that all students have been exposed to the same rules of communication: they may have different images, symbols, and values for things.

- To learn that people respond to their own mental creations, not necessarily similar to "reality."

- To note that verbal communication and other outward behaviors are the only ways we can understand a student's thought.

- To present some basic questions that the teacher needs to raise about his theoretical function in the classroom.

- To learn that to the extent that communication alternatives expand in the classroom, learning possibilities also expand, for the student has a variety of ways of being rewarded by the teacher and other students.

- To understand that most all that we do or say is rhetorical, since it is aimed at evoking a particular response from someone else.

4

Understanding What Happens When Humans Communicate with One Another

Overview

We take a look in this chapter at the complexity of the communication process. Often we assume that others understand us most of the time. If they do not, we assume that they aren't "with it." This may be one possibility, although teachers ought to know that there are many possible reasons why we may confuse others. Such things as differing rules for talk, values, expectations may cause confusion.

This means that teachers need to look closely at the communication of individual students in their classrooms to assess different rules of communication that appear to guide their talk. Once this is done, understanding student goals becomes an easier task, for goals can be seen in a broader context of how the student views events in the world and what values he places on them. In turn, the teacher must find some way of expressing his own goals to the students, outlining his particular view of the world or "rules" of communication that have created this view.

All of this questioning helps the teacher maintain a more effective posture for the rhetorical task he needs to carry out in the classroom, and it also aids him in responding to the rhetoric of his students as they seek to fulfill their needs. It may make him a better teacher.

BY OBSERVING human behavior, it is possible to build a model that explains the complex process and relationship of communication. The model we present here attempts to include the major variables involved when people speak with each other. It applies to both formal and informal situations. The model is "systemic." This means that the people represented in the model are bound by norms and rules of behavior. The model is also based on the premise that communication is both a process (which can be observed externally) and a relationship (an emotional commitment mutually made). The model is relatively limited in that it can only confirm observable events; the material about what goes on inside the mind is conjectural. It is the best model we can present to you at this time, but it is subject to revision as new data comes in. It purports to describe what we can observe happening when humans talk with each other. Used carefully, it can serve as a diagnostic; deficiencies can be located in the diagram to clarify what needs to be improved in the process. It has been examined by several thousand classroom teachers and has been used to generate classroom communication strategies with considerable success. The model can be

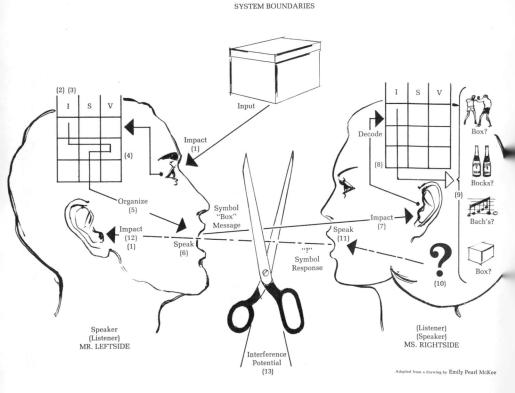

A Complicated Model of Two Humans Communicating.

followed by noting the numbers on the diagram and comparing with the following text.

The two participants are connected in a relationship. They have formed a system. It has boundaries. The boundaries are the norms and rules that they agree on for their system. Other people entering the system must abide by those rules and norms. The system is open to permit information to get in. Information might be perceptions, comments from other people, any influence on either of the people communicating. Incidentally, there could be three, four, or a thousand people inside the boundaries.

By following the numbers on the diagram you can get an idea of the complexity of the process. Note that neither person is *always* speaker or *always* listener. They take turns subject to the control of their norms.

1. *Communication starts with a feeling.* Communication is purposive and responsive. It is purposive, for it expresses some feeling state, desire, or goal of the communicator. It is responsive, for it starts with something perceived or felt by the speaker. Our communication here starts with the perception of a small container and with the "feeling" that Mr. Leftside wants the container.

2. *The perception or feeling is associated with a previous image or symbol or both.* The brain stores information. The grid in the diagram represents this storage capacity. The brain can store records of previous perceptions and experience in an organized way, and it has rules for retrieving the information. We cannot store every experience in a separate place, so we create "cells" or storage bins and locate them with labels. Thus, we can have a bin for trees. If we are tree specialists we might have bins for conifers or deciduous trees. We might even reserve cells for special trees, like the one where we carved Sally Ann's name. Each new perception is checked to see what cell it fits into, and it is associated by giving it the label that is on the cell. We sort information into image, symbol, and value categories. *We need names, for without them we cannot communicate anything.*

3. What we have in memory removes specific characteristics. Once we give a thing a name we associate it with a stereotype or prototype that exists in our image, symbol, value storage cells. New perceptions may alter the prototypes, but mostly new perceptions are stored where they fit best even if they have to be altered slightly to make them fit. The process of association enables us to select a symbol to be spoken to our audience.

4. Every image and symbol we have in memory is associated with an evaluation. We assign "+" value to things we like, "−" to things we dislike and "?" where we are uncertain or have mixed emotions.

5. We combine symbols and values to fit together a communication. We need to know something about our audience (the one other person in this case) in order to make this selection, and we need to proceed according to the rules for arrangements of symbols we learned from our society. When we do not follow the rules, people cannot understand us. In this case, we have options. We can say "bring me the box," or "the box, bring it to me," or we can simply point our finger and say "box?"

6. Once we have our message put together, we send it to the other person. We follow some rules here. We do not turn our back. We try to look at the other person. What we want to do is get the goal image we have in our thought into the mind of our audience. We want him to see things the way we see them, and it is necessary to say our words in ways calculated to do this. The clearer we are about what we seek, the more likely it is that our audience will understand us.

7. Once Ms. Rightside gets the message, it becomes a perception for her, and she must process it the same way Mr. Leftside processed it. Because she agrees to respond, she has made a relationship through the process of communication.

8. Ms. Rightside must process the symbol until she finds an image that fits it. If she heard only the word "BOX" and didn't see Mr. Leftside point, she might think of two men fighting. Or, she might interpret this as "*Bocks*" and agree to have a glass of beer. She might also hear "*Bach's*" and think, "sounds like Mozart to me!" She might be uncertain. She searches her grid for a symbol for uncertainty and responds with "huh?" The original speaker then has the obligation to clarify his message.

9. Once an agreement has been made to relate, the rules of the system offer alternatives for response. Ms. Rightside can act, question, or ignore.

10. If she chooses to question, as she did in this case, she must question in some way that Mr. Leftside will understand.

11. The minute she starts processing, she becomes speaker and Mr. Leftside becomes listener. The basic rule of their relationship is to take turns.

12. Whatever is sent back to Mr. Leftside starts the process all over again.

13. The process can be interfered with in seven basic ways. There can be interference from outside sources; hammering, a lawn mower, and Ms. Rightside just did not hear (PHYSICAL INTERFERENCE). Ms. Rightside may have had plugged ears, an upset stomach or be paying attention to her headache (PHYSIO-LOGICAL INTERFERENCE). Mr. Leftside may have pronounced his words poorly (PHONETIC INTERFERENCE). Mr. Leftside may have put his symbols together poorly (SYNTACTIC INTERFERENCE). Mr. Leftside may have selected words with many possible meanings and Ms. Rightside didn't know which to pick (SEMANTIC INTERFERENCE). Mr. Leftside may have insulted or threatened Ms. Rightside (PSYCHOLOGICAL INTERFERENCE). Mr. Leftside or Ms. Rightside might have violated the norms of their system (SOCIAL INTERFERENCE). If all goes well, Ms. Rightside will get an image in her head something like the goal that Mr. Leftside had for her, and she will behave in ways that Mr. Leftside approves of. If this doesn't work, Mr. Leftside can keep trying to persuade her to behave the way he wants her to. Ms. Rightside, of course, has the privilege of trying to persuade Mr. Leftside to leave her alone, clarify the message, change the subject, or any other goal that is legitimate within the boundaries of their system. *Thus, the model shows us*

COMMUNICATION is a process carried on for a purpose in a relationship which has a purpose which is carried on through communication which is a process etc. . . .

The process of human communication starts when some sort of stimulus makes contact with our senses (eyes, ears, nose, mouth, skin) or when our mind sends a message that effects us internally. Once we have received information it may not make any sense to us, so it has to be processed through our memory of experiences and symbols. It is necessary for the brain to accommodate and generalize the information, since if each perception were handled individually, we would soon run out of storage capacity and retrieval would be virtually impossible. Thus, cognitive processing is a primary element in communication.

Cognition demands that before the brain stores anything, a sufficient number of unique qualities of things and events are removed until the information can be made into prototypes, associated by a common set of characteristics and identified by a symbol that can be used to identify new perceptions received. Each image or relationship is stored and identified by some symbol so that it can be retrieved or transmitted. Furthermore, a governing set of principles is also stored, so that the brain has procedures to follow in processing data, selecting informa-tion to transmit, and putting together symbols into transmittable form. Deficiencies in cognitive development, thus, hamper the whole process of thought and speech. Inability to abstract, poor memory, distortions in the rules of symbol connection all reduce the capacity to communicate. For example, none of us can remember all of the different trees we have encountered in a lifetime. We have a storage area in our brain called "tree" which is open to all objects associated with the characteristics of the prototype for which the symbol "tree" stands like trunks, bark, leaves, needles, cones, etc. We may also have some substorage areas for particular kinds of trees, so that we are able to discriminate "pine" from "palm" and "Christmas tree" from "tree of knowledge." Associated with these categories we have some associated spaces so that we can remember particular, significant trees like "the old oak in our backyard" and "the tree that fell and smashed my garage during the tornado."

We do not necessarily store "small tree" and "large tree" as such. Rather, we have concept categories for "largeness" and "smallness" which enable us to make a series of judgments. We can process information so that we can compare the elm tree with our own height and pronounce it, "large," or we can compare it with our memory perception of a sequoia tree and pronounce it, "small." "Large," "small," "pretty," "ugly," and similar concepts are relative evaluations and can be plugged in to provide judgmental categories which apply to things and events we hold in memory. This is of particular importance for classroom teachers who deal with concepts like "originality" and "creativity." Often, we lose sight of the judgmental quality of these words, and thus forget that a product similar to what has been produced by other students might be totally original to the student who produced it. Something cannot be original only when it is first produced, for there would then be little originality in the world. "Creativity" also is a judgment we apply to the quality of work produced. It is not so difficult to teach students to produce something or other, but it is impossible to teach them to be "creative," since we would only know if they were after the fact. A recent study of the concept "creativity" shows that there is no agreement about its qualities and thus, it cannot be used as a noun (state of being), but rather as an adjective (expressing a state of mind in relation to another quality).

The process of perceiving, analyzing, and communicating seems to follow rules. We carry it on as we do because we have learned to do so. If we do what we have learned, we should have a sort of guarantee that other people around us who learned in the same way are doing roughly the same thing. That is, we can assume that when they receive data similar to what we receive, they will use symbols similar to what we use when they classify it. We can also assume that they will use similar rules to connect words for transmission and make their judgments in roughly the same value categories we employ. What we cannot tell, of course, is whether or not people have learned what we have learned. It is dangerous to assume that this is so without evidence. The nature of home life and neighborhood can produce vast differences in acculturation. One of the hazards of inner-city education is the fact that most of the teachers are acculturated quite differently from their students. It is easy to identify with people who share a common symbology, but such identification cannot be extended to unfamiliar people until we have "cracked their code" and understand their system. We have noted in previous chapters that the ability to take the role of the "other" is essential to rhetorical development. Rhetoric can only be effective if the audience can be understood. Without effective rhetoric, teaching cannot be effective. We have also noted that ability to understand a common symbol system is the basis of identification. Thus, almost as an admonition to teachers, it appears unwise to assume that any given student uses words in the same way we use them. We can only expect reasonable compatability in understanding when we have ascertained that abstract dual perspectives are the same.

Another important problem we face in our communication is that we do not react solely to external stimuli. The human brain has the capacity to process information without reference to external fact, and consequently we can develop internal motivations unique to ourselves. We can literally create a world of events in our own minds. The rules and ideas each of us operates by are sensible and rational to us at the time we employ them, but it is not safe to assume that another person understands them.

A computer operator can present you with a handbook about the operation of his machine and the language it responds to, and if you are willing to do the work, you can learn to make the machine behave the same way he does. This is not the case with humans, since we cannot explain our own internal programming to others, and if we could do it for one set of circumstances, there is no guarantee that it would remain the same for others. In order to remain fully aware of the complexity of human communication, it is important to remember three propositions.

1. Despite the fact that what goes on in your mind may appear similar to what goes on in the mind of another person, your mind is unique in content and only partly similar in its rules of operation to another mind.

2. Whatever goes on in your mind is logical and reasonable to you at the time, despite the fact that it may not look logical and reasonable to anyone else and that it might even seem foolish and defeating to you after you behave.

3. Every communication behavior affects the person who perceives it and influences his next behavior. Thus, communication is a dynamic process of relationship.

In our diagram, if we were to spin the grids so that each column and each row could rotate independently and at different rates of speed, virtually anything retained in one row or column could be connected with virtually anything in any other rows or columns. Thus, any word we possess can be connected with any other word, and any image to any other image. We can connect our image of horse and horn, and then connect our symbols "uni" and "corn" and create a "unicorn." People create such entities in their mind much of the time. Humans have the capacity to manipulate what they have stored in their heads according to rules of culture, rules of their own making, and sometimes just at random. We may, if we like, refer to this process as thought. We refer to its results, i.e., what is communicated—the whole process is a composite of images and symbols manipulated somehow by the individual—thus, verbal output is "evidence" of thought.

We may refer to the process of manipulating what is stored in the mind as "thinking," "daydreaming," "creating," "wheel spinning," "wool gathering," "hallucinating," or by many other names. It is possible for humans to create a horse, put wings on it, give it a name, "Pegasus," make up stories about it, and take those stories quite seriously, even though no such animal appeared before their senses. It is possible for humans to make up other people, endow them with personalities, sets of values and behaviors, bring them into contact with each other, and report the results. We know that all people tend to manipulate the material they hold in their minds. We know that generally, humans are capable of thinking almost anything; they can commit criminal acts in their minds, and they can do great deeds of courage.

As long as the mind is able to abstract and store and manipulate, the grid has infinite capacity. Both rows and columns are open-ended, and sometimes they can intersect and relate in peculiar ways, indescribable by any diagram.

Humans can block memories from their minds, and they can make events look like something they were not. It is possible to build a wall around parts of memory and to add and subtract details to make events more palatable. It is also possible that hidden and blocked parts of the mind can take over activity and move and motivate the person, and it is possible that truth can intrude on repression and bring about anxiety and guilt. Though these are matters sometimes treated by a psychiatrist, we need to know about them, for we never know when a person is operating under control of his unconscious mind.

People often respond to their mental images rather than to real objects. A girl meeting a handsome man for the first time, knowing little about his personality, can endow him with a personality so charming that she ends up marrying him in her mind, even when he pays no attention to her at all. A student can endow a teacher with the qualities of evil incarnate and respond to him accordingly, even though the teacher never gave him cause for emnity (we call this prejudice). Because of the infinite capacity of manipulation in the grid of memory, it is relatively impossible to predict what people have on their minds at any given moment.

We can add to our grids indefinitely. We can add new perceptions, new words, and new methods of putting words together. If we discover new words with no images, we can construct images for them. If we encounter images for which we have no words, we can discover or invent words. We can learn other languages and grammars. Furthermore, we can vary our particular values depending on what is important to us at a particular time. A stimulus that evokes a mild response on one occasion is capable of evoking a much stronger response, if the conditions are different. Thus, the human has the capacity to react in ways that may appear unpredictable to other people, even though they could be explained logically, if we could perceive what was going on inside the person's mind. The ability to predict individual behavior with a high degree of accuracy is denied to us, although most of us eventually develop regularities in some of our mundane behavior that lead others to believe us predictable. For the most part, however, it is dangerous to assume that a given communication strategy will evoke consistent responses, either from one or more people. Allowance for possible variation must always be made. For the teacher, this means that adjustment to uncertainty is imperative. He must be prepared to make individual adjustments as he perceives variation from his expectations in the responses of given students.

How most naive observers regard the communication process can be discovered by watching an American attempting to communicate with someone who does not speak English. When the American receives a look of bewilderment in response to his words, he may repeat his sentence in a louder voice. Then he may try to shout the sentence, conveying the impression that sheer sound will break the cultural barrier. When he discovers that his words have no effect at all, the speaker may finally resort to gesturing, pointing, and repeating English words that represent his acts. He finally gets to the point where he begins to build a common experience based on what he knows the other person agrees with and associates it with symbolic representations. Between the two, people from both cultures can build agreement about the meanings of the words used. Until there is a first agreement, communication between the two is virtually impossible. The problem suggested by this analogy is that cultural differences often exist among people who ostensibly speak the same language.

Often we conclude that we are being disobeyed and resisted when the real fact is that our listener or audience cannot understand what we want of him. This concept is of particular importance to teachers who face the disadvantaged, but it is also important to remember that children of different families will be products of different cultures as well; we never know where the significant differences lie until a disagreement has been generated. It is imperative that the teacher help bridge communication gaps wherever they exist. This is usually best done by cracking the student's code and using it to lead him to understand that of the teacher. The teacher must be attentive to unique rules of communication revealed by his students. If he is skillful, he may use these rules to acculturate the student into normal classroom behavior.

Every culture (including families) strives to get children to learn to communicate according to the rules of that culture. Thus, since the child must learn to communicate in a variety of settings, he often finds that his communication rules of one culture conflict with those in another culture. This may be a reason why some students resist school with such vigor; if the student learns what the school wants him to learn, he may no longer be able to function in his home or his neighborhood. Clearly, he will choose to communicate according to the code of the group most important to him. If peers are most important, then school may be rejected. The task for the teacher is to point out that rules are not always the same, and it is necessary to act according to rules of a given situation rather than to try out one set of rules in all situations.

Grown-ups, however, often do not remember that a child's memory banks may be incomplete, or his experiences limited, and thus, they may tend to expect more adjustment from him than he is capable of giving. Most children struggle to accommodate, and if they are rewarded for their efforts, their capacity to use symbols expands. However, in this process it is possible for a child to suffer enough penalties so that the urge to communicate is suppressed. Even people who are ostensibly wise and sophisticated often do not understand that they must take into account the acculturation of the other before their words will make sense. Professors talk to laymen in terms that are incomprehensible, and yet ascribe to the laymen willful resistance to their talk. Specialists in all fields remain locked into their jargon, and confuse the daylights out of people who have to listen to them. This idea is of considerable importance to teachers, particularly those who have been at it for a while, and who have achieved real familiarity with their subject matter. After several years, the teacher may forget that his students are encountering for the first time materials so familiar to the teacher that he can talk about them with little conscious effort. The teacher sometimes loses sight of the fact that the students who come to him new each year have not had the experience of the students that preceded them, and that, therefore, the teaching process must start at the beginning, on a very simple level. New professors, just out of graduate school, make this error when they try to teach their beginning classes everything learned during the preparation of their dissertation.

COMMUNICATION, THOUGHT, AND THE TEACHING-LEARNING PROCESS

Since communication involves the *results* of internal processing of symbols, images, and values, we cannot regard it as a simple linear function of symbol processing such as that performed by a computer. Often we find ourselves connecting images in our head and living through future events. We can, in that way, "rehearse" for what might be about to come. We can also relive the past; enjoy past recreations and suffer through past miseries. Often, we can do this at will; sometimes we cannot prevent a flood of memories from the past or apprehensions about the future from taking over our minds. On occasion, we will be overwhelmed by emotion, suffering a flood of feeling from some unspecified source. In any case, when we are required to respond to communications coming at us, *we will respond in terms of whatever our mental state happens to be at that time.* Regardless of how hard we try, we are not able to conceal our thoughts very well from an adept observer. We reveal our agitations, distractions, concerns, angers, and joys with the words we speak and the way we speak them. To our listener, therefore, our communication is the end product of thought. For our purposes here, we can regard thought as the process in which symbols, images, and values are associated for the purpose of transmitting information; descriptions, inferences, evaluations, concepts, directives, associations, and so on to others with whom we interact.

Description of the communication process thus tells us little about thought, but it is our only clue to what goes on in the other's mind. We may conjecture about what goes on inside the mind of another person, but we can never determine this absolutely. We can only infer what is taking place. Everything we say here, for example, about thought and its association with communication is inferential. As teachers, it is our task to approach students and get them to think in some orderly fashion in order to direct them to some goals. We must have some conceptualizations from which to work. But most of us fail to inquire about the nature of the assumptions on which we act toward others, and consequently, we lack an adequate theoretical framework from which to evaluate our teaching.

In school, we are mostly concerned with "reporting out." We generate input by engaging in some activities in the classroom, and we expect the student to give us evidence that the experiences have had some impact on him. We get this information by requiring the student to respond for us in the form of recitation or test. We then proceed to judge the response, because we infer that there is a relationship between thought and verbalization or written output. We do not believe that a student has learned until he does some task that we feel measures his learning. It is questionable, when we do this, whether we are really inquiring about what the student now knows, or feels, or can do, or whether we are testing our own capacity to control his output to make him fit our expectations. There appears to be a tendency for

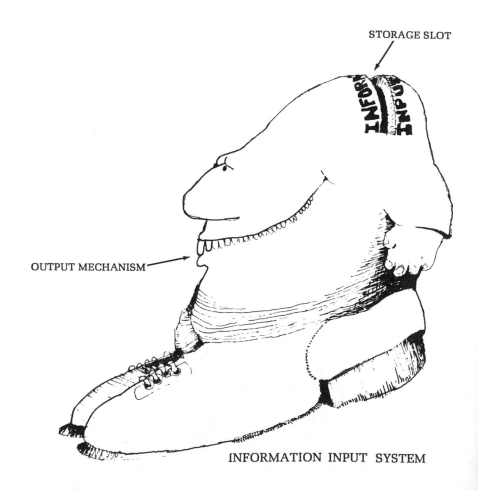

STORAGE SLOT

OUTPUT MECHANISM

INFORMATION INPUT SYSTEM

teachers to specify what a learning student will look like and then attempt to regulate the behavior of all students so that it will conform to that specification. There is little effort to discover how a student has changed as a result of the activites carried on in school. Yet, based on what we know about cultural variation and individual uniqueness, it is quite reasonable to assume that each student will change in a different way, thus providing minimal use for generalized test or measurement.

When teachers test a student, they require him to perform orally or in writing at a specific time and place. The assumption appears to be that all students have equal dexterity at writing, equal skill in speaking, and thus, what they produce will appropriately represent their learning rather than their skill at writing, or speaking, in general. Once we have their output, we attach some evaluation to it. We set limits on the student's behavior toward acts we can evaluate because they describe *what we think we have communicated to him.* When we evaluate his response, we do not really know whether he had learned substantively, whether he has learned what our expectations are and decided to comply with them, or whether he has done his best but is limited by lack of skill at responding. Teachers attempt to persuade students to learn things and behaviors that can be reported out in ways that the teacher evaluates as "good." Thus, a rhetorical teacher will try to make the student into a rhetorical student, for if the student seeks the approval of the teacher, he will devote his learning efforts to the discovery of behaviors that will evoke the response he seeks from the teacher. The student can also choose to employ a negative rhetoric and engage in behaviors calculated to disrupt the teacher and evoke noncontrolled behavior from him. For some students, the ability to agitate the teacher is more important than earning an "A."

It is hard to conceive of a teacher acting in any way other than rhetorical, however, for *the purpose of teaching is to change behavior* through the use of communication, and when anyone tries to change behavior through communication, he is engaging in rhetoric. Even in a totally "free" classroom environment, students must be persuaded to take advantage of that freedom, and somewhere in the circuit there must be contact between teacher and student to "sum up" what has been learned. The imposition of a free environment in the classroom is itself a rhetoric designed to persuade the student to take greater advantages of the experiences available to him.

There are a great many options that are open for the imposition of rhetoric in the classroom. *Once the teacher honestly accepts his role as persuader,* there are some basic questions that he must raise about what he does in the classroom.

1. What behavior do I seek from the student that tells me he has

learned something? What reason do I have to believe that this behavior is relevant to learning? Is it reasonable to expect that the student can demonstrate this behavior? Will demonstrating the behavior injure him in any way?

2. What must the student know and be able to do before he expresses the behavior I seek? What alternatives are there that I will find acceptable?

3. Will the activities I am carrying on bring about the desired behavior? What do I need to know about the student (students) in order to bring this about? What do I know (from research or experience) that leads me to believe that my method will work?

4. Of what use is this particular behavior to the student? How can I make him understand its use?

When the teacher raises questions like these about his subject matter he must put himself into closer relationship with the students in order to discover answers. He may see his students more individually and may even discover that his role is to persuade students to learn on their terms rather than on his terms or on terms of the curriculum.

It is important here to distinguish between compliant behavior and learning behavior. Most teachers know that the student who comes to school only to disrupt, and the student who stays away entirely, are not learning (at least in the standard definition of it; they may well be learning about what a hateful place school is). What most teachers do not understand is that the students who are present and obedient may also not be learning, they may only be complying. Much behavior that teachers evaluate positively and thus reward can be classified as "compliance behavior."

1. Compliance behavior is characterized by the ability of the student to pass the tests that teacher devises with high marks according to the teacher's evaluation. The compliant student will be equally adept at objective and essay type tests.

2. The compliant student will conform to the rules of the classroom. He will speak when he is invited, he will remain quiet when others are speaking. He will not violate school rules.

3. The compliant student will do things that please teacher and he will do them solely for that purpose.

4. The compliant student will rarely threaten teacher with questions he cannot answer or with requests for help that he cannot fulfill.

5. The compliant student is generally neat and clean and comes from a "good family."

While it may seem cynical to say so, it is students who fit that description who receive the maximum rewards from the school system. However, while it might be desirable to have compliant students in the classroom, and while it is not necessarily true that compliant students do not learn, there are other indicators that provide a more valid evidence of learning than do the above behaviors.

1. A learning student is able to think and express different thoughts about what he has been exposed to, and he will be able to argue for the subject matter with a reasonable degree of success. He will seek opportunities to read, listen, talk, and write about topics of interest.

2. A learning student will want to do something about what he is learning. He will not want to sit passively and receive information. He will want to take an active part in acquiring it.

3. When a learning student shows lack of interest and elects not to participate in a particular activity or exercise, he will have reasons for his lack of interest and he will be willing to talk about them.

4. A learning student occasionally resists the teacher's attempts at measuring his ability through tests, but he will be willing and able to display what he knows, believes, and can do in alternate ways.

5. A learning student puts considerable pressure on teachers and peers to move on, either to more sophisticated concepts in the subject under study, or to new topics about which his curiosity has been raised.

The main characteristic of the compliant student is that his learning takes place mostly on the cognitive level and he is able to display it only in ways devised by the teacher. He does not become this way out of choice, but because he is offered few alternatives by the teacher. The learning student may, but not necessarily will, show excellence in measures of performance devised by the teacher. *The compliant student responds to the rhetoric of the teacher. The learning student will respond to the rhetoric of the teacher, the subject matter, and his own personal involvements and commitments.*

This leads to the main declaration about the teaching-learning relationship that is the substance of this book: *the process of learning is best described in communication terms.* To the extent that the willingness, opportunity, and alternatives of communication expand, learning also expands.

The alienation of young people in our society; the rising crime rate, the increase in use of drugs, new sex norms, epidemic apathy, all seem to indicate that there has been some failure in our society to provide young people with knowledge about ways to live a satisfactory life. There is, indeed, the gnawing feeling that the kind of life we, as adults, would regard as satisfactory, seems unpleasant to many young people. Adult society has spent its generations expanding science and technology for purposes of security and comfort. Wisdom and cognition have been almost synonymous throughout this process, to the point where intellectualism is now closely associated with symbolic behavior rather than with the capacity to perform acts to solve problems. Our expanded population and technology confront our young people with a world of problems that seem unsolvable. They seem to have the urgency to find out either how to solve those problems, how to live a satisfactory life in spite of them, or how to stop the world and get off. Because of this, there is urgency to find ways of relating to other human beings that are supportive and gratifying. Relationship between humans now becomes an end in itself, rather than a means to an end. Our schools are confronted with legions of young people who need to find out how to get along with one another. It cannot be assumed that this is a process that comes about automatically, merely because of desire. It is necessary to learn something about the art of relating, and to take steps to activate our learning into activities and instruction that will help students learn what they need to know to survive in the future.

The psychiatrist Jordan Scher once said, "man is born alone and must acquire twoing." The acquisition of the capacity to relate to other people becomes more and more important as the society demonstrates its capacity to destroy itself. Many people in our society are concerned with survival. Some "know" that we will survive. Others are not so sure. But survive or not, there is no way to cope with the problems of the future if we remain locked into ritual routines that are not relevant to the problems that society and individuals face. And to complicate matters even further, there are those who inquire if there is a purpose in seeking survivial at all, if the quality of life in the future is to be dehumanizing. The message given us by B.F. Skinner in *Beyond Freedom and Dignity* suggests that only conditioned robots will survive. The message given us by Rollo May in *Power and Innocence* suggests the alternative; man taking control of himself not only to solve the problems of our society, but to solve his own problems as well. It is to the latter task that the diligent efforts of the schools need to be turned.

It does not take much experience for the student to discover that making harmonious relationships with others is not necessarily assisted by the kinds of things that are formally taught in school. He knows that he has to survive in his family, on the street, with his peers. Schools teach little about this. Social scientists have dealt extensively with socialization and interaction but talk little, if at all, about friendship and loving. There is, perhaps, little that can be known, cognitively, about human relationships. They seem to rest on affective bases. But presumably, like most attitudinal and behavioral issues, they can be materially affected by supervised experience of the type legitimately given in the schools.

In the light of these demands for new kinds of learning, some modification needs to be made in the traditional approach to teaching. The modification we have in mind is not revolutionary. It starts with the understanding that some kinds of learning and skills cannot be taught except in an authoritarian framework. A student cannot have choice in how to pronounce the letters of the alphabet or in what numbers mean. However by the same token, rigidity in instruction in social sciences and humanities is tantamount to indoctrination. What is needed is some understanding of the wide variety of possible outputs from students which demonstrates that learning has taken place. Traditionally, teachers have asked students to produce what is acceptable to them (the teachers) as evidence that learning has taken place. All other outputs have been ruled out. Our view of change is to provide alternative channels for students to use to demonstrate knowledge. In a sense, *it would be to rule out what is unacceptable, and rule in all other contributions.* Thus, in some areas there would only be one possible output, such as associating sounds with letters in print, or knowing number rules. In other areas there could be a variety of outputs. Certainly there are other ways to demonstrate a knowledge of U.S. geography besides reciting the names of the state capitals in alphabetical order. Perhaps a student could demonstrate that he knows how to follow a road map and interpret its symbols. Perhaps another student could write descriptive essays about the topography of a state. The point is, when the teacher applies his rhetoric to motivate the student to learn, he must take into account the student's rhetoric directed at satisfying some of his personal urgencies. The provision of the widest possible range of alternatives represents an effective way to allow for the joint functioning of rhetorics which might otherwise clash.

The model would be an alternative-filled classroom with students making choices and taking the consequences of them. There would be opportunity for talk between students, and between students and teacher. Students would not necessarily all be doing the same thing at the same time. Yet, the classroom would not be devoid of structure or goals. Definition would be made of what students need to learn, and opportunity would be allowed for them to learn what they want to learn. Legitimate exchanges could be made between teacher and student so that the privilege of following one's curiosity could be traded for the task of learning fundamentals defined as necessary. Each student would be seeking identity through achievement of capability and acquiring subject matter, learning skills, discovering how to manage feelings. The goals of this kind of classroom would be compatible with the philosophies of George Herbert Mead.

Mead's philosophy is that people find their identity through the responses that others make to them. The more important the other person is to them, the more influential he is in shaping their personality. For all of us, if a behavior is rewarded consistently, it becomes part of our permanent repertoire of behaviors. If it evokes penalties, we tend to suppress it. If it is rewarded by an important person, we are even more likely to use it. If it is punished by that person, we feel guilt about it. We make decisions about who we are and what we are capable of based on our assessment of what works and what does not in achieving our goals. The only data we have on which to base this judgment are the responses beamed at us by other people. If a child enters school with the notion that the teacher is an important person, then the way the teacher responds to that child is crucial in determining his identity as learner. It may even affect the entire course of his life. Thus, acquiring ethos, that is, appearing important to the student, is an important part of the teacher's rhetoric.

If we accept this idea, then the job of teacher is much more than that of disseminator of knowledge. His task is to build his own image, to manage and manipulate environments, to moniter the behavior of each student, to attempt to persuade or motivate him to try various ways of expressing what he knows, and to make sensible choices among alternatives. Persuasion must be directed toward moving the student into activities where he can succeed, for each success is its own motivation, pushing the student to select increasingly more difficult modes of operation.

This is, admittedly, an idealistic view of what can go on in a classroom. The authors are well aware of the strictures that prevail in the typical school. Still, with the record as spotty as it is these days, it seems worth the risk to attempt to provide more realistic learning situations and experiences.

By permitting a range of choice, and encouraging interaction among the students while they are at work, the student can be helped to come to grips with his own capabilities and thus develop his personality in a way that is most productive to him. As we have noted, the interaction process is the medium through which this kind of development is most effectively brought about. Learning about working and interacting with others must be more than superficial. To tell the student what is expected of him when he deals with others may provide him with a set of cognitions, but what he learns will make no sense to him until he has the opportunity to test his behavior under relatively natural circumstances. As far as interaction is concerned, "knowledge of," is far more important than "knowledge about." Those skills that support the whole curriculum, reading, writing, speaking, listening, are not learned for their own sake. In a sense, they are not cognitions; they have no subject matter of their own. They are, rather, the supportive instruments that permit all other instruction to go on as well as everyday existence.

If the student's opportunity to communicate is restricted unnecessarily or suppressed, he is denied alternatives for personal development. To require only one kind of activity, for example "show and tell" or book reports, suggests that there is no relationship between communication in school and life outside. The child needs all four communication skills in his life. It may be necessary to build from skill in one area to motivate acquisition of skill in the others. Thus, if a student is a skilled speaker-interactor when he enters the classroom, this skill can be used to encourage the growth of competence in writing, reading, or both.

Even though the school may not be able to control the kind of interaction that goes on in the home, with peers, or on the playground, constructive interaction situations can be built in the classroom. We can never make the classroom into a home, but it can be sort of a neighborhood: students do spend six to seven hours a day in school, and thus, skills can be acquired in a setting natural to the classroom, which can be carried over into other dimensions of life. To be natural to the classroom means that the situations designed aid learning and implement the curriculum, but still provide contact with others in the working out of problems, learning of applications, and sharing of experiences. There is no reason, for example, why most assignments need to be solitary tasks done while seated at a desk. Most subject matter throughout the grades and into high school is sufficiently complicated (and often exciting if handled well) to permit mutual activity geared toward involvement with the material.

If the student's communication in school is restricted only to performances deemed necessary by the teacher, his opportunities to grow are limited to the directions specified. Often these are not compatible with the kinds of communication the student is using in contacts with people outside. Therefore, even if he learned performances well, there would still be no reason for him to apply what he has learned outside of the classroom.

We dare not assume that all student goals will be compatible with teacher's. When a student tends to behave other than in ways approved by teacher, he becomes dissonant, and if he cannot reconcile his dissonance to discover some sense of fit between his goals and the goals specified for him, he may elect either to pull out, or to resist the system. When this happens the school has lost, for rhetoric has failed. Interestingly enough, there is an aura of failure that pervades all the experience of the failing student. A failure in one aspect of life will affect behavior in other aspects. The student who is not making it at home or in the streets cannot be expected to make it in the classroom unless he is provided with special opportunities to achieve—which may, under certain conditions, strengthen him so that he is better able to cope with home and street.

THE RHETORIC OF SCHOOLING

At the beginning of this chapter we offered a model of thought-communication which consisted largely of a hypothetical grid or set of storage "bins," into which information can be put. We have identified the information as images, symbols, and values. We have talked at length about images and symbols, but we have said little about the nature of values and the way they are shaped, and how they influence the way the student learns and grows. Values make the difference in the way a child matures; the rhetorical impact that the teacher has on his values is most important to the student. Thus, for any given teacher, it is not so important how much substantive knowledge has been pumped into a student's head, but how that student feels about the knowledge and what it means to him. If the student can develop a positive attitude toward a subject area, he will be well equipped to get his own information as he needs and wants it. It is our value system that underlies our rhetoric which determines what we will do or say.

It is possible to feel very strongly about some image or idea, either positively or negatively; it is also possible to have no attitude at all, or to have mixed attitudes. What is clear, however, is that whatever we select to communicate or act out, we have some feeling about. The precise way our system of values operates to control our choice of goals is still a mystery, but there is reason to believe that we make choices based more on how we feel than on rational appeals. People who are important to us tend to shape our values. If we are hostile to someone, or if he has no importance, we are likely to reject his wishes or ignore him. This has some direct relevance to the criticism of performance as it is practiced in the schools. There is an assumption that if the teacher offers criticism the student will improve, and if he does not, it is because of his willful resistance. But most admonitions offered by adults to children tend to fall on deaf ears because, in the value system of the child, the adult is not important enough to warrant agreement or the value system of the child is antithetical to the value system the adult is offering. Children can be compelled to behave "appropriately" if tight control is maintained, but there is little hope that the behavior will be carried over into everyday life.

As an example of how values might operate, suppose we have stored in our minds an image of "father" working long hours in his store trying "to make ends meet" and perhaps to send his teen-agers to college. We may have a strong positive orientation to this image. We may have made a connection between this image and the set of symbols, "American private enterprise system." Because of our membership in a radical group, however, we may have a negative value assigned to the verbal concept. When we get our image and our symbols together, it is necessary to reconcile the conflict between the values. We must either revise our image of father, or change the symbols associated with the image, or change our values assigned to the original symbols, or change our values assigned to father and his activity. This is a process known as "resolving dissonance." The necessity for us to make this kind of reconciliation frequently keeps the "wheels spinning" in our heads. We try to get our images and symbols into some kind of harmony with our values, so we can look ahead and make some fairly accurate predictions about what we want to have happen and what influence we might exert to make those things happen.

The simple act of selecting a restaurant at which to eat is an illustration, for in order to make the selection we have to examine our images of past experience, symbols about experience, and values assigned to all of them. We define an image of a "pleasurable experience," and we try to make our selection based on what we think might bring about this pleasurable experience. Thus, we select a restaurant based on symbol and image processing. We do not make empirical tests of several restaurants prior to our selection. It is our experiential memory from which we build our selection.

When values assigned to images and symbols are concordant, then the actions we choose appear clear and definite. If we value negatively both the image of the insect and the word "spider," and we assign a negative value to the act of being bitten by an insect, then we can elect squashing the spider as a course of action without causing ourselves very much trouble at all. Our concern is primarily with doing something to avoid being bitten by the spider. Later on, however, another set of values may plug in, and we may want to alter our actions toward spiders.

Other actions we might take are not always harmonious with the values of others around us. We may see a beautiful "chick" in the classroom and project an image of "me and her together in the moonlight." The "chick" may not have the same image, however. She might resent the use of the word "chick," our physical appearance may not accord with the type to which she assigns value, and so on. Our problem, once we discover that our values are incompatible, is to get her images and values consonant with our own. When we attempt to beam symbols at her in order to bring this about, we are using communication as rhetoric; we are attempting to exert some control over our environment through application of symbolic behavior.

The preceding model is directly applicable to the classroom. Teacher, following his plan (to which he assigns high value) says, "it is reading time," to which Joseph assigns low value. Joseph resists reading. Teacher then says, "it is time to study airplanes," to which Joseph assigns high value. Teacher hands Joseph a book about airplanes and suggests that he read it. Joseph is perfectly happy to do so, because he prefers that to "reading." As absurdly simple as it sounds, this is essentially the process of rhetoric; teaching involves discovering what moves the student and using it to motivate the student to participate in useful activity. For some, the act of reading may have high value. Others may need to be appealed to through their own interests. As the teacher proceeds to make his appeals, he is practicing rhetoric.

Virtually anything that we do or say is rhetorical. To be rhetorical there must be a listener or receiver in mind and an intent to do something to bring about some response from that person. Traditionally, rhetoric has been applied only to those communications that are directed at some specific outcome. We broaden the definition somewhat to include those communications that are directed at differential outcomes, like the communication of the classroom where teacher wants to have some effect on all the students, although often he cannot specify one effect that should come about in all of them, or a specific effect for each student.

Most of our communication is designed to bring about some kind of response from others. The nature of the response we receive to our rhetoric is the crucial variable in becoming a mature, competent human. We get our idea of who we are and what we are capable of achieving by examining the responses to our attempts to influence others. Any communication that can be examined against the criteria of "effective-ineffective" can be considered rhetorical. Let us examine some of the kinds of communications we use to see how this principle operates.

1. The simple act of greeting someone on the street is rhetorical. The goal is to receive acknowledgment from the other. To say "hi" and receive no response makes the message ineffective. If the other person greets you in return, then the rhetoric has been effective.

2. The act of giving information of any kind under any circumstances is rhetorical. The essence of persuasion is the latent message that the information being presented is worth having and should be accepted by the other. Giving directions to a stranger, a list of instructions about how to do something, a classoom lecture, a narration of a personal experience—all are rhetorical. Instruction in a school setting is particularly rhetorical, for its goal is the modification in behavior of the learners.

3. The act of offering therapy to a troubled person is rhetorical. Even though the therapist may have no more specific goal than "helping the

client to function or feel better," the goal is still a behavior change, and consequently the talk that goes on to achieve that end must be considered rhetorical.

4. Telling one's problems to someone who can help is rhetorical. The recital of problems is a clear request for help, even if the image of "help" is of the other person listening.

5. The advertiser is engaged in rhetoric when he seeks to induce the public to buy his product. Any effort at exchanging goods for money is rhetorical for it seeks an action from the receiver of the communication. The resistance offered by the potential customer is also rhetorical, for it seeks to have the seller modify his price (or go away entirely).

6. Any political message is rhetorical because it seeks to change attitudes resulting in a specific action at voting time. Discussion of social issues among friends can even be rhetorical, for the goal is to modify the beliefs of those who listen.

7. A husband and wife carrying on a family argument is rhetorical for each is seeking acceptance of his opinions. Any family dispute or discussion may be considered rhetorical according to this view.

8. The sexual suasions and resistances carried on between men and women are rhetorical, for both the male message and the female message seek a behavior change in the other.

9. The comedian entertaining in a nightclub (or anywhere else) is rhetorical for he seeks the response of laughter from his audience.

10. The work performed by the student in the classroom is rhetorical for it seeks a behavior in the form of an evaluation or reward in return.

In general, then, we consider communication to be rhetorical when it has a purpose. When a speaker has something in mind (even when it is not clearly in mind) that he wants from another person, any action that he takes to bring about the desired response (or any response at all) is rhetorical. By this definition, virtually everything that goes on in school is rhetorical. School seeks to modify human behavior in many ways and, as a formal institution, it can exert control over the ways it seeks to bring about modification. Schools sometimes employ "inartistic rhetoric," that is, they seek to bring about change through force of regulations or punishments. According to Aristotle, inartistic rhetoric is any attempt to persuade through means other than language.

The student has his own reasons for engaging in rhetoric. Regardless of his commitment, or lack of it, to school, he is there involuntarily. There is, in most students, a kernel of resistance that motivates them to attempt to induce others to view the school as unpleasant. Only rarely will students totally commit themselves to the goals of the school system.

Once acculturated to the involuntary system, however, a student often discovers that survival demands that he try to get teachers and classmates to act in ways that are compatible with his goals. He may generate the idea of becoming a "top student," and thus have to persuade the teacher that he is worth the highest possible evaluation. He may also wish to achieve status with his peer group and may decide that one way to do this is to convince the teacher that he is a troublemaker; thus each negative reinforcement from school results in positive reinforcement from peers.

In this sense, the relationship between students and teachers could be regarded as a sort of rhetorical competition, in which each is trying to win rewards at the expense of the other. Good sense says that if the rewards can be won collectively, that is, if both teacher and student can act in ways that are mutually rewarding, then school would be more profitable for all. This means, of course, a wide variety of alternatives for behavior available to teacher and student alike so that the student can develop feelings and achieve skills in addition to the cognitive material that he takes in as the school's prime offering.

When the student wins at the expense of the teacher, school is ineffectual. When the teacher wins at the expense of the student, school is authoritarian. Therefore, there is a real necessity to develop a system of exchanges of rewards that can make school a gratifying experience for all parties concerned. To do this, the student would have to be aware of the teacher's goal, and the teacher would have to be equally aware of what the student seeks. When this happens, rational exchange can take place, and learning, rather than compliance, can be a feature of the instructional arena. Presumably, such a condition would start with the teacher imposing rhetoric on the student to convince him that his (the student's) goals can be met in some way in conjunction with the goals of the teacher. This means that the teacher needs to be able to assess his own goals, those of the school, and those of students and find compatibilities among them. Demonstrating these compatibilities to students is the rhetorical task of the teacher.

The implication in this chapter is that any exchange between humans has an element of competition in it, and the most satisfactory state of affairs is to work toward a mutual victory for all parties. Since winning at communication has so much to do with the development of a total personality, this becomes imperative for the school system and everyone participating in it.

The focus of this book is mainly on talk. However, art, writing, music are all acts of communication and are part of our concern. We direct our attention to talk because it is the activity most frequently engaged in—the main means by which people exchange rhetorics. Furthermore, we believe that most other modes of communication are based on talk. For your purposes, as reader, if you are more concerned with writing, feel free to substitute the word "write" for "speak" any time it seems reasonable.

SUMMARY

In this chapter we laid some communication groundwork by explaining what goes on when one person attempts to exchange symbols with another and be understood. Throughout, our goal was to look at the ramifications of this process of communication in the context of the classroom, for it is here that exchange of symbols is most often confused. This confusion results for a number of reasons. Primarily, all people have slightly different rules of communication which they have learned. These differences in rules may be seen to a major extent when teachers from one socioeconomic background instruct students of another; or when there is a mixture of cultural, racial backgrounds represented by students in any classroom. Even the most homogeneous grouping of students is likely to illustrate some family rule differences which have ramifications in the classroom behavior of the students.

In order to respond most effectively to this variation, the teacher needs to make a number of experiences available to students so that they have maximum opportunity to express their ideas and learning. A student whose needs are blocked by generalized restrictions becomes frustrated and defiant or simply compliant with little carry-over of learning into his everyday life. The teacher needs to make assessments of student communication with an eye toward differences and how these differences can be accommodated in the classroom. Both students and teacher operate rhetorically in that both seek to meet needs with the other. Our aim is to help teachers become better rhetors in the classroom, while aiding their students to gain the same capactiy.

WORKS CITED:

May, Rollo. *Power and Innocence, a Search for the Sources of Violence.* New York: W.W. Norton, 1072.

Mead, George Herbert. *Mind, Self and Society.* Chicago: University of Chicago Press, 1934.

Skinner, B.F. *Beyond Freedom and Dignity.* New York: Alfred A. Knopf, 1971.

WORKS RECOMMENDED:

For an introduction to the general semantics system see Harry Weinberg, *Levels of Knowing and Existence.* New York: Harper & Row, 1954, and Gail Myers and Michel Myers, *The Dynamics of Human Communication,* New York: McGraw-Hill, 1973.

A good introduction to general systems theory in communication can be found in Paul Watzlawick, et al. *Pragmatics of Human Communication*, New York: W.W. Norton, 1967.

For some excellent insights into the influence of families on communication behavior, see Jules Henry, *Pathways to Madness*. New York: Random House, 1971.

A contemporary view of rhetorical theory is summarized in Lloyd Bitzer, "The Rhetorical Situation," in Richard L. Johannesen, *Contemporary Theories of Rhetoric*. New York: Harper & Row, 1971.

Futurologists interested in some possibilities for life tommorrow can check Alvin Toffler, *Future Shock*. New York: Random House, 1970, or Herman Kahn and B. Bruce-Briggs, *Things to Come*. New York: Macmillan, 1972.

The notion of social exchange as an explanation of human behavior is found in George Homans, *Social Behavior: Its Elementary Forms*. New York: Merton, 1961.

• To learn that all animals have four basic needs: survival of the species, stimulation, homeostasis (security), and territory.

• To note that in addition, humans have symbolic identity, sense of time, sense of mortality, and ability to meet their needs through negotiations with others.

• To remember that humans use rhetoric to meet their needs.

• To learn how human organizational systems develop from human needs and how the school operates as a survival agent for society.

• To recognize that school systems need to direct their rhetoric toward helping students learn how to develop effective rhetoric to cope with problems of the present-future.

• To realize that human competition involves psychic as well as physical survival.

• To learn how games function as structured stimulation designed to teach problem solving.

5
Human Needs and the Responsibility of the School

Overview

In order to use rhetoric effectively in the classroom, the teacher needs to be able to assess the needs of the students he encounters. In this chapter, we explore one possible group of needs common to all animals and attempt to relate these general needs to students functioning in the school system. We take a careful look at symbolic needs that operate for humans only: the need to acquire and defend personal identity and to make decisions in line with changes in situations as time progresses. The schools undertake great responsibility in preparing students to utilize rhetoric to meet their needs effectively in the face of increasing societal and personal problems. We hope to help in this task by offering a look at human needs as they exist in society at present as well as to speculate on their development in the future, and suggest how the classroom teacher might respond to these needs.

WE HAVE EXAMINED a communication model that explains the process and relationship of human communication. We have generated from that model an understanding of the concept of rhetoric and noted some ways that rhetoric operates in the teaching-learning situation. We have also pointed out that rhetoric proceeds from intent, the desire to accomplish some

117

goal with the person or persons who receive the rhetoric. In order to understand the nature of possible rhetorical intents, we must discover what humans need and how needs are generated into wants and wants into goals and assess the communication stake: the nature of winning and losing. In the following chapters we will discuss how strategies can be employed to make winning more likely, and what the consequences of losing are. In this chapter, we will turn our attention to human needs and where they come from and attempt to show you how human needs underlie the rhetorical transaction.

One useful source from which to understand human needs can be discovered in the work of students of animal behavior in its natural state. These scientists, referred to as *ethologists,* state that there are basic goals which all animals seek.

Survival of the Species. Animals behave in ways that regulate the number of animals that survive and control which animals mate with which others in order to balance the size of the herd or pack against the ecology. Animals that are subject to depredation breed more rapidly than their predators. In general, among all animals, modes of survival of species can be discovered.

Stimulation. Animals need excitement to stimulate them to seek food, shelter, breeding grounds, and so on. Animals also need some time for play, exercise, and recreation.

Homeostasis. Animals seek a sense of security, protection, safety and consequently build nests, explore feeding grounds, watch out for enemies, and so on in order to maintain a sense of safety.

Territory. Animals need a sense of place, a habitat, a feeding ground. In some cases, this territorial urge is very strong and individual animals contest for chunks of territory which they "own."

The process that keeps animals seeking survival, stimulation, homeostasis and territory is called "aggression." In its characteristic form, aggression keeps animals seeking what they need and defending themselves.

Each species of animal has some characteristic quality or behavior that is *specific,* that is native, to the species only. The human animal has only one quality that is not present in other animals. That is his capacity to exchange meaningful symbols, i.e., to communicate. The ability to exchange symbols provides man with additional capacities other animals do not have.

Humans can have a sense of self, an identity. They know their own names and they can separate self from other. For this reason, when we discuss basic human needs, we must consider protection of the self as a need that is not found in other animals.

Humans have a sense of time. Because of their sense of time, they are able to manipulate symbols in such a way that lessons from the past can be applied to current problems, and plans can be made to meet future problems. Alfred Korzybski referred to this process as *timebinding* and called it the most important human force. Because of timebinding, human homeostasis-seeking is materially affected. Much of human behavior is characterized by learning from past experiences and discovering how to apply them to future problems. We call this process "education."

Humans have a sense of mortality. While some animals may respond to some physiological disturbances at the time of death and separate themselves from the pack when they are about to die, there is no evidence that animals, in general, are aware of death. Humans are aware because of their timebinding capacity, and consequently much of human activity is spent protecting against possible threats and preparing for eventual extinction.

Humans may aggress directly or symbolically. We may seek goals or solve problems by direct action or by using symbols to engage the collusion of others. This latter capability, to seek goals by using symbolic communication directed at other humans for the purpose of helping us seek our goals, is called "rhetoric."

Thus, we can generate some basic human needs with rhetorical communication as the prime force designed to meet them.

1. Humans use rhetoric to organize society against physical and psychological threats. Humans also use rhetoric to protect themselves as individuals.

2. Humans use rhetoric in order to find pleasure and excitement. Most personal and social motivation falls into this category.

3. Humans use rhetoric in order to gain understanding of the world in which they live and in order to use that understanding to make themselves feel safer or more secure.

4. Humans use rhetoric in order to identify some sort of role they can occupy in society, and thus derive a unique human identity.

Most of what goes on in society (and in any classroom), can be understood in these four categories, which offer a great deal of "wisdom" about why human animals behave as they do. The four basic needs offer the substance of goals. We can infer what a person's goals are by observing his behavior and referencing back to these general categories.

PROTECTION OF SELF AND SOCIETY

Rhetoric is used to organize human society. To withstand threats to existence imposed from external forces: floods, tornados, predatory animals, and so on, it is necessary for humans to work together. Because of our physical fragility as human beings, it is necessary for us to group together to build protections against death and destruction. Our infants are so frail that they must be protected for many years before they are able to function on their own. In nature, the more complex the animal, the longer the protection period for the infant. Species that need longer protection periods show the most marked socialization.

Organization of society against natural forces is still an imperative. Early in his history, man found it necessary to organize hunting groups, agricultural communities, and so on to provide food and protection. Today our social organization has become so complex that the grocer who sells a can of beans, perhaps, does not recognize his role in the organization. But the act of raising food, processing it, transporting it, merchandising it, and preparing and eating it all represent social organization for preservation of the species. This organization is tied together through the communication of technology, science, advertising, and simple exchanges of money for goods. All of this is part of the communication process. Without the ability to exchange complicated ideas, our very complicated society could not function.

Threats from natural forces are as much with us as ever. Our own organizations, industries, towns have so interfered with natural forces that we find we need to reorganize to defend ourselves against our own organization.

Humans use rhetoric to group themselves for many purposes. The family was organized to protect the helpless neonate. Tribes developed to protect families and organize acquisition of food. Cities were organized to protect tribes and clans physically and economically. Larger geographic units were organized in order to meet the increasingly complex needs of the smaller social units.

States and nations are too complex to permit people to relate in any way they choose, so they are connected through complex communications called "laws." Laws are used to structure the behavior of people, to reconcile their differences, punish violators and predators, and regulate commerce. Through law, the tendency to vengeance can be controlled, predatory attacks can be discouraged, and people can be assisted in living together without unnecessary interference from one another. Thus, the communication network called law tends to reduce the potential threat that people pose one another, while it organizes those same people to resist external threats.

People within geocultural units are held together through common sets of verbalizations, traditions, customs, mores, and religions. To ensure the survival of the culture, aggregates of initiates are set up in units so that they can be trained in the cultural tradition and values. These units are known as schools. The school is primarily a communication unit. It is used as the agency of time-binding, through which the culture transmits information that young people will need to know to survive as members of the culture. Presumably, school should also help young people to discover a personal identity capable of withstanding attacks from the natural competition from others in society.

Our traditions are made specific and permanent by phrasing them in language and writing them in books. Thus, in order to become a functioning member of the society, the child must learn the language, and through the language he must learn what behaviors are approved and which prohibited. Furthermore, the operation of the school in which this learning takes place is a model of the society the student is slated to enter when he attains adulthood. School can be considered a microcosm of society, developed to maintain the continuity of existence of a society grouping, employing communication as the tool of cohesion. Those who declare that what goes on in school is "unreal" and not like it is "out there," have probably never considered how closely the essential features of school parallel the essential features of the society. In school there are both authoritarian and democratic systems of activity, systems of relationship, laws with attendant punishments, norms, social customs, traditions, and so forth, exactly as one might find them in the society at large. Sharing this information with students might help motivate greater participation in school.

We maintain conformity by organizing students through the school. As dismal as the prospect may seem, this is precisely the case, and *it is necessary*. The schools are the survival agents for society. As long as they are tuned with society and can adapt to meet changes in it, the schools perform the function of holding the society together. However, when the schools lose touch with society, students begin to behave in ways that are threatening to the school as an institution and to society itself. If students perceive that what they are offered at school has little or nothing to do with life as they experience it, they will resist its teachings. They will communicate their discontent with the life-training they are receiving.

It is here that the exchange of rhetorics becomes most crucial, for it is the teacher's task to motivate the student to participate in school, while the student seeks to persuade the school to provide for his needs. The clash of rhetorics decides the balance between the needs of society for a conforming population and the needs of students for specific instruction.

We noted in Chapter 2 that children are expected to reach biological maturity, a reasonable level of cognitive development, and certain skill levels at socialization before they can be deemed socially mature. What is most paradoxical is that once biological maturity is attained, there is absolutely no guarantee that the other maturities will develop. The recent Katz and Sanford studies of college students showed that there was no consistent gain in social maturity attributable to "growth." A characteristic pattern, for example, is to set goals in a fuzzy way, and to suffer frustration and often demoralization from it. If we presume that communication is purposive, there is no way to measure its effectiveness except by comparison with goals. If a person has not achieved sufficient maturity to be precise at setting goals, the rhetoric is applied in a haphazard and often self-defeating way. A major function of a communication teacher must be to help the student learn to specify goals for which his own rhetoric is applied. When students cannot reconcile their goals with those of their society as expressed by schools, they tend to become restless and employ their rhetoric to seek relief from what they see as despotism in the system.

The ethological goals described in this chapter represent a baseline of needs. There are many alternative views one can take of goals. Our hope here is to suggest some fundamental possibilities. The admonition that personal goals must be inferred from observed behavior is relatively worthless without a baseline against which to judge. By attempting to specify both teacher and student goals in the same terms, it is possible to work toward a rhetoric of reconciliation and exchange, where students make their needs manifest and teachers attempt to show how goal accomplishments in school terms help them meet their needs. Rewards would come when the student discovers that what he learns in school is important in his own life. It is not sufficient for teachers to say "learn now, no questions asked, and it will be useful later." Learning proceeds best when rewards are immediate.

From the standpoint of the young, society offers few rewards that make sense. Young people can look about them in the school and realize that there is little payoff for the behaviors the school requires of them. Memorization and drill do not offer ways of coping with personal problems of identity and effectiveness and how to be alive in a society of computer banks, instant retrieval, mechanization, pollution, overpopulation and social conflict. In frustration, students may form their own societies to try to cope. What is needed is a realization by schools of their function as instruments of social acculturation, and adaptation of curricula to the needs of society. If our society presents students with problems of loneliness, identity loss, dehumanization, overcrowding, crime, and so on, then the rhetoric of teaching must be directed at the students' learning a rhetoric that will help them cope with these problems in the future. What we have said earlier about providing alternatives that permit differential tracks to success is of crucial importance here, for only adults with a strong sense of identity and competence will be able to contend against the kinds of problems that will afflict us in the future. Furthermore, if we will need to make supportive relationships in order to survive in a "future shock" society, and if the society itself does not teach the young how to make these relationships, then the schools must fill the gap.

Propaganda and persuasion are the tools that enable a society to survive. Our young people have learned to resist them and to develop their own messages. Cultural myths are transmitted symbolically in the schools, but children are asked to accept them as truths. When a student discovers that, for many people, America is not the "land of the free," then he begins to doubt the credibility of the institution that told him it was. Theoretically, the student in school must accept the social myths in order to learn to live by the same values as the adults around him. Presumably, when all the social myths are learned, the student is ready to become an adult and enter the world of work in a fashion that will not threaten the society. Apparently, what has been happening in recent years is that young people who learn from the school that it is proper to criticize communism as a form of government, also learn the art of criticizing their own government. If the school permits no outlet for talk and writing about the results of such criticism, then students become mistrustful and become its enemies. In short, when a school exists to acculturate students to living in a democracy and then proceeds about the business in an undemocratic way, it will take little genius on the part of students to recognize the paradox. If they are not cognitively and socially mature, they will seek disquieting and often violent means to resolve the paradox.

In our society today we glorify the appearance of youth, but we have found no way to integrate youth productively into society. Adults admire and fear youth, so that our society tells us to look young and our economic interests suggest that we exclude young people from the main stream of society. It is precisely in this kind of milieu that rhetoric is most important. Rhetoric has as its purpose resolution of uncertainty. It works most effectively when all who use it are skillful. To learn to speak in ways that contribute to the solution of society's problems represents a major need for students.

The rebellion of youth and the resistance of age are characteristic of the kind of dissonance that can pose survival problems to individuals and the society. Man is apparently the only animal that can generate stress out of the methods he has used to combat stress. By organizing society into aggregates of people too large to manage, man has built a kind of life in which people threaten each other within the society, often without violating its rules. In order to find groups that are easier to handle, men split themselves into subgroups with which they can form an identity, and these subgroups then compete with each other for influence in the society at large. Allegiance because of occupational interest, age, race, economic status, and so forth, is characteristic of human groups. What is most detrimental is when these allegiances supersede the basic allegiance to the society at large and thus threaten to destroy the society. Once again, the art of using rhetoric to resolve social conflict is essential to survival. These kinds of issues are not normally dealt with in school. If social conflict is characteristic of our society, then the school must teach the students how to live with it and deal with it. From the generation of alternatives through which students can develop rhetorical skills, schools could regain their position as prime acculturation institutions in our society.

RHETORIC AS A TOOL OF COMPETITION

Most animal social structures permit competition. It is in the best interest of the pack to have the strongest and most competent animals lead. The leader can be challenged by other animals, winner take all, but the fighting does not culminate in the death of the losing contender. The loser may be relegated to lower status in the pack, but his value is recognized and he is not destroyed. Human competition is often lethal. Young people, observing the kind of competition that goes on in society, may reject that as a value; yet they cannot escape the need to compete, and so they generate spurious issues. The rewards go to the most rebellious, the best stud, and so on. Thus, there can be a denial of the *kind* of competition that goes on in society without a denial of competition itself. Certainly, there is a need to change the kind of competition that is characteristic of society today. There may be some significance in the fact that humans seem to need to make a new label to dehumanize those they kill. The use of "gook," or "nigger," or "pig" to refer to various enemies tends to take from them their human image, and thus they can be fought. Most animals (exceptions: rats and men) do not kill their own kind. It is almost as though our competition has become so furious that we need to define something not human to compete against.

The fact remains that people are potential destroyers of each other.

Part of survival in society demands resistance to the depredations of fellow human creatures. Psychic death can be brought about by forcing a person into a position which he does not want to hold and forcing upon him behaviors associated with an identity he does not wish to have. Black people have been subject to this force for generations, and young people are now beginning to discover (as they see it) that they, too, have been subjected to a kind of pressure that tends to make them into something they do not wish to be. More recently, women have been making the same discovery.

Symbolic designations, thus, represent a deep psychological threat to most people. Classifications used in school like "slow learner," "Special Ed.," "low track," or "Sparrows Reading Group," while, perhaps, convenient for the teachers who use them, force children to hold unfortunate images of themselves. Many students try to fight back by relegating school to an unimportant position in their lives rather than take the designations seriously.

People, in general, tend to fight symbolic depredations as furiously as they fight physical ones. Whatever frustrations and threats we encounter from others in our daily existence, we can put into perspective symbolically. We can curse at our opponents, joke them into nonimportance in our minds, or make plans (never realized) to fight against them. We can develop ploys to use against the companies that send us "please remit" notices. We can find ways to harass the teacher, to render him impotent, so he is not able to challenge our self-esteem with quizzes we can't pass, recitations that bore us, and drills that are a waste of time. We can make defeat into victory by changing our language. The Chicago riots of 1968 illustrate this. Though the peace demonstrators were obviously beaten by the police, they turned their physical defeat into a symbolic victory by declaring that the police had behaved like "animals," thus proving that the demonstrators were right in the first place. Teachers in inner-city schools know that punishment for classroom failure is ineffective so long as the students have an arsenal of invective at their disposal. Failure in school is not failure at all, so long as the student can make school into an irrelevant institution staffed by "copouts."

We can make symbols in our head and develop a fantasy world into which we can retreat in order to recoup our psychic identity. This kind of withdrawal represents a childlike state of conceptual ability. If the school pushes students toward these types of withdrawal, then it is clearly not meeting its obligation to help them achieve conceptual maturity.

Even in the students who do not fight back, and do not use mental fantasy as a weapon, there is a withdrawal tendency. The daydream, for example, is a powerful weapon, used by almost everyone, to withstand the onslaughts of a society that is not very comfortable. Every young man who has failed to make the team can see himself as Joe Namath leading his team to the championship. Every middle-aged man who lives with the frustrations of job and family can imagine himself to be a George Blanda. Every young girl who recovers from a lover's quarrel is helped to do so by her dream of Prince Charming coming to take her away from all this. The quiet man can use the retreat of Walter Mitty and, in his mind, put down everyone who stands in his way; the student can imagine destroying the teacher with a lethal quip. Sometimes daydreams serve as rehearsals through which we can examine our goals and plans to implement them. Sometimes daydreams function as a means of releasing hostilities. The daydream is symbolic activity. Every man can be hero or villain in his mind. It is communication with self that reveals some of the hidden goals we never knew we had.

Traditionally, in law-governed, organized society, rhetorical communication has been the means through which men have solved their problems, made their decisions, resolved their differences. By systematizing discourse, by learning skill at persuading others, people become more competent. They build the reservoir of personal power that Rollo May tells us is essential to individual survival. Rhetorical skill is the defense against social threat. Rhetoric employed haphazardly and ineffectively represents a social threat.

To handle rhetoric demands maturation on three levels: biological, cognitive, and social. When such maturity is not present, it is imperative that students be trained or treated for it. There is little that the schools can do about biological deficiencies, but there is much that can be done to help students acquire communication skills that will help them take realistic action against their problems. Preceding or concurrent with such training is training in socializing and cognitive processing. Communication with others helps us to cooperate, to withstand external and internal threats; it helps us compete for prizes in society; it helps society by permitting us to make a relevant contribution; it helps us sustain the image of ourselves that makes us feel relevant. It is essential to our survival. Improvement of communication may well make humans more peaceful, accommodating, and productive. We cannot know until we have tried.

COMMUNICATION TO STIMULATE: GAME DEVELOPMENT

Communication is often used to stimulate people, to provide them with excitement, sensuous pleasure, recreation, and escape. It seems that every animal in some ways attempts to find recreation and enjoyment. Robert Ardrey describes how colonies of lemurs simulate fights, get worked up, chatter at each other, and look for all the world as though they were going to tear each other apart, yet never touch each other. Humans also engage in this kind of behavior with the formal and social games they use to put variety and challenge into their lives.

The word "game" should not be taken as synonymous with recreation. Game refers to a system of regularized, rule-following verbal or nonverbal communications that limit the scope of the behavior of a person and tell him clearly whether he has won or lost. Games are sometimes difficult, often painful. The pleasure, more often than not, lies in the winning, not in the playing. Activities such as painting a picture, running an experiment, making a business deal could be considered "games" even though they generate very little joyful laughter. Rhetorically speaking, a game is an exchange of persuasions by people, each of whom has some goal to achieve, often, but not necessarily, at the expense of the other.

What goes on in the classroom could be considered a game. There is an object: to get an "A." There are activities required of everyone; to read a book, to memorize some words, to write a paper, to recite some answers aloud in class, to say pleasant words to the teacher, to pass a test. All of the activities are communicative and persuasive. The teacher judges which communication is "best" (more persuasive) and rewards it. The winners are awarded the designation "A." The losers are designated anywhere from "B" to "F." Consistent losers may drop out of the game and start their own game called "resistance." They generate their own rewards and punishments, and the teacher is not permitted to play; he becomes one of the playing pieces. The object of the game is to make trouble for the teacher. He becomes an unwilling participant in a game he may not understand. When confronted with this kind of threat, the teacher may respond with the game of "discipline." During the teacher's off-hours, he can go to the coffee room and play the game of "complaint" with his fellow teachers. He also competes in a broader system game called variously "merit rating," "salary negotiation," or "job tenure." Whenever we find a human encounter where the activities carried follow some rules and where there are rewards or punishments meted out, we can identify it as a game. The purpose of the game is to stimulate the organism to action. The stimulation is needed in order to generate the physical and mental energy needed to solve problems. Game-playing represents the basic structured form of competition in a society. College students deplore "gameplaying" and in their attacks on it, they develop a game. Without the stimulation that comes from game-playing we would be impotent in the face of our problems.

People would sometimes like to investigate problems without playing the game of "research," but there is no way of evaluating the quality of research unless some judgment is made on conformance with technique. Some people would like to talk to one another without playing the game of "social etiquette," but there is no way to protect people from encroachments on their privacy without applying some rules. Some people would like to release their tensions and hostilities and get away from the game of "inhibition," but if they were permitted to do so, others might be injured. Thus, the game offers us a model in which we can understand that the ways that people use communication to stimulate themselves have a great deal to do with their survival in society, as well as the survival of society itself.

The word "game" should not be construed as negative. There are productive recreations where rules are important. Writing poetry or playing football are good examples. In poetry, the rules of the game specify that the writer must make his point by arranging words together according to a variety of prescriptions which can be evaluated by critics who determine whether or not the poem is worthy of reading. Conformance with the rules provides the double satisfaction of getting something said and the honor that comes with publication. In football, the payoffs are clear cut. A winning team puts money into the school treasury and the members of it win national fame and lucrative professional contracts. To accomplish this, the players must become skilled in the implementation of rules or, at least, in concealing their deviations from the rules. Obvious deviation from the rules is punished, and the game becomes harder to win. Those who cannot comply with the basic requirements of the game do not get to play. Thus, there is a difference in quality between a high school football team and the professionals, even though the rules are the same. There is also a great difference between the high school literary magazine and the *New Yorker*. Thus, we can see that games have levels; each level has its standards which the players must achieve. The tension that comes from attempting to meet the standards generates the force which permits growth in the individual. In this sense, games are vital to human existence.

The productivity of a culture, its literature, art, music, drama, function to stimulate individuals. They are symbolic in nature. They are produced to provide pleasure to both producer and consumer, although the act of producing them might be arduous in itself, eventual consumption rewards the artist for his productivity. Art may not be necessary to life, although life would be dull without it. Some people are capable of using their productivity to make an income. Considering, however, that every fifteen-minute newscast includes a five-minute sport review and every newspaper, however small, includes a theater and art section, occasional book reviews, and advertisements for events, recreations seem to be an important element of our society. There is no society so primitive that it does not use games for recreational purposes.

Use of leisure time is becoming more and more important as our society expands its technological capacity. Less time needs to be spent on the survival of the body, thus more time is available for the survival (or destruction) of the mind and spirit. The increasing incidence of boredom, alienation, loneliness, and simple unhappiness that appears to characterize our times seems to indicate that the stimulation aspect of living, as well as the quest for security, will receive more and more emphasis in years to come. We are experimenting already through the use of drugs, sex, violence, and destruction as recreation. X-rated films, riots, and constant drug-induced "bliss" are recreations that can be considered destructive of the human spirit. Certainly students growing up into this society need to be persuaded to attempt some options for the use of their leisure; options which lie somewhere between the natural state options of the street, and the lofty literary options presently offered by the schools.

Communication skills represent an important defense against boredom. The man who can talk with others effectively, write his thoughts down, paint, make music, participate in theater, enjoy reading, will have powerful defenses against boredom and its attendant gloom. Far too little emphasis is placed on this aspect of living by the schools. Many educators are still trapped in the Calvinist notion that if it is enjoyable, it can't be learning. Even though learning takes place through tension, the release from tension that comes with accomplishment needs to be pointed out as one source of reward. Training of students to communicate to satisfy their own urges for pleasure will be one of the challenges faced by our schools in the future.

COMMUNICATION TO UNDERSTAND: MAINTAINING SECURITY

All animals seek a sense of security in the world they occupy. A dog moving into a new home will sniff about and explore, and he will be uneasy until he finds out where the food will be served, where the water supply is, and where he can do what dogs do after they eat and drink. When given an opportunity, he will explore the neighborhood, identify danger areas and "look over" the other occupants. Wild animals show this same behavior, seeking a food supply, a water supply, and preparing a warm nest before they settle in to live their lives.

Humans also seek a sense of security, or homeostasis, both physically and mentally. Communication is the device used to organize for physical security and to understand for mental security. In addition to guarantees that the necessities will be available, humans also want explanations of what they see around them. Because man has the capacity to imagine the future, he needs to develop for himself some kind of prediction apparatus to enable him to assess how things might come out if he did this or that. He needs theoretical propositions that will help him choose individual actions, and he needs to understand the unexpected and find ways to resolve dissonant perceptions. Because man recognizes his mortality, he needs some way to contemplate and adjust to this grim reality. He even needs an explanation of what will happen to him after he dies. In formal terms, humans manipulate their symbols to develop concepts that help them understand complicated relationships. They develop theories to explain how events and ideas are connected. Much of their behavior depends on hypotheses generated out of these theories and concepts. As we have noted earlier, we rely on the images, symbols, and values stored in memory to make our predictions of what a particular behavior might evoke from a particular person and how a given plan might work when tested against a specific problem. Thus, we are all researchers in our daily living.

The development of rhetorical skills demands that we learn ways of evaluating argument directed at us, as well as learn ways of making argument. We need to know what evidence is reliable, how to select trustworthy authorities, how to interpret the accuracy of generalizations—both those phrased in words and in numbers. Much of the rhetoric that is beamed at us is generated solely out of the authority of the person who speaks it. Teachers often rely heavily on their position when they offer information to students. Consequently, students, in some ways modeling teacher behavior, do not learn to provide reasons for their own rhetoric. Without a logical component, rhetoric becomes sophistry, a purely emotional appeal. In building homeostatic skill, the student needs careful instruction in interpretation. He needs to learn to listen critically to develop the ability to speak skillfully.

In a world that confronts constant change, one aspect of homeostasis is crucial. One of man's most vital needs is the feeling of security he can find when he is able to trust and be supported by his fellow human beings. The search for affection and trust is a lifetime quest. It is the substance of friendship and marriage. The exchange of affection, stroking, cuddling, sharing intimate secrets represents so strong and vital a drive that most people risk a great deal in search of it. In our technological society, where men feel less relevant because machines do so many jobs, the exchange of trusting affection represents a crucial means of survival. It also represents one of the main sources of human hurt and psychic injury. Because of the desire for closeness, for example, humans have confused the search for affection with the sex drive. Sex lies under the heading of survival of the species. It is not biologically designed for the same purpose as exchange of affection. The confusion of the two has resulted in a serious distortion of interpersonal relationships. The exploration of what is needed in supportive relationships has only just begun. Animals seem to do very well in their mutual grooming and nuzzling, but there is a relatively limited human counterpart for this behavior. It is something we have been seeking but have not yet found, except, perhaps, in those units of people which still maintain extended family norms.

When we consider homeostasis, we usually find ourselves examining science, philosophy, religion, and human relations. Each attempts to offer us ways to live securely in our world. Science generates propositions that technology manipulates in the form of machinery that makes our lives easier (and sadly enough, sometimes threatens to destroy us). Science and technology not only offer us a defense against hostile forces, but sometimes become hostile forces in themselves. The science-technology that gave us our high standard of living also gave us nuclear weapons and the hydrogen bomb. Governments, presumably, function to protect us against these threats, but for the individual, philosophy and religion may offer more.

Science does more, however, than help us cope with threats or be more comfortable. It explains thunder and lightening so we need not fear them. It helps us predict eclipses. The forces of nature that were once a source of fear to men, now can be understood, and hence become manageable in our minds.

Religion offers us a method of coping with life and death. It provides us with moral precepts which we can apply so that we can lead a "better" life. This, in turn, if we accept the major premise, will guarantee us a life hereafter. Philosophy secularizes these propositions and focuses on matters like why we must suffer pain and why we live the way we do. The formalization of this kind of explanation indicates that men need to understand themselves and their world in order to live in peace with it.

Human relations represent the core of our homeostasis. When all else goes wrong, the presense of loving friends and family can do a great deal to make us feel more secure. So important are these relationships that many futurologists say that they spell the difference between sanity and insanity.

Security is often necessary in order to survive the mundane lives that most people lead. It seems that men are more interested in their daily lives than they are in cosmic questions of morality and mortality. Society barrages us with information designed to make us feel safe and secure in our day-to-day relationships. People are sold toothpastes to induce sex appeal, deodorants to feel more virile, apothecary drugs to ward off physical hurts. We are sold guarantees, seals of approval, lists of ingrediants, anticipation of well-being, political formulas, true beliefs of all sorts. We pick our way through a barrage of stimulation and security cues and purchase for ourselves what we think we need of each.

The verbal delusions we can build out of symbols are another source of homeostasis. Our daydreams sustain us against frustration. Adorning ourselves with clothing, jewelry, hair arrangements makes us feel more secure in dealing with others. We cannot be denied if we look as we are supposed to look. Furthermore, the causes we believe in, the political and social beliefs we count on, give us standards of judgment that help us evaluate the new people we meet. Sometimes we can get excessively involved with our homeostatic mechanism. We can be so convinced of our understanding, so sure that our information is right, that our friends can do no wrong, that our religious beliefs are the only ones worth having, that we prevent new information from entering our heads. Then we become fanatics or fools, and we are threats either to society or ourselves.

The schools have always offered formal training in philosophy and science, though often without ferment and controversy, the revelation that there are opposing views that are worthwhile considering. An explanation of this phase of instruction through rhetoric is not hard to imagine. In the realm of interpersonal communication schools have done little. The urgency will become steadily greater to help students find ways of judging and relating to others so that more satisfactory human relationships can be developed to nuture them against a threatening future. In the following chapter, we will present some analytical questions useful in assessing relationships. These might be considered for use in groups in classroom discussion of human relationships and how they meet needs.

COMMUNICATION FOR TERRITORY: STATUS AND ROLE

According to a distinguished social psychologist, if you ask a man, "Who are you?" he is most likely to reply by giving you the names of the group he is affiliated with or by telling you his occupation. People

People tend to rank each other on an up and down scale

tend to identify themselves by where they fit or what they do. They seem to need a niche, a specific location in society, and even in their groups there is a competition for position so that every organization has some sort of hierarchy. It is an axiom of small group sociology that members of groups tend to develop ranking procedures by which position in the group can be mapped out and through which the leaders can be clearly identified.

Whether or not all animals are territorial, or whether man is a completely territorial animal, is a disputed issue. It is clear that some animals have built into them an uncontrollable desire to possess a piece of territory. The ethologists Robert Ardrey and Niko Tinbergen have described the phenomenon in detail in their books. Man seems to need to define his territories. In any classroom, experienced teachers often know that a seating chart is often unnecessary. Given a chance to sit where they please, students will tend to stake claims to particular chairs, and they will return to them consistently, resisting interlopers.

Man tends to think of his territorial position vertically instead of horizontally. People tend to rank each other on an up and down scale. In a discussion of colleges, for example, conversants will talk of comparative rankings of the football team, who has the best chemistry department, which has the highest enrollment, and so forth. None of the criteria by which these ranking decisions are made are necessarily clear, but they might be related to personal desires to have your particular school come out on top.

We talk often of the merits of our automobiles, our neighborhoods, or our wives. We struggle for position and power within organizations. We constantly seek promotion to a "higher" position. We accord respect to a man depending on the status of his job, so that physician is regarded generally as more important than sanitary engineer. Isn't it ironic, that on a similar scale of measurement, teacher is rated on a par with shop foreman, considerably below salesman or bank teller.

We identify with in-groups and out-groups. We hold contests to pick the most beautiful, the most talented, the most everything. We display our grade averages, generate dean's lists, grant honors designed not only as rewards but also as indications of where we fit in whatever hierarchy is important to us. Every organization seems to have a "man of the year" competition sometime during its history. We give testimonial dinners to confer rank, and we have a passion for organization charts and diagrams of association; we are particularly pleased to see our own names high on the list. The man above us occupies our goal. The man below us is a threat to our position.

The classroom tends to follow this pattern in its grouping of students. Each small social set or clique will understand where it fits into the social hierarchy of the school. We may be the last in studying, but we are the first in fun. It is very important to the student to find out what group he belongs to and what rank he holds in it. The teacher can also confer status by conferring grades and rewards and by assigning merit groups. The reading group system characteristic of most elementary school classrooms, or the tracking system indigenous to our high schools, formalizes this sort of organization. There are hazards here, of course, for if a student is formally put into a group, he will take on the coloration of it simply because it is his. We wonder how many special education students could have "made it," if they had remained in regular classrooms or if they had been called something else.

Furthermore, those to whom low rank is assigned may decide that they no longer have respect for the system that assigned them that rank and may decide either to overthrow the system or find a new one in which to compete for rank. Thus, our rebels and our dropouts!

Since much of our identity is conferred on us by our membership and rank in groups, when our position is challenged, we tend to react aggressively to defend both the group and our position. Ethologists point out that an animal fights more effectively on its own territory than does the attacking predator. In human affairs, it appears that much depredation is unconscious. It is usually carried on by those who have not made the sociocultural transition referred to in Chapter 2, who have not become aware of the feelings of others. Most of us really do not know when we are threatening someone else, and we often react in suprise when some of our actions evoke hostility in the people they are directed toward. The commercial with the line, "mother, please, I'd rather do it myself!" is a good example. The parent who wishes to help the child function often seems like an aggressor to the child, and he will fight in many ways to have his identity left alone. The child who will not clean his room but resents his mother cleaning it is an example of this phenomenon. In bureaucracies we maintain channels and people learn not to "rock the boat," which simply means, you accord to each position on the chart what is due it, and you do not interfere or criticize, for to do so may mean encroachments on your own position. To interfere on someone else's territory means that your own territory may be vulnerable. The nature of this defensiveness and the ways to communicate about it need to be understood by people who seek to function well in society. Little or none of it is taught in the schools, however. It is our contention that each student needs to know the nature of the competition he faces and his stake in it, for when he communicates, as we will note in a subsequent chapter, he risks a good deal of himself and his identity.

Our physiological capacity for aggression helped us resist animals and organized us against threatening forces in an earlier day in history. It was necessary to be physically aggressive to find food for all, and in the event that there was not enough food to go around, the stronger got the food and the weaker died out, thus keeping the species strong. Competition for mates, special living areas, and so on are in some ways matters of survival, but there also seems to be the tendency for possession, latent or active, in all of us. We are like bowerbirds, for once we find a nest, we decorate it uniquely and resist attempts to alter it or take it away.

So deeply rooted is territoriality in human personality that many of our games can be understood territorially. In baseball, teams compete for ranking in the won–lost column and individual players compete for position in a vertical list of names representing ranking at various skills. They are paid based on where they stand. Our preoccupation with spaces, our concern about privacy, all of these strivings confirm the hypothesis that man is territorial. Some respect for this basic urge, then, must enter human relationships. Certainly teachers must understand this urgency in their students, for they must feel it in themselves. Surely each student must learn about the competitive nature of his society if he is to live in it successfully.

SUMMARY

We have offered a premise that man, as animal, uses comunication rhetorically as a mode of behavior to satisfy his needs rephrased as goals. We have discussed the competitive context of communication, and we have shown that combat of one sort or another seems to enter every communication relationship; symbols are the weapons used. Looking at communication this way represents a clear challenge to the schools to devise methods where people can be helped to communicate more productively so that their position both in society and within themselves can be enhanced by what goes on in the school room. In a time of increasing violence and physical threat, the school remains the only organized force equipped with the capability of training young men and women to work toward the kinds of interpersonal relationships that are characterized by mutual gain. For schools merely to reiterate the combative and aggressive aspects of interaction or to ignore them would ensure that society would remain the threatening place it now is.

WORKS CITED:

Ardrey, Robert. *The Social Contract.* New York: Atheneum, 1970.

May, Rollo. *Power and Innocence, a Search for the Sources of Violence.* New York: W.W. Norton, 1972. (See Chap. 4)

WORKS RECOMMENDED:

Reading more of Ernest Becker will provide a framework for understanding the anthropology of human communication. Try particularly *Beyond Alienation.* New York: George Braziller, Inc., 1967.

A good concise work is Anthony Storr, *Human Aggression*. New York: Atheneum, 1968, for the study of the role of biology in shaping human communication behavior.

A basic understanding of human interaction for the layman can be found in Eric Berne, *What Do You Say After You Say Hello?* New York: Grove Press, 1972.

Objectives Chapter 6

- To note that we cannot reward a person by our responses to him unless he knows what his goals are and somehow shares this knowledge with us.

- To learn that the rhetorical view of communication trys to systematize behaviors in a relationship so that both parties can realize what is possible and what is unrealistic.

- To learn that the most effective relationship rhetorically is when both people achieve their goals and know they have achieved them.

- To present some questions, or heuristics, that can be applied to any opening encounter between people to help determine appropriate actions.

- To learn that the child needs experiences of both failure (losing) and success (winning) in relationships with others, though he needs to be taught ways of protecting himself from failing too often.

- To recognize the need to open more choices of experience to the student in the classroom so that he may be directed to evaluate experiences against his goals.

6.
Winning and Losing: The Rhetoric of Goal Seeking

Overview

Our goal in this chapter is to examine the need for developing and raising questions about our actions with others so that we may fulfill our human goals. It is necessary that we achieve our goals in conjunction with other people in some way, but given the need for competition among all animals, human beings are often thwarted and emotionally injured in their quest for goal accomplishment. It is the need for some sort of cooperation as well as the potential dangers of competition with others that we must teach the child to handle. The human has at stake his fragile self-image when he encounters others and attempts to exert rhetoric to make some sort of bargain or deal with them so that goals may be met mutually. Raising critical, analytical questions about what behaviors might meet with the most mutual gain in a given relationship is a good start in the process of teaching effective use of rhetoric in the classroom. As students are offered expanded choices of behaviors and methods of evaluating the impact of their behaviors on others, we might expect increased competency in personal goal seeking through rhetoric.

THE TEACHING of oral communication is a goal directed activity. Unlike many other subjects in the curriculum, the thrust of the teacher of oral communications is toward providing the student with skills useful in learning other subject matter. While "advanced" courses in college may well deal with theory and experimentation, for most students contact with oral communication is through training in skills. In the secondary school, as we noted in Chapter 1, virtually the entire focus is on advanced skills, with little effort to generalize instruction in basic skills.

Up to this point in the book, we have been dealing with generalizations. We have focused on learning some of the basic propositions about how communication develops in the child and how communication operates as a process and a relationship. We have stressed the notion that virtually all communication is rhetorical, that is, focused on goal accomplishment. And, at the conclusion of the last chapter, we suggested that to the extent that goals are not known, rhetoric tends to be ineffective. This holds for both students and teachers.

In this chapter, we will deal with the process of goal setting and its ramifications. We will attempt to show how the process of setting rhetorical goals fits into the normal life of humans in general and teachers and students in particular.

THE RHETORICAL SITUATION

Lloyd Bitzer, in a recent, widely acclaimed article, pointed out that rhetoric arises from a feeling of urgency when an individual is confronted with a situation in which his assessment is that some changes ought to be made. Bitzer's formulation was directed more at messages delivered from the public platform, but its propositions are equally applicable to the informal rhetoric employed by all of us in our daily lives.

Goals. We are all seeking to meet our basic needs. However we regard our needs, whether based on animal needs as described in Chapter 5, or whether we use some other formulation, the Freudian "Pleasure Principle" for example, all of us somehow translate our needs into symbolic goals, and use speech to achieve them. Since it is impossible to project inside the minds of people, it is necessary for us to infer the goals of others. What is even more difficult to cope with is that most of us are not consciously aware of the goals we seek. When someone is not fully aware of what he is seeking, it is difficult to reward him. If we accept the basic proposition from learning theory that people learn best through reward, then it is difficult to figure out what might constitute a reward in the case of the person who does not understand his own goals.

We have a choice in goal seeking to accept reality or appearance of reality. Sometimes a particular behavior is rewarding; sometimes we need to be convinced that it is a reward. Sometimes the learning of a concept in science is rewarding, and sometimes we need the persuasion of an "A" in order to drive home the reward. When we seek a change in a person's behavior, what we really seek to do is find out some behavior we can offer him in exchange for the behavior we seek to change. Rhetoric is directed at convincing him that what we offer is worthwhile and that he ought to deliver what we seek from him. The exchange is imperative, for without exchange people are bribed or intimidated into performance and become unreliable people with whom to deal.

Within the school, our capacity to specify goals is limited by the roles we must play and the norms of behavior we must follow. These constrain both our goal setting and the methods we can use to seek goals. Part of rhetoric, therefore, is a careful analysis of situation including the people at whom we beam the rhetoric. Most of us understand, instinctively, that we must take individual differences and preferences into account when we direct behavior at others, but we lack a systematic way to plan our own behavior. The contemporary student mood, for example, advises people to "go with the flow," to be "spontaneous," since, apparently, they despair of ever finding rhyme or reason in their dealings with others.

The rhetorical view of communication seeks to systematize the behaviors of which relationships are made by offering modes of analysis, heuristics of analysis, and alternatives in both goals and strategies.

We can, for example, seek approval, acceptance of information, changes in behavior, extension of services, use of goods, good humor and goodwill from the other person. Our understanding of what it is possible to seek must be based on an analysis of what the other is likely to be willing to part with, what limitations there are on his behavior, and what we can do for him and how much he values it.

We are further limited by situation. The assessment of what is possible here and now vs. what is possible some time in the future may also affect our goal setting. More explicitly, what teachers can expect from students depends to a large extent on how they see each other's roles and what the situation in the classroom might permit. Teachers are not able to cope with blandishments to outside interaction; students are not likely to be willing to put up with gross interference in their lives. In short, setting rhetorical goals is the process of discriminating the *doable from the desirable*.

Heuristics. Because situations are variable, roles are fragile, and the life experience of each person is different, there is no possibility of generalizing about strategies and methods that work infallibly, or even with a high order of probability in every case. Each rhetorical relationship is unique, although there are components of each that are similar. Consequently, teachers and students alike would profit by having a handful of questions that can be raised in any case. By any case, we mean public performance before the class down to the most private and intimate rhetorical relationship one can conceive of. There is no human experience with another in which goals are not operating, in which strategies are not used to achieve goals, and which is devoid of constraints imposed by roles, norms, and the limitations of the situation. The questions we need to apply in any case must be relevant to these issues. The answers to the questions, presumably, can provide us with some kind of "game plan," and a way of knowing who wins and who loses. We operate on the assumption, furthermore, that there is no human experience with another in which both are unable to win and in which both must necessarily lose. In fact, we could stipulate that the optimum rhetorical relationship is one in which communication has been employed so effectively that both parties emerge victorious— that is, both have achieved goals and *know* that they have achieved them. It is to this purpose that rhetorical training is directed.

We might start our heuristic questions by examining any two-person relationship. At the moment of meeting, certain questions emerge:

1. I see a behavior. What does it mean about the goals of that person? Is it worth spending more time to investigate? (If both parties answer "yes," we can move on to . . . .)

2. Seeing more behavior, am I attracted, repelled, or neutral? Do I want to see more behavior? Does the other person indicate that he wants to see more behavior from me? If yes, then . . . .

3. What is it in the behavior that I find rewarding? What must I do in order to keep it coming? Does it injure me to do that? And finally,

4. What are my goals in this relationship? How do I read the goals of the other person? Are my goals and his compatible? If so, how deeply can I get into this relationship? Am I impeded by differences in role? Are there clashes in the norms we follow? What are the limitations of the situation? Are there third parties that might be involved and how might they react?

These are calculating and strategic kinds of questions. Utilizing them keeps the mind continually focused on goal accomplishment, and provides for the person asking them a continual stream of options about his own behavior. Two people skilled at viewing the world through these questions are capable of making a good bargain, for they will move in ways that prevent themselves from being injured, thus sparing interpersonal hurt and the guilt that comes when you discover that you have hurt the other. The questions can be adapted to the school situation:

1. To what extent must I share time with this person? If there are obligations, what are the penalties for violating them? Is the situation so bad that I would take the consequences of violation?

When school, for example, becomes nothing more than a matter of complying with the law, there is little exchange that is possible. If the student can be taught, however, that affirming behaviors on his part will evoke affirming behaviors from teacher, it may be possible to improve behavior on both sides.

2. What will be the effect on me (the student) if I learn (comply or commit) what teacher wants me to learn? What use can I make of this learning? If the answer is "little," then, what can I do to demonstrate to teacher that I need more motivation?

3. What is the most effective set of strategies I can devise to signal the teacher about my own needs, and how can I fit these needs into the constraints around the teacher? That is, without making teacher into a parent, lover, or friend in my mind, how can I derive benefit from his behavior?

For the teacher, the questions operate another way.

1. What change do I seek in this student as a result of my teaching?

2. How can I justify that change in terms of student needs and requirements of my system (teaching plan, syllabus, and so forth)?

3. What strategies must I use to bring about this change?

4. What reason do I have to believe that the strategies will work?

In each case, using the question format, teacher and student alike are pushed to establish norms for their rhetoric based on careful analysis. The norms ensure greater possibility for talk without threat. There is little change in basic internal demeanor implied here. We all continue to want what we want and seek what we must seek. What is provided through a formalization of the rhetoric is a chance at greater satisfaction with the results through the operation of a mutually rewarding exchange.

HOW GOAL SEEKING OPERATES

We must now examine how we learn our rhetorical skills and how they operate in society.

1. The human communicates to organize others around him to

protect him from attacks. He must also learn to communicate to play his role in protection of the society in general.

2. The human communicates in order to develop a personal identity. He attempts to strengthen this identity by feeling unique and competent. He uses his identity to make relationships and to ward off loneliness and boredom.

3. The human communicates to make relationships with others that are rewarding and nurturing, relationships that induce growth in his personal identity and provide protection from psychological attacks.

4. The human communicates to stimulate himself into action, problem solving, defense, excitement, or just plain fun.

5. The human communicates to discover and understand so that he may feel secure.

6. The human communicates to achieve a position in a system of organization, preferably the highest position possible.

The child learns generalizations about what works. He continues his strategy into adulthood. What worked in childhood becomes part of his repertoire of behavior. He files away both negative and positive responses. If he gets few messages that he might regard as positive, he might draw away from communication altogether, avoiding human contact, seeking privacy. He will discover an identity as a solitary person and thus sacrifice the possibility of gaining support from others. Furthermore, society will be denied his contribution.

In an extensive survey of 20,000 school children, kindergarten through twelfth grade, done in central Pennsylvania and the Bay Area of California, it was discovered that in the elementary schools, 14 percent of the children demonstrated this withdrawal from communication; in junior high 24 percent displayed it; in high school 12 percent. Surveys done over a period of six years on the campus of a large university show that even 5 percent of college students show symptoms of "reticence," which disables people in their attempts at oral communication, particularly in a social vein. It is not clear what happens to students who cannot communicate well along the way, but it appears likely that many of them are to be found in the ranks of dropouts and failures. There is no evidence to indicate that spontaneous remission takes place. The high proportion of reticence in the junior high school may be attributed to the biological-sexual changes taking place in children of that age, but the 12 percent figure in high school is sufficiently similar to the elementary school figure so that we might presume that a good proportion, more than half of the reticents, drop out after high school and never reach the university. It is clear that if schools can help to provide these people with rhetorical skills, they would be doing a great service both to the people and to the society at large.

In addition to the role that communication plays in interpersonal communication, it also is very important to the process of internal symbol manipulation. Most of the time, children and adults live in a world of nonreality. Nonreality is not unreality. Nonreality is a state in which the ordinary things and events of the world are stored in memory in such a way that they can be reviewed and manipulated even in the absence of the stimuli that evoked the images in the first place. This process provides humans with the ability to plan ahead to cope with anticipated events. We have referred to this phenomenon earlier as *goal setting*.

Goal setting is a probabilistic activity. The skill with which it is carried on depends mainly on the skill in symbolic processing (cognitive development) acquired in childhood. The child who learns that his communication is ineffective may have some real difficulty when he seeks to process nonreality. He may prevent himself from doing what he is really capable of doing, or he may reward himself too much internally by playing an omnipotent role in his own mind to compensate for his real inadequacies. In either case, the result is ineffective action, which only serves to weaken his capacity to communicate and thereby achieve his human goals.

One way of measuring maturity in a human is to determine how dependent he is on others for the meaning of his symbols. As Ernest Becker pointed out, the ability to assign values to experience confers the ability to take independent action. When a child is able to interpret symbols and exert control on his own communication output, so that he can make choices of what to do with problems with which his environment confronts him, he can be regarded as mature. When he no longer has a need to depend on rigid dogma or the direction of others for his decisions, he has achieved symbol mastery. When we look at the adults around us, it is clear that not many humans achieve this kind of maturity, which depends on how the person uses communication to achieve a sense of competency.

The act of communication with others implies the existence of a sort of social mirror in which people can see themselves in order to make adjustments in behavior so that what they see looks better to them. It helps when you like the person you have to live with, and it is necessary to live with yourself. The image of self stored away may be a composite of successes and failures, but successes are often emphasized and failures rationalized. Your personal image of self may define outcomes that are gratifying to you in line with the "Pleasure Principle."

The Pleasure Principle stipulates that the human will act in ways that minimize pain and maximize pleasure, although sometimes the decisions about what is pleasurable and what is painful may be distorted. Thus, if gratification does not come from the external world, your internal world can distort the data and make you a winner. In a fully functioning adult, however, there will be a tendency to examine reality to see what works and to select those behaviors that evoke positive response for future use. If only a few behaviors are defined as effective, then a person can become restricted in his behavior.

If you accept these ideas, it should be clear that adults have a great deal to do with a child's eventual success as an adult. If the child is rewarded only for a few behaviors, then his options for behavior will be limited. If he is not assisted in making decisions about what is effective and ineffective, he may not be able to develop criteria by which to judge his own effectiveness. He will not know the satisfaction of achieving goals. This means that somewhere in school, the child must learn about situations, roles, and norms; that what is appropriate communication behavior at one time and place may be ineffective at another.

People do not preplan their interactions like chess players or theater directors. This does not mean that interactive behavior is random, however. People have choice in the behaviors they use. Communication behavior is selected from available alternatives. It is neither random nor directed by outside forces beyond the control of humans. As we have noted earlier, behavior is rational, that is, there is a reason at the moment of action for any behavior that is selected.

The foregoing suggests that human communication is a form of competitive activity. In communication the inner selves of people are projected. We seek goals. The tools of goal seeking are communication behaviors. The process is aggressive. Everyone seeks to gain something through communication and often goals conflict. In dog-eat-dog competition there are many losers. But communication is not necessarily a "zero-sum" game where there can only be one winner and one loser. It is possible, through intelligent use of communication, to make a suitable exchange, so that all parties win.

Unfortunately, people are not equally skillful at communicating. As a result, the more powerful often take advantage of those weaker than themselves and win consistently without considering the cost of losing that others must pay. Teacher-dominant classrooms illustrate this. Teacher is more concerned with holding and protecting his position than with developing the students. For the student, each loss results in a reduction of self-image. Each loss makes victory harder the next time. It seems cruel that so many students in our schools are forced into interactions in which they cannot possibly win. It also means that our society receives many adult citizens who are not able to participate effectively.

Interactions can be mutually successful if some care is taken to analyse goals, to discover mutual commitments, and to find out if it necessarily means a loss to one person if the other person gets what he wants. Sometimes clash is inevitable, but most of the time it can be prevented if the parties take care to show some concern about the goals of the other. It would be helpful if we understood the risks involved in interaction. If teachers could learn how students can be injured in interaction, they might be able to devise ways to make it possible for them to acquire sufficient skill to survive.

If we regard our communication behavior as aggressive, we might become more aware of the hurt that results when a person fails. The combat between self and others is perpetual. It begins at birth when the infant seeks to assert his demands and maintain control over the household. It stems from our essential sense of self as the center of the universe, the necessary egocentrism of a self-aware organism. It continues through life as husband and wife vie for ascendancy in the family, as professional colleagues struggle for position in the hierarchy. Though there is aggressive content in every contact we make with others, a mature communicator can control aggression and get much of what he seeks without jeopardizing the goals of others. There is still little attention paid, however, to the goal of working out relationships so that everyone can come away feeling somewhat successful as a human being.

People let themselves get trapped in idealism about human relations. Because we believe that altruism is not only possible, but likely, it is impossible for us to administer the kind of training that people need to cope with the competition indigenous to society. The social arena is where we strive for selfhood. We struggle against each other in order to form an identity in the same fashion as we struggle against our environment to survive. We have the choice of preserving or destroying our environment, and we have this same choice about people with whom we come in contact.

Children display grossly what adults do with subtlety. Children seek to find out how much control they can exert over others. As youthful cave men they seek to find out how much of the cave they can own, and they continually contest with adults for more authority and a broader range of control, both of themselves and others. When a child is conceded some authority by an adult, it is often defined as a defeat for the adult, yet the act of watching a child grow in competency can be very gratifying. The child wants to extend his influence, and he can be taught to make deals in order to do it. Through negotiation and concession, the adult can teach the child how to take the needs of others into account. This is one way the child can be helped to cognitive maturity.

In their social contacts, children develop heavily structured peer arrangements. We all need heros to emulate. We all need information about what is expected of us to maintain our roles in the group. One way of achieving this information is to invite children to participate in the planning of their learning experiences. This only works where there are many options offered. Formal games or competitions may provide such options. Games like "research" may be played for the joy of the game, while "test" may be played to earn a reward. Children will tend to model themselves and their games on the adults around them. When teachers use the game of "rhetoric" on their classes, it is reasonable to expect the students to pick up the rules and compete with teacher on his own turf.

Children need to learn the symbols of winning and losing. If they cannot identify victory and defeat, they cannot set reasonable goals or employ effective rhetoric. How does a child know when he is socially acceptable in the group he aspires to belong to? How does he decide which group might accommodate him? How can he learn to conform to the norms of his selected group? What must he do to achieve respect and position in the group? These questions are the core of personality growth in the child, and they are not very different for adults. In every case, the answers lie in some communicative activity. Acceptance, support, friendship are the rewards for victory.

Responses to rhetoric are recorded as either victories or defeats. If we get the responses we seek, we win. If we do not know the responses we seek, we cannot win. Therefore we are constantly trying to discover where we stand in relation to others, to determine who is above us and who below us. We select our relationships, at least partly, on a basis of the rewards we see in them. A student needs to discover how to win, to savor the satisfaction of winning, and how to do so without injuring other people involved. Furthermore, the child needs to understand that any given loss does not disqualify him from subsequent victory at another time and place. Paul Goodman refers to this quality as the courage of failure. The growing child needs to be able to test his skill without being destroyed in the process.

Schools need to equip students with perspectives on combat. The child needs to know about words and sentences, not as systems of grammar, but as tools he needs to develop himself as a person. He must obtain a wide range of techniques which he can use to meet his basic human (animal) needs as discussed in Chapter 5. He must understand how to bargain with others, that there are some services he can perform in exchange for the services he seeks. If a child gets carried away with a lust for winning, he can turn into a totalitarian who destroys others. If a child loses too often and too drastically, he may be destroyed by his own feelings of inadequacy.

Rhetoric is the tool through which all of this is carried on. Our identities and roles are developed through responses to our own rhetoric; our methods of achieving goals are rhetorical strategies, our survival mechanisms are through rhetorical exchanges. It almost seems as though rhetoric is the core of learning, without which everything is irrelevant.

CONTROLLING AGGRESSION THROUGH SOCIAL RULE

Part of growth is coming to understand the rules imposed by members of a society to control the aggressions of the people in it. A realistic view of human society tells us that aggression cannot be totally eliminated. Therefore, it must be controlled; channeled into activities that benefit the community. Where this cannot be done, rules must be imposed to prevent people from doing damage to one another. This kind of practice is difficult enough just in the realm of physical damage. There are no laws that could control psychological damage that people can do to one another. People attempt to protect themselves from psychological deprecations by inventing techniques of conflict resolution and methods of keeping interactions on a nonthreat level. People play interaction games in which they can carry on regular moves and thus avoid loss. When moves are regular, people can plan ahead and not feel uncertain about what behavior they might evoke from others. Society also provides outlets for aggression in the form of structured games, sports, and contests. In extreme cases, war is used as a means of utilizing and channeling aggression. In school, no matter how we try to avoid it, students compete for grades, for notice, for social status. Teachers' rhetoric directs the development of the norm for these competitions.

Societies that offer their people nothing to struggle against, no national goals, no outside "evil" forces to hate, no internal threats to worry about, seem to make little progress. Without reference to the benefits of the homeostasis that might prevail in such a society, there appears to be a correlation between struggle and success; progress without stimulation is impossible. Progress in task accomplishment and personal growth seems to be a function of tension. According to one authority, the most effective learning model is one of alternating states of tension (stimulation) and gratification (homeostasis). Tension is a function of the threat that comes from confronting a problem, an impediment. Tension and threat are the foundations of conflict. Students in school will develop their own norms about what to struggle against. They form cliques that compete with each other. They involve themselves in interscholastic rivalries. Often they declare teacher to be the enemy.

Adult competitors seek identity through aggressive behavior. They work for position in the family, for economic and political power on the job, for relevance through social acts, for pleasure through competition with peers. The field of combat can be the kitchen, the cocktail party, the office, or the PTA meeting. Each interactive combat carries with it a set of formal rules, which, if observed, can lead to all contenders emerging with some kind of victory. Learning to play these rules and make the appropriate trade-offs, however, is very difficult, and cannot come about without considerable practice under direction. Within a school system teachers vie with each other for merit ratings, positions on committees, and choice class periods.

Any attempt made by a person to dominate interaction leads to dissidence and conflict. It is interesting that in societies, like schools, that are subject to authoritarian controls, there is little outward dissidence. That may be because students perceive the futility of fighting against an overwhelming force against which they cannot win. They may concede the battle, but that concession may, in itself, defeat the goals of the authorities, for all they receive in exchange from students is superficial and compliance behavior (*ressentience* in Friedenberg's terms). Outside the school, the students regard the whole business as irrelevant and they go on about their business of meeting their human needs. It seems that people will only compete when they think they have a chance to win. Repressive societies felt their revolutions when they began to make reforms, not at the height of the repression. Thus, excessive control (total victory) is dangerous, even though it may appear convenient to the person who has power.

Students follow the pattern of competition they observe in adults, and often parents do not know how to respond to it. If a child is raised permissively, the parent often has to sacrifice the trappings of control. If the child is raised in an authoritarian environment, the parent often loses the child through rebellion: if he remains under control, he grows into an apparently docile, though tension ridden, adult, ready to impose the same kinds of controls on his own children. The combat relationship is so natural in families that often neither parent nor child is aware that it is going on. The parent needs control, for the demands of the child can disturb his calm and thwart his goals. The child must compete to develop his self-image by displaying uniqueness and showing skills at control over parts of his environment. The same pattern appears true at school. To carry on his tasks in the classroom, the teacher needs to maintain discipline and control. But often his tasks have nothing to do with what students need, and so students resist, preferring to seek their own goals. The excessively permissive teacher finds himself overwhelmed; the authoritarian teacher finds himself in control, but if he looks carefully, he can see little progress in his students.

People do not normally seek democratic socialization, although they may employ it to heighten their chances of winning. People normally seek autonomy, although sometimes they will subordinate themselves to an institution or its leader in order to find some form of identification. Erich Fromm contends that people seek to escape freedom, for it is simpler to have choices and decisions made by others. Students will, at times of stress, submit completely to the will of the teacher or the school. Living under control, however, does not teach a person how to live without control. Thus, we confront a major paradox of our schools: the goal of school is to train citizens for a democracy, but for the most part it is done in an authoritarian manner. Children learn about democracy, but they do not learn to live it in schools as they are presently organized. Since they do not learn democracy, they cannot develop autonomously, and they emerge with blurred and confused self-images. It is small wonder that a recent (April, 1972) Associated Press dispatch cites a government report which classifies nearly half of our middle class as mentally ill.

What seems appropriate as a change is not necessarily the sacrifice of the teacher's authority, but a broadening of choice for the student. This can be efficiently accomplished by individualizing learning goals and devising methods that might enable the student to commit, to choose, to try, to defend with argument, so that he can learn the rewards of winning as well as the reactions of failure in ways that will help strengthen rather than defeat him. We will suggest some of these possibilities of instruction in the final chapter.

GOALS IN RELATIONSHIPS

Man cannot exist as a human except in relationship to other men. Man cannot interact without aggressing. Thus, men must accept this essential element of being together and engaging in competition while they are together. Achievement of our animal goals requires mutual participation; acquisition of our personal goals requires competition. In our society, the only legitimate means of interactive competition is rhetoric. While there are many alternative forms of rhetoric, the goals of communication are universal to all contacts.

1. Each person attempts to discover through interaction who he is in relation to the other person and what capabilities he might have in evoking responses from him.

2. He wants to know what the range of possible responses is that he can expect from the other person.

3. He wants to be able to develop a plan of communicative behavior that will enlarge his feelings of security and reduce potential threat.

He seeks these objectives because they are necessary steps toward accomplishing the animal goals of survival, stimulation, security, and territory. He accomplishes them to the extent that he can satisfactorily deploy power.

We are constantly engaged in tests of our power. "Power" may be an unpleasant word, but it describes what people seek in their interactions with others. When we interact, we attempt to make changes in the behavior of others so that they will provide services necessary to our seeking of goals. In order to succeed (survive) in social relationships, it is necessary to know what we seek, and what it is that we can say or do effectively. In order to get this information, we must know how others respond, so that we can sort out what is reasonable to expect from others and thus make some decisions about which of many possible behaviors we shall select.

We must understand human behavior horizontally and vertically. *Horizontal behavior* refers to behaviors in general; how people in general display anger, affection, and so on. *Vertical behavior* refers to the totality of behaviors by a single person. If we understand this, then our goal setting has a high probability of utility. That is, we can do a better job of predicting which of our behaviors will evoke a desired response from others. We have already stated that interpersonal relations are fundamentally rhetorical. Basically, a form of instruction in interpersonal rhetoric would include information about the nature of the person as communicator, the nature of the communicator's audience, the style of communication that can be applied, and a method of analysing and drawing inferences from responses. Suggestions from which such a curriculum can be built are offered in the final chapter. For the individual teacher, this means helping students understand what their goals might be, how others seek their goals, how people can combine their goal-seeking behavior (cooperate), what can be feared from others, and what the individual can do to avoid hurting others and to convince them not to hurt him.

Our concern here is with the goals of interpersonal relationship. Most of these goals have been structured for us through acculturation. We have experiences, and the people around us teach us which are worthwhile and which are defeating. Through these experiences and our evaluation of them, we become able to select some goals that will help us achieve satisfaction in relationship. Usually these goals have something to do with survival, security, stimulation, and territory.

A successful response from a parent, for example, might be nothing more than a nod of approval. From the boss, the nod may mean that the

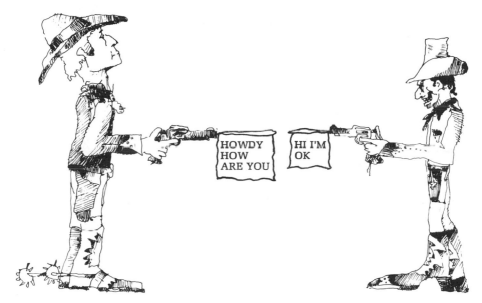

Probing in social conversation

work has not been quite satisfactory. For some people, a nod is the maximum positive reinforcement they can muster. From others, a nod may be a dismissal, a total rejection. Any tendency to universalize the response of nodding disables a person as a communicator, for nods can mean different things to different people. While there may be some probability that several people mean the same thing with their nods, room must be left for individual differences in the meaning of the gesture.

Thus, in any engagement with others, we are confronted with the need for some personal analysis. We need to know, for example, what we define as a gratifying response, and then we must determine whether the person who gives it to us means it in the same way. Furthermore, data must be analysed instantly, so that we can continue communicating. We do not have time, in an interpersonal situation, to ruminate about the possible meaning of a response we may have received. Society does not help equip us with standard criteria against which to judge the responses of others. Most of the time we tend to interpret intuitively, and often let wishful thinking dominate our conclusions.

Our perception apparatus functions as an antenna. We communicate with others and pick up data in order to determine whether we want to continue the interchange, and if so, what direction it should take. New people represent a threat to us, for their response styles are unfamiliar to us. We learn to inquire, prod, probe, and define, and during the opening period of a conversation, usually confine our talk to nonthreatening topics, so that we can gain time to size up the other person and discover how he may help us achieve some of our goals, and what we may have to give up in order to get his cooperation. Observe the following:

(Scene: A cocktail party. Jim, a salesman, meets Alice, the wife of someone else in the company.).

JIM: Hi there! I'm Jim Johnson.
ALICE: My name is Alice.
JIM: Are you enjoying the party?
ALICE: The Carlsons always throw a good party.
JIM: This is my first time here. I don't think I've met Mrs. Carlson.
ALICE: Take my word for it, they always throw a good party.
JIM: Are you with the company?
ALICE: My husband is.
JIM: Has he been there long?
ALICE: Several years.
JIM: I'm in sales.
ALICE: Excuse me, I must say hello to the Blacks.

Alice had control over the situation. She was obviously more familiar with the people and the milieu. She knew what she wanted to accomplish and who could help her accomplish it. Her contact with Jim was a probe, and was apparently nonproductive since she excused herself rather soon, but she did not make Jim feel uncomfortable. Jim, on the other hand, presumed on the relationship. He asked for too much information and tried to give away too much about himself. He accomplished little because he had not thought through some questions. Was Alice his hostess? Did Alice's husband have power over him in the company? How had he played it? Did he impress someone he wanted to impress? Would it have been better if he had not made the contact in the first place? How does one go about doing and saying the right things at these parties? How do you find out who you have to talk to and in what ways?

Lest you believe this is an overstatement, think back over the judgments people have made about you as a result of very little communication. One psychiatrist has alleged that the first five minutes of a therapeutic relationship can determine the entire course of the therapy. The initial encounter between student and teacher often sets the mood for the whole year. This premise applies to all human encounters, for once we have made a judgment about the worth of a person or the possible benefits to be derived from him, it is very hard to reverse that opinion.

Consider the first few days of a new school year from the perspectives of teachers and students. Schools are often open to rumors about both faculty and students. On a first day of classes, participants enter with a number of ideas about what their experience will be like that year. Oftentimes, expectations about the personality or competency of the teacher are thwarted. Also, teachers find that students perform differently from what they had expected after having listened to comments about them from past instructors. Most students realize that their expectations may be thwarted, so they are wary for a few weeks in the classroom; they need time and experience to test their behaviors against teacher responses. Of course, the teacher is engaged in the same tentative process. New teachers may be surprised when, thinking that their demeanor is friendly, students do not engage in conversation with them during the first day. Questions are often answered minimally; sometimes deviant behavior is tried and quickly retracted, given the teacher's response to it. At any event, students and teachers engage in the same kind of communication probing we all find in social settings.

We determine our attitudes toward other people based on our evaluation of their communication to us. We are also judged that way. We have few criteria on which to base our judgments. For teachers, this is a particularly crucial concept, because the students in our care have to suffer through the relationship, whatever it is, with no power to make rules about it. Students are in a state of doubt when they encounter a teacher. When people are in a state of doubt, it usually is not possible for them to react with perspective. They need to know if there is something in the relationship that will benefit them or if they will be required to do what the other wants with no possibility of exchange. If children cannot find benefit, then they will comply, withdraw, or rebel, none of which is desirable in a learning situation.

If we were all to confine our relationships to people we know well, we would do little with our lives. While people crave homeostasis, they also know that they can make little progress if they confine themselves to the familiar and the secure. This is very important to the classroom teacher. He can maintain some control over interaction by regarding all children as the same. When he does this, he may be able to regularize their behavior in the classroom, but he has no way of knowing whether he has stimulated learning.

But if he opens himself up to the wide range of differences in his students, the teacher faces the responsibility of responding to their human characteristics. His chance of gain in any given case is vastly increased, although his failures will be much more obvious to him. It is not at all clear whether the close-contact style of teaching really induces more failures than successes. It is just that it is more threatening to know about students so directly. When we can get students to commit themselves to personal goal seeking compatible with the teacher's goals, then we have optimum learning.

To withstand the risks that come from encountering too many people as individual human beings, we tend to develop stereotypes of behavior to deal with people in general. Despite our understanding of differences in people, it is much more secure to respond to a category than to a person. However, when we do this, we eliminate the opportunity of rewarding the individual directly. Only to the extent that he is bound up with his category can we make him respond to rewards. If the student who seeks identity as a person is responded to by relevant adults around him only as a student, he does not receive specific nurturance for his self-esteem.

Our school system is built to reward the unusual. Despite the fact that schools were developed to provide the greatest good for the greatest number, in practice, they mainly serve the needs of those who succeed in them and usually serve the convenience of those who structure and run them. Thus, the child-student rarely emerges as child, John, or child, Sally, except during those rare moments when he and teacher succeed in breaking through the barrier of social role. The memory of those moments, for those of us who have had them, keeps us seeking similar experiences. But for those who have never experienced a positive moment of interpersonal contact in the schools, there is no possibility of defining a positive outcome from any kind of interaction. Probably, no one has told them that school can be satisfying, and no one has shown them how it can be.

Often, we have problems of relating when we cannot assign a clear label to the stranger with whom we are talking. Our initial attempts in conversation are to determine the group to which our protagonist belongs. Is he a teacher, a salesman, a member of the military-industrial complex, a good kid or bad kid, a troublemaker? *What* is he—rarely, *who* is he? We have social rules to cope with labels. We have few rules to cope with people.

Society has structured some routine dialogues we can go through when we meet strangers. But going beyond this initial talk is often distressing to strangers who may not have made the same decisions about us that we made about them. Revealing personal information too early in a conversation may push people away. Initial contacts between people are designed to be superficial. If both parties decide to continue and change this style, the option needs to be exercised later on.

Initial conversations are not necessarily satisfying, but they enable us to make decisions about whether we want to continue, to risk some future contact. They are the first steps on the road to relationship. What is not often told to us as children is that making relationships is very complicated and difficult; that it proceeds through stages and takes time. We do not learn, for instance, that what makes relationships is an exchange of services; nurturance traded for stimulation, cooperation traded for status. We are taught to assume friendship or friendship potential in all cases, and we are thus led to expose ourselves to ridicule or abuse. Not all people are exchangers. Some would do us harm, intentionally or unconsciously. Each of us has trusted a teacher with some personal information only to find it displayed publicly to just those people we did not want to know it. Hardly anyone has reached adulthood without experiencing some kind of betrayal. Often this leaves us suspicious, unable to make satisfactory relationships. Sometimes, however, we continue to proceed naively and blindly into relationships where others use us for their own purposes, and we have no weapons with which to fight our way out. In the survey of college seniors referred to earlier, respondents noted that they would prefer a defeating relationship to no relationship at all. It seems sad that they could not see the possibilities of trying again with someone else, using the information they acquired from defeat in order to bring about victory.

Often it is necessary for us to interact with people who are unpleasant because their communication style confuses us or they have the power to make us feel threatened. Teachers confronting students from other cultures often develop some dismal feelings about them. When we deal with this situation, we try to preserve what we can of our self-image. We can do this by changing the image of the others inside our head, by reducing their importance to us. "What does the boss know? He's just another pushy jerk." "Anyone who would wear a skirt like that would. . . ." If a person has no significance for us, he cannot hurt hurt us very much. The only caution, however, is that it is unwise to invest a person with no importance in the internal world if he does have the capacity to hurt us in the real world. To solidify opinions too strongly or too soon offers the risk of making reality out of nonreality and interferes with behavior options.

Some parents seem to understand instinctively the win–loss potentials of human interaction. When they train their children to play formal games, like checkers, they are careful to let the child win a few. The child cannot be permitted to win all the games at the beginning, for then he will understand that the parent is "throwing the game" and his self-image will be demeaned. But the child must win enough to encourage him to keep trying, so that he will understand that acquiring skill will pay rewards. It is imperative that rules be followed in formal games, for without rules there is no way to determine winners and losers. In the interaction game, it is also important to master rules; however, they are not published in a handy book to memorize before the game starts. They are written in the cultural code, and they develop out of the relationship of every two or more people in contact. They must be inferred and they must be tested.

Once a child gains enough skill to win on his own, he poses a threat

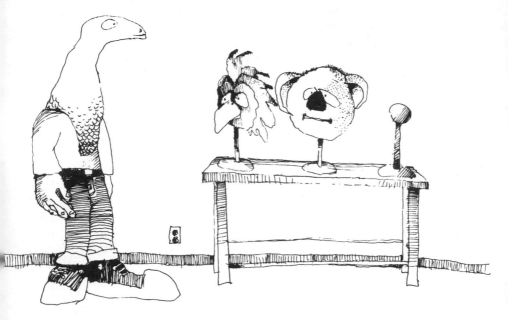

Selecting an alternative behavior style

to the parent, who now does not have full control over the game. The parent may then decide that play is not important, for he cannot afford to concede that the child has mastery over him. The parent sulks and refuses to teach any more about interaction. The child learns that it is necessary for him to be controlled until he is strong enough to control. He submits to the parent's tantrums, goes along with the gag, until it is possible for him to work things around his way. Sometimes he asserts his power by doing things that annoy or hurt the parent like growing long hair or joining the newest "Movement."

Thus, the home teaches socialization in the form of games. When the child learns to exert some controls over his parents, he attempts to apply them, where he can, with teachers and peers. Thus, as noted in Chapter 2, the child learns about role functions and control on some level, even before he gets to school. If he has learned that blind submission is the best course of action, he will present himself that way in school. If he has learned strategy, he will attempt to adapt it to the teacher. What the school has to do is provide alternatives so that whatever strategy the child brings with him can be utilized and then modified as a result of the school experience.

Because the child cannot spend all of his time with familiar people, he also needs to learn some social rules that will help him bridge the gap between himself and unfamiliar people. He must learn that there are alternative styles, and that it is unwise to submit himself to one course of action or to one set of beliefs. Value diversity calls for an accommodating spirit, which is built out of rewarding interaction experiences. Positive interactions where the child feels gratified will help him risk contact with the unfamiliar.

The successful communicator is usually one who knows what it means to win and lose, who knows when he has won or lost, who knows what he needs to do in general in order to win, and who can profit from losing by acquiring behaviors that may be used differently later on. The successful communicator will know that if he wins at the expense of another, the next encounter, which may be necessary, may not be so pleasant. The child who comes from a home that has encouraged him to risk attempts will learn more quickly, but parents in this kind of a home must take care to protect and buttress the child against penalties he earns when his risking action is inept.

Each victory increases the chances that the next encounter will be victorious. In order for a person to do well at communication, he must have an image of himself succeeding in interactions. He must know that he can't win them all, but he must know that some victory is available to him. Life is actually very bleak for the small child. He does not have sufficient physical force at his disposal to intimidate anyone. The world is designed for older and bigger people, and hardly anyone understands that he can get emotionally involved in his own concerns and activities. Consequently, few adults really know how much a child can be hurt from the defeats he suffers in interaction. Failure to listen to the child when he "babbles" about the bug he caught; failure to take a child's tears seriously; reliance on authoritarian control and corporal punishment to maintain order; failure to provide opportunity for the child to do both childlike and adultlike things tends to reduce the child's self-image. When he grows to adulthood physically and learns more of what the world requires of him, he will be less and less able to cope with interaction because his childhood has given him the feeling of ineffectuality. He may learn to believe that accomplishment is impossible and that he is not able to cope with interaction, and he may withdraw and move physically away from humanity. We will discuss this kind of person in detail in the next chapter.

Thus, the school has no choice but to build on what the child brings to it, and attempt where possible to modify both the process of concept-making and the process of exerting influence. The school is, perhaps, the only place where a child can get an orderly and safe exposure to communication training. But it is difficult for the school to compensate for defeats that the home may have administered. A child who has had no success at home may perceive the rewards the school offers him as spurious. He will compete for them only if he sees them as making his life more comfortable elsewhere. What the school can do best is to teach the child about interactions with teachers and peers, discussing feelings derived from interactions and demonstrating possible alternatives in behavior, and then attempt to relate this knowledge to situations important to students outside the classroom. A kindergarten youngster, for example, will need to know how to develop a peer group, how to respond in the classroom, how to work with others to plan the solution to a problem. An older child may have to learn something about communication with people of the opposite sex, how to impress future employers, how to play the social game.

Communication learning must proceed through reinforcement. The child needs the opportunity to risk and to fail without excessive sanction. He must learn how to develop internal rewards and penalties. The teaching of rhetoric cannot proceed as regular cognitive instruction with grades as the usual reward. That would make rhetoric an irrelevant game.

Children do not grow automatically to adulthood with rhetorical skills adequate to meet their needs to fulfill themselves economically or socially. All we need to do is listen carefully to the adult talk around us. There are few adults who can engage in sprightly social conversation; even fewer can do a sensible job of group problem solving with others; fewer still are able to stand up and state what is on their mind with cogency and persuasive impact. Few adults know and understand the art of friendship. Intimacy and love are quests for most adults, but they raise few questions to aid them in obtaining a closer relationship. Most adults even find it hard to express their problems to people who potentially can help them. Thus, even though there is as yet no specific method of doing it, teaching students to play the communication game well is a vital task for which the schools must assume responsibility.

SUMMARY

Both child and adult, student and teacher, engage in winning and losing interpersonal situations daily. Sometimes the students encountered in the classroom have psychic battle scars which pose a real challenge to the teacher; sometimes they have such limited experience in dealing with others that they need to be protected. We have introduced a closer look at the meanings of "winning" and "losing" in relationships and have posed some heuristics that can be applied in analysing given encounters with individuals to help determine the possibilities for mutual goal fulfillment between these individuals. We have explored some needs of students and teachers so that teachers might begin to see how rhetoric can help them and their students become more competent in their communication situations in the classroom and outside.

WORKS CITED:

Becker, Ernest. *Birth and Death of Meaning*, 2d ed., New York: The Free Press, 1971.

Brenner, Charles. *Psychoanalysis*. Garden City, New York: Doubleday & Co., Inc., 1957.

Fromm, Erich. *Escape from Freedom*. New York: Rinehart & Company, Inc., 1941.

Pedersen, Douglas. *Report to the Alameda County School District on the Incidence of Reticence*. Hayward, Calif.: Alameda County PACE Center, 1968.

WORKS RECOMMENDED:

For the most definitive discussion of instructional objectives obtain the *Mager Library*, Belmont, Calif., Fearon Publishers, 1968. Particularly useful to teachers and students alike is Robert Mager, *Goal Analysis*, Belmont, Calif.: Fearon, 1972. The classic in this vein is Benjamin Bloom, *Taxonomy of Educational Objectives*, New York: David McKay, 1956.

For additional information about the use of heuristics in interpersonal communication see Gerald Phillips, *Communication and the Small Group*, 2d ed., New York: Bobbs-Merrill, 1973, Chapter 5.

Objectives Chapter 7

- To reaffirm that human beings cannot have positive identities without effective communication relationships with others.

- To note that people develop communication patterns based on expectations and responses from others around them.

- To learn that we need to acquire skill at setting and analysing goals as well as selecting rhetoric designed to help meet these goals.

- To note that ineffective communication leads to decreased humanness and to emotional illness.

- To explain the progression of setting idealized goals, becoming frustrated, and finally becoming demoralized which leads to emotional illness.

- To describe essential behaviors which characterize "healthy" communication.

- To describe specific communication behaviors which are signals to emotional distress.

- To elaborate one particular distress behavior, reticence, and compare it with the problem of stage fright.

7.

The Clinical Responsibility of the Speech Teacher

THE PERSONAL QUALITY OF COMMUNICATION

Overview

We have alluded throughout these chapters to the ineffective communicators who surround us on all sides. Because communication behavior is so closely tied to "winning" or "losing" as a *human being*, to creation of a positive or negative self-image, we have concentrated on the importance of the teacher utilizing rhetoric designed to help meet the daily needs of his students, as well as his own needs.

In this chapter, we will make it even clearer that ineffective communication has great emotional illness potential. We will outline some specific behavior patterns that may be found in the behavior of your students, as well as in your friends and loved ones that signal the need for some form of help. As teachers, we have a responsibility to meet the needs of students in the most effective way possible without jeopardizing our own goals or those of the school system. Therefore, when someone "reaches out to us," communicatively, we need to know some possibilities for response. We will explain some goals that are essential to increased effectiveness in communication which might offer one realistic alternative to the person who is not "making it" in his general relating to others. The reticent student is one who is most likely to emerge in the classroom as having a communication-relationship problem, so the last part of the chapter is devoted to description of his problem, how it develops, and what pedagogical responses seem to help most.

COMMUNICATION is an identity building device. Society pressures us to conform to its norms and standards. Our need for territoriality, role, and status push us into an identity. When we see ourselves in a glass mirror, we are only aware of our physical self—and even that is distorted by what we expect to see. If we have been told by others that we are unpleasant or ugly, we will see lines and pimples more vividly than if we expect to see a handsome creature reflected. People who are concerned about being fat may look considerably larger to themselves than they appear to others. Thus, even on the most fundamental level of perception, we are who we are because of the way others respond to us.

Thus, it is not possible for humans to have identity without relationships with others. Our need for nurturance, part of the homeostatic drive, is much too strong. Man must acquire nurturing relationships if he is to be truly human. The most fundamental use we make of communication is to deepen relationship. Our most crucial rhetoric is directed toward the exchanges that result in intimacy. It is important for each of us to develop personal competency so that we can evoke the responses we need from others and exchange the kinds of responses they seek.

We learn to communicate because we need to. It is the only way we have to influence the world around us. People do not know who we are unless we communicate it. We are not restricted to verbal communication. Our whole body communicates. Body movements, hand gestures, facial expressions, clothing, the way we arrange our possessions are all vehicles for expressing who we are to others. People respond to us as totalities through these communications. Through their responses, we are able to assess our impact, evaluate our effectiveness, and develop a repertoire of communicative choices which can be employed as we meet new people in new situations.

Who we are is a blend of our roles and goals. We have no single authentic self. There is no situation we can imagine in which we are not involved in playing a role and through it seeking both long and short-term goals. The only real self we have is a result of success and failure at persuasion of others to support us in our goal seeking.

We begin to learn about ourselves, what we need and what we can do to get it, early in life. It begins when we learn to symbolize and it matures when we can take the place of another in our minds. We experiment with identity through plans. Our culture tells us which games are permissable and we try them out. Little girls learn about womanhood by playing dress-up or mommy. They teeter on high heels and trip on long dresses while they temporarily become actresses or nurses. They make mommy-talk with each other and with their dolls. They know it is a game, and this is very important to them, for a game played in the imagination is a game they cannot lose, and through it, they can find out about themselves. Little boys become cowboys, baseball players, and other hero-type people almost in random order. They alternate daddy scenes and hero scenes. They put a pipe in their mouths and curse at other drivers when they ride in the car. To the extent that the behaviors of play are approved, they become part of our repertoire.

What is important to understand is that identity and communication are inextricably bound up with one another. As long as play is not interfered with excessively and the child does not incur penalties for it, he will move toward a kind of communicative behavior that works for him. This does not mean that parents must take an entirely permissive attitude toward what their children do. If a child is doing something dangerous to himself or others, he must be stopped in order to protect him and to permit the superego to develop so that he will not injure others. On the other hand, if a child is doing something the parents

Communication and identity are inextricably bound up with one another

regard as trivial, he should be permitted to go ahead, for it is his own experimentation with the world. It is even more important for the school to recognize that children will need to work out some of their learning activities in line with their own needs, to make commitments, and take the consequences of them.

Our stake in communication is huge. When we communicate, we invest our entire personality in the act of discovering who we are. Our identity is defined by the way others respond to us. Our repertoire of behavior is defined by the responses we receive. If others respond to us in positive ways, we store a memory of the behavior and use it again. Someone has just given us information about who we are. If we get a response that is ambiguous or negative, we store the behavior in an "avoid use" category. We must either modify our behavior or change the way we regard ourselves or the other person. We cannot function with dissonant material. We must resolve conflicts inside our minds or we are not able to function at all. We may choose to define the person who transmitted the negative response as a fool. But if we do this and the person holds some power over us, we have committed an act which jeopardizes our personal growth. Thus, we constantly employ rhetoric to motivate reinforcement from others and we respond to the rhetoric of others as they seek their goals. Some examples of this process are in order.

MARILYN, a slim thirteen-year-old decides she likes the role of "hippie." She revels in tight bell-bottom pants and see-through blouses. She wants to tell the world that she is a creature that has power over men. The responses she receives are suppressing. Her teachers comment on her morality, the boys avoid her, and her parents give her advice about her dress. She responds by altering her behavior and trying a hostility role. She antagonizes old friends, teachers, and parents. She fights back, employing verbal weapons she has found most disruptive to others. She wants a positive response, but she has begun to define negative as positive. At least it is a confirmation of her existence. Thus, when she succeeds in irritating people, she feels reinforced. This kind of behavior may be defeating in the long run, but because of her failure in her defined role, she needs to develop strength so that she can believe she altered her role playing by choice.

BILLY, in the fourth grade has been trained by his parents who believe that "children should be seen and not heard." When Miss Cummings asks for volunteers in class, Billy keeps his hand down. He has learned that silence is his most effective role. It is the only thing that pays off for him at home. When Miss Cummings calls on him he has nothing to say. (His father "can't stand 'lippy' kids.") Miss Cummings has read somewhere that high verbal skills are correlated with high intelligence. She assumes that the reverse is also true. Her come-on with the class has been to encourage talking and most of the class has taken this cue and talks a good deal. Billy cannot play this game, however, for he knows *he* is not supposed to talk. The penalties that accrue for him at home when he talks out supersede any reward that Miss Cummings can provide him in the classroom. He is trying to protect himself. But he hears Miss Cummings (of whom he is very fond) talking to another teacher. "Billy," she says, "is a slow learner." Now Billy has an identification of his role. If Miss Cummings wants him to be a slow learner, he is willing to play the part, for it will confirm her expectations and thus satisfy Billy's need to exert influence. He has found a role that is approved by relevant and important people. Billy succeeds in playing the slow-learner role so well that he never acquires verbal skills. He is destined to remain a "slow learner" for the rest of his life.

The point we are trying to make here is that people develop characteristic communication patterns depending on the expectations of the people around them, particularly the people defined as important. Part of belongingness is persuading others that you know the style. A characteristic of ethnic group members, for example, is to overplay the style of the group to which they wish to belong. Furthermore, groups of people who interact assign roles and ranks in the course of an interaction. The technique and skill displayed controls the role and the ranking an individual receives. Participation between people is a continual exchange of rhetoric to improve rank or master role. People who wish to change groups need to learn a different communication style suitable to the new group. Most people manage to learn several roles. They can play a family role, a job role, a social role, a civic role. They do not play them all well; usually, they do not play any of them well. They adjust, as best they can, to the requirements of the society in which they find themselves. Their success at adjustment is measured by their ability to cathect the proper role at the proper time. A man may change his name from Golembiewski to Gill, but he generally retains the style of his prior culture.

The ability to perceive what is expected in communication and to comply with expectations is an important ability for people to learn, at least if they do not wish to feel alienated from their fellows. Everyone needs to feel "in" somewhere. Everyone seems to need the homeostasis that comes with membership in a group. A good part of our life is spent trying to find some group with which we can fit comfortably. We are all concerned about our relationships with friends and family, about our status on the job. "Does my husband still love me?" "Is Smedley a good enough friend for me to borrow money from?" "Will Burns vote for me as president of the club?" "Should I date Johnson if he belongs to the wrong fraternity?" "If the Smythes invite us to dinner, does that mean we are moving up? If so, what does it mean if they don't invite us over?" There is some tendency to suspicion in our relations with others. We seek their nurturance and reinforcement, but we are afraid of the damage they can do us. No one knows that better than the new teacher making his first incursion into a school system. He seeks the approval of students and peers. He uses rhetoric to convince the students that he is a "good guy," and to convince other teachers that he is a disciplinarian. He also uses rhetoric to evoke the highest possible merit rating from the principal.

We all want to know where we are and what we can expect from others, and we want to know what we can do about it. The only way we can find these things out is from analysis of our rhetoric and its impact on others. We have already demonstrated that the main part of our self-image comes to us this way. But it is also clear that without training, we have very little equipment to make the kinds of decisions we need to make. We do not normally learn how to analyse the rhetoric of others, and what it demands of us, nor are we trained to assess adequately our own competence at interaction. We are not taught how important rhetoric is, nor given opportunities to practice its techniques. Some of us learn informally and develop a "good personality" or "high social skills," but there seems to be a tacit hypothesis operating that interactors are born, not made. If this is so, it offers a very sorry prospect to young people, for it means they can never aspire to more satisfactions from communication than they have right now. Our presumption in this book is that rhetorical skill is necessary to satisfy the most basic needs of man, and consequently, considerable teaching is necessary to help people to rhetorical adequacy.

Some possible alternatives for this teaching are laid out in the taxonomy in Chapter 9. For the most part, we need to learn:

1. Precision and realism in setting our own goals.
2. Methods to analyse others and their needs.
3. Methods to analyse situations in which we find ourselves.
4. Methods of acquiring and testing rhetorical strategies.
5. Methods of evaluating our own effectiveness.

Without these skills our communication is haphazard. Chance determines the outcome of our relationships, unless, of course, we run into a skilled and unprincipled communicator and then—we lose.

WHAT HAPPENS WHEN WE LOSE

The simplest thing we can say about the importance of communication skill is: when a person stops communicating, he stops being human. Such a statement warrants considerable explanation. It can be found in the diagnosis procedure for emotional illness, which seems to focus on communication cues as evidence of emotional disturbance. Some psychiatrists go so far as to say that the person who is mentally ill ceases communicating in symbols and proceeds to communicate in actions. This, in itself, is considered to be a mark of illness. If, however, the capacity and ability to communicate symbolically is a specifically human characteristic, the incapacity and inability to do so would render the human less human or nonhuman.

It should be clear that there are many varieties of emotional illness that are the result of physical pathologies. Any physiological involvement, in fact, will have some effect on personality reflected in communication style. Severe pain causes concentration on pain and conversation may be distracted and disjointed, but, in cases like this, the cause of the communication disturbance is clear and often can be treated. We are concerned here, however, with minor problems, neuroses, the disorders characterized by ineffective behavior and communication which brings little fulfillment. Characteristic of neurotic people is the tendency to keep doing acts which result in little reward, often intensifying the degree to which they are done. We believe that there are a number of minor emotional problems, like neurosis, that can be handled in the classroom, if we accept the premise that they are largely problems in interaction. If the communication climate in the classroom can be changed, then *people can be trained to interact more effectively, their image of self can be expanded and they can, perhaps, be spared at least that part of emotional illness that has its origin in ineffective communication.*

Many neuroses are dependent on our language system. There seems to be a cultural style in neurosis, that is, certain socioeconomic levels and various life and vocational styles seem to generate more of one type of disturbance than another. It seems that people select among alternatives for displaying their emotional pain, and come up with one that has meaning in terms of their own life style. The element of choice is crucial. Thomas Szasz believes that people choose emotional illness as a means of resolving their problems, because when one is "ill" he is spared the responsibility of coping. Thus, a man on the "way up" may choose a peptic ulcer; the poverty-stricken person may simply withdraw. The executive will choose a neurosis that will help him on the job, like mild paranoia, and the wealthy person who can support his neurosis economically may choose hysteria or a psychosomatic ailment. This cultural definition of emotional disturbance not only applies to socioeconomic levels, but also prevails across societies, which seems to indicate that we are not dealing with an exclusively physiological problem, but rather a response to ineffective behavior in interacting with others.

Szasz believes that the body will take over to communicate distress if the person is not able to verbalize about it, and that is why there is often a physiological involvement associated with emotional distress. Certainly, the ability to talk about tensions with sympathetic friends helps to prevent them from getting in the way of behavior. One clear indication that a person is in trouble is a change in his style of communication. Contrary to folk belief, when people become disturbed, they do not change flamboyantly, but rather intensify some behavior that is characteristic of their normal interaction. The person who is naturally quiet will become withdrawn; the loquacious person will babble incessantly.

We tend to become neurotic when our rhetoric is ineffective and can no longer evoke the kinds of responses we seek from others. Part of our failure may be because what we seek is unrealistic. Part may be because we are inept at seeking it. Both of these problems are reflected in symbolic output. The thwarted person may need only to adjust his communication about his goals, however, or learn to talk coherently about himself and what he seeks. He also may need to cultivate skill at analysis and rhetorical control in order to make his behavior more effective. The person who cannot achieve his goals may need first to find language that will make his goal setting more realistic.

Wendell Johnson offered the concept of "IFD" syndrome characterized by:

1. Idealization of a goal.

2. Frustration in achieving it.

3. Demoralization as a result of failure.

According to Johnson, people whose expectations are either unspecific or too high cannot receive the rewards that come from success. The student who has been persuaded that an "A" grade is the only sign of academic success might be demoralized by a "C." A teacher who equates silence in the classroom with learning may be demoralized by a productive discussion.

If a person thinks about goals consistently in abstract terms, he may never know whether he has achieved them. If the person who wants to "help others" or "do something socially useful" has no criteria by which to judge whether or not he has done what he wants to do, he can never feel the gratification that comes from achievement. People who reflect this kind of abstract goal setting in their talk need to be helped to define goals in smaller and more specific units so that they can derive regular rewards through the knowledge that something has worked out well. A human cannot exist permanently in a stimulated or excited state. He needs, periodically, to come back to homeostasis. What happens when there is no release from tension is a pervading feeling of apprehension called "anxiety."

The risk that comes with defining goals specifically is that it is also possible to spot failures; usually, if goals are realistic, they can be achieved anyhow and, compared with the advantage of being able to discern success, the small jolt one gets with failure at a minor goal is not very disrupting. The person who seeks goals that cannot be defined will never win. Teaching him to impose goals on himself may alter his perception of himself so that he can eventually achieve success in his own eyes. For this reason, development of options in the classroom is of very great importance. The teacher of communication needs to have strategies available and to permit each student to select from among a number of goals. A report, for example, can be delivered to a class or to a small group. Conversation can be practiced privately in groups of three. The student needs to be helped to skill through small steps, and the option of the size and kind of step needs to be negotiable.

When a human is not able to get the response he wants or cannot communicate well enough to achieve the goals he has set with others, he needs to take some kind of refuge. One possible recourse might be for him to adjust his behavior so that he becomes more effective. Unfortunately, society offers little to this end except psychotherapy. It is more likely that some internal adjustment will be made and signals of distress transmitted to others. The signals may be quite subtle, designed to be received only by people with whom the distressed person is familiar, or they may be gross signals. The person is seeking relief from anxiety, but in sending off his signals he often intensifies it, because people respond awkwardly to others whose communication is out of phase with their expectations.

Sooner or later the person begins to expect failure. He thus gathers some esteem for himself as a predicter if he enters every transaction knowing he will lose. It is easy to manipulate any encounter with another into something painful and defeating. Failure is easier to engineer than success.

Goal setting seems to be the variable that determines how effective a rhetoric is. If goals are specifically set, they can be analysed and questioned. When you know what your goals are you can ask whether the goal is worthwhile seeking, and whether it is attainable, and who is most likely to be able to help with it, and what you might have to do to induce that person to help. The problem is that people's goals often conflict, and as one person tries to attain his goal with another, the second person seeks a counter goal from the first. Thus, it is possible that in a given relationship, neither party gets what he is after. Sometimes one man's goal means the destruction of another person. To become an executive means that someone has to be deposed. When one is possessive about a friend, then competititors for the friend's favors have to be defeated. For one child to become popular, another child may have to be made unpopular. Behavior may then direct itself to the destruction of another person's self-image. The aggressive quality of human communication reflects itself in the way we seek our goals. We are not always considerate of the other. When we fail to recognize that the other person is also seeking his goals, we may lose sight of the necessity to exchange and our rhetoric may be destructive.

When goals conflict, there is the possibility for victory of one person at the expense of the other, the possibility that both can achieve what they are after, and the strong possibility that both will lose. In any case, to most people, failure of rhetoric is synonymous with failure of person. At the very base of human behavior is the quest to avoid failures. We try to influence others, and if we fail, we endeavor in our minds to make them seem unimportant.

We are normally not aware of the risks we take in interpersonal relationships. Most of us approach others blissfully unaware of the damage that can be done to us. When we consider the state of our self-image, however, we find it to be the composite of our interpersonal successes and failures, and so it is possible to retain in memory the image of failures as well as successes, in order to avoid the techniques and people that let us down. The person who cannot perform as a public speaker might blame it on "stage fright," and avoid subsequent contact with the public platform. The person who fails at interpersonal communication, however, is unable to live up to normal and natural public expectations, and is consequently evaluated by his associates as some kind of deviant. It is possible to live a good and happy life without ever giving formal public speeches, but the day-to-day requirements of human interaction demand a certain degree of skill at coping with the requirements of meeting the social norms of talk. When a student, for example, does not perform well in the classroom in an activity in which he is required to participate, we negatively evaluate him and reduce him to a lower station in the classroom society. Such evaluation and its attendant downward social movement may have serious effects on many students. It is hard to reconcile the conflict between the necessity of rewarding excellence and the urgency of avoiding excessive punishment of those not so competent.

When we examine interpersonal communication in rhetorical terms, however, the issue seems much simpler. The rhetorical model can be managed in school. It is possible to teach children skills which will improve their public performance, and it is also possible to teach them some understanding of what is required of them in the social domain. By combining exercise in socialization with the normal work of the classroom, often doing little more than to use social groupings as task and problem-solving groups, we can acquaint each child with some of the social urgencies in a situation that enables the teacher to monitor behavior and provide advice and correctives where warranted. If it is possible to do more, then, presumably, it should be done, although we confront another paradox in seeking to avoid a kind of sensitivity-training atmosphere in the classroom. We know that formal modes of teaching communication in the classroom presently hold little promise for carryover into mundane activity, but there is no reason why they cannot be carried over, if the teacher specifically directs his activity toward this goal. What he needs to know is what needs to be present in a healthy communication transaction, so that he will have some specific goals toward which to direct his efforts.

ESSENTIALS OF A HEALTHY TRANSACTION

We have already asserted (*several times*) that communication is both a process and a relationship. It is the process that people use to transmit information, beliefs, feelings, directions, conceptual relationships, personal commitments from one person to another. It is the relationship developed between them as a result of this activity. The procedure for establishing a communication relationship is still pretty much a mystery. College students, when asked if they recalled what it was that made them classify people as "friends" could not recall specific events; most declared that it "just sort of happened." Careful analysis, however, leads to the conclusion that friendships grow out of perceptions of satisfaction in an exchange of rhetorics.

While there is no infallible formula for "healthy communication," we can phrase the essentials in the form of communication goals.

- When we learn to phrase our goals with others specifically, our communication tends to be healthy.

- When we learn to separate idealistic goals from attainable goals, our communication tends to be healthy.

- When we are able to analyse and discover what the other person seeks and respond to it, our communication tends to be healthy.

- When we are able to communicate within the norms of the situation in which we find ourselves, our communication tends to be healthy.

●When we have a large repertoire of strategies from which to select in order to achieve our goals, our communication tends to be healthy.

●When we are able to distinguish success from failure, our communication tends to be healthy.

●When we are able to succeed, without jeopardizing the success of others, our communication tends to be healthy.

●When we are able to fail without being demoralized by it, our communication tends to be healthy.

Within the communication classroom, theoretical learning, exercises and activities, criticism and comment, all need to be directed toward the accomplishment of these goals. The student who learns them well acquires sufficient personal power to become an effective and productive citizen of his society.

THE EFFECTS OF COMMUNICATION FAILURE

When communication fails, frustration sets in. When frustration sets in, people are not as capable as they would like to be in their relations with others. Incapability with others usually results in incapacity to perform effectively in most situations, which in turn results in failure to achieve our human objectives. Most people who suffer from communication failure consistantly emit signals of distress. Most of us will behave in these ways some of the time. What we must be concerned with is the person whose repertoire is so scant that he behaves consistently in one of the following six categories.

1. When an individual speaks *consistently and frequently, to the exclusion of all other topics, about one and only one topic,* he is indicating a kind of fundamental insecurity. If he is not able to respond to change in conversational topics or take into account the conversational needs of others, we might consider him to be disabled in his communication process. He is regarded as a bore and usually ignored or rejected.

2. When a person is *chronically depressed in his talk, and confines his remarks to gloomy, foreboding topics;* when he denigrates the comments of others and seems disquieted by anyone else who is feeling joyful, he is signaling some deep psychic involvement. Such a person needs considerable help, for he is probably indicating a psychic depression. When a student is encountered in the classroom who does not seem to be able to smile and participate in joyful activities, some outside diagnosis should be sought.

3. There is another kind of problem communicator who is the counterpart of the depressed person. Usually female, it is the person who *confines conversation only to the light and bright.* She is able to find something "nice" to say about everybody and everything, although she attempts to prevent people from talking about serious subjects or topics that would offend her sensibilities. This kind of person may be escaping from reality and setting herself up for incalculable suffering when reality finally breaks through.

4. Some speakers are unusually aggressive. They *try to "win" every interaction by overpowering their opposition.* Although it is often necessary to be aggressive in conversation, these people chronically overstep their bounds by imposing their will on the people around them. They make accusations, offer insults, declare that their belief is the truth and anyone who opposes it is a fool. Often they compensate for lack of facts by the vigor with which they attack. There are usually some severe inadequacies felt by this kind of person; and in extreme states, he is far beyond the ability of the classroom teacher to cope. What has to be watched is the tendency of this person to be a bully and harass those who are not as proficient as he is at talk.

5. A communication disorder quite prevalent among young people is verbal evangelism. This is the *expression by a person that everyone else ought to be doing precisely what he is doing.* This person gets "hooked" on things. When he "digs" movies, then everyone else ought to. When he has discovered a new idea to believe in, everyone else needs to believe in it as well. He is particularly dangerous when he discovers drugs. A great many young people attempt to compensate for their own uncertainty about what they believe by sanctioning it through persuading others to do what they do.

6. The recent growth of sensitivity training has brought a new kind of problem speaker on the scene. This is the person who *seeks instant intimacy.* He will *tell you his innermost secrets within fifteen minutes of meeting you,* and if you do not respond with secrets of your own, he will accuse you of being "repressed" or "inauthentic." In the early teens and into the twenties, the tacit inference made by this speaker is that physical intimacy brings about psychological intimacy.

THE RETICENT SPEAKER

7. Perhaps the most frequent cue given off by people in trouble is silence. Our society is filled with grey, shadowy people who operate around the fringes of social groups without ever being noticed. They look like people who are not really there. Sometimes they are known as

daydreamers or "good listeners." We have referred to them earlier as "reticent."

Not all quiet people are troubled. Some people prefer not to talk very much because they do not have a great deal to say, or because they can accomplish their goals without it. We are concerned here with people *who cannot communicate effectively even though they want to very much.*

Communication may be construed as a skill to be learned, but unlike most other skills, it is deeply rooted in human personality and essential to human survival. Most of us can get along nicely even though we lack skill at playing tennis or doing chemistry experiments. But it is virtually impossible to live in our world of interaction without having basic, minimal skills at interpersonal communication. We are not concerned, particularly, about the ability to perform in public. That, too, is elective, and those who wish to learn to use the public platform can do so through practice and the application of a rigid training discipline. Our concern is with communication by people in day-to-day situations. We are concerned about the child who cannot recite when called on in class, the man who cannot tell another about his needs and dreams, people who cannot find satisfaction in being with others. Generally, these are people who are desperate to communicate, but whose efforts have been so consistently ineffective that they no longer can get an image of themselves communicating at all. As a result, they withdraw from contact, or they learn some ploys to get attention turned from them and on to someone else they think is more competent. They prefer to be classified as "poor students" rather than try to respond in class. They would rather take a dull job with no future than risk on a job that requires interaction. Thus, society is denied their skills, and they deny themselves the opportunity for fulfillment through interaction with society. Our schools are filled with these people (as earlier noted, 24 percent in the junior high grades) and they require a major effort by teachers to get them back into the main stream of human interaction.

Most teachers are familiar with the phenomenon of stage fright, a syndrome that affects many people before they perform on the public platform. Stage fright is mainly a situational problem that can be overcome through familiarity with circumstances and specific performance training. For those interested in performing in public there are many approaches to performance training which have been demonstrated to be effective. Most public speakers feel apprehensive when they approach an appearance no matter how often they have made it. A skilled performer learns to utilize his tension and release his energy in the performance in ways that help him succeed with the audience. Those who cannot overcome stage fright need not elect to appear on the public platform. Children in classrooms, however, cannot avoid being called on to talk in class, nor can they escape mandatory formal reports in front of the class. None of us can escape the requirements of interaction with family, friends, peers, and work associates. Consequently, disability at carrying out mandatory tasks because of a communication deficiency is a serious problem for the person who suffers from it.

Stage fright is of particular concern to those who teach public speaking. But fear of performance pervades all human transaction, and thus, is of concern to all teachers. The techniques used in schools to teach public speaking tend to make the skilled and committed even more effective, but also tend to increase the apprehension level of those not skilled and not committed. One need not require public speaking, however. Even with the skilled, there seems to be very little carryover from training in public speaking to interpersonal performance. Thus, communication training in the schools, for all children, needs to be directed to general performance; training should be directed for carryover. Special training can be offered to those who want to acquire specific skills.

The withdrawn person has something like stage fright, but he encounters it every time he tries to talk with another person. For one reason or another, he is so convinced that he is unable to handle what he must handle, that he triggers in himself a kind of hypertonic apprehension. He fails at interpersonal communication because he is so fearful of it that he fears his fear. In a sense this is very much like the etiology of stuttering as described by Van Riper, except that the reticent student does not often block or stammer. He merely finds ways to avoid talking.

To avoid his fear, the reticent fails, confirms the prediction he made about himself and reinforces his resolution to avoid verbal contact. His inadequacy soon becomes pervasive, for each failure diminishes his self-image, and the inept speaker learns that "for sure" he is not able to handle any kind of communicative situation. He may be capable of making a few secure relationships, but these become so important to him that he becomes dependent and a drain on the persons on whom he must lean.

Reticence manifests itself in many ways. Some people report feeling a shaky nervousness, butterflies in the stomach, physical symptoms such as perspiring, throbbing in the temples, audible heartbeat, and headache when in communication situations. Others suffer a tension block that prevents them from making all but the simplest statements and forces them to confine their remarks to monosyllables. Some may stammer a bit, though it is not clear that stuttering is a form of communication inadequacy. Some are able to initiate talk but are unable to finish it; they abort their conversations without ever getting to the point. Some can get statements out, but find themselves unable to cope with disagreement or questions. Most can speak to animals or children, and often they tend to assert dominance over younger people, though they are thoroughly intimidated by their peers and superordinates. A few manage to cover their inadequacy by adopting one of the six patterns discussed earlier. There are even some who can mask their interpersonal difficulty by acquiring performance skill which obscures their inability to relate in ordinary ways.

As noted previously, many times quiet or nonparticipatory behavior of a student is interpreted as a sign of boredom, resistance to instruction, or lack of intelligence. Interpreting the meaning of or reason for any behavior is difficult when dealing with humans, because we can never know what a person intends and whether or not his visible cues demonstrate this intention or contradict it. Furthermore, the human being is such a complicated animal, with a symbolic capacity that opens possibilities of thought which can never be shared with others, that trying to trace behavior back to intention directly would be impossible. So, the teacher is left with the job of "gestalting" behavior of students in his classroom, over periods of time in different situations, and he must consider the scope of possibilities of why a given student acts the way he does.

The reticent student may behave the way he does for a number of reasons which may never be determined specifically. But knowing some of the possible explanations for reticence can help the teacher understand possible changes in his own behavior, and in the structure of his classroom, that might give the reticent student more of a chance to participate.

We have talked a great deal in this book about the influence and function of language in the home. Some children are exposed to limited use of language as a medium for need recognition and fulfillment: talk may be restricted and little value placed on its use in situations. Also, styles of communication differ from family to family within the same racial, cultural, and socioeconomic group, which means that children often experience different orientations in their view of objects, space, time, and so on. So, even without basic cultural differences in the use of language in the home, children learn some idiosyncratic ways of handling talk. Studies of elementary school children from rural areas attending semiurban schools demonstrate that they act reticent in the school environment because expectations of conversation differ from what they have learned at home. Children from bilingual homes may experience difficulty in understanding language appropriate to the classroom, and may act reticent because of their uncertainty about whether or not they will sound like the other children. Sometimes cultural or social marginality, therefore, may be a source of reticent behavior.

Related to marginality as one possible explanation of reticence is the question of learning in general, which we have elaborated previously. Children may never learn to extend their perspective of language to understand the manner in which it influences others, and may therefore be confused about how to handle conversation to supply needs. If the child does not become aware of talk as having impact on others, he may not learn what behaviors are appropriate to what situations, therefore opening himself to ridicule and rejection by others. Some people never teach children what is expected of them in certain situations, yet they punish inappropriate behavior. The teacher who does not explain his expectations or how they should be carried out by the students in the classroom may evoke reticent behavior from some children. Sometimes reticence is a result of not having learned how to do something that other people expect you to be able to do.

In addition to these explanations of reticent behavior, there are considerations of physiological disorders such as those related to voice, articulation, fluency, and emotional problems. These are problems which a teacher is most often not equipped to diagnose on his own, yet they need to be considered in understanding why a student might act as he does in the classroom.

Studies have shown that the state of physical health affects emotional health and communication behavior, and vice versa. Teachers often note communication behavior differences in their students and themselves at different times of the day, often revolving around hunger states, states of physical discomfort, and tiredness. A student who is withdrawn in the classroom may be chronically ill, suffering from malnutrition, continued lack of sleep, and similar problems. If the teacher suspects physical involvement in communication behavior, he should suggest that the student have a physical examination without delay.

A child who is aware that others react negatively to something about the way he talks may develop a reticent posture in the classroom. Children are often quick to make fun of what is different, particularly before they develop (if they ever do) a dual perspective necessary for them to consider the needs of others. Thus, a child whose speech is hard to understand because of articulation problems which affect pronunciation and diction (lisps, sound substitutions, and so on), or voice problems (a voice too soft to hear or in some other way difficult to listen to), or fluency problems (stuttering and complete blocking of certain words) may choose reticence as an escape from ridicule.

Some of the authors have encountered reticent college students who reflected back to their days in elementary school when "people laughed at the way I talked, but I didn't know why" and "people always told me to speak louder because I sounded like a 'mouse'." A teacher who suspects that a child may be reacting self-consciously to the way he talks or to the way others evaluate his conversation, may want to consult a speech correctionist to aid in one aspect of a possible reticence problem. This does not mean that many children in early elementary school should receive speech therapy to avoid negative reactions from others and possible reticent coping; young children typically mispronounce words, stammer, or substitute sounds ("wabbit," for rabbit, "wif" for with, and so forth), but they most often alter their pronunciation as they become more proficient in conversation. It is the negative reaction from others that necessitates correction of talk, though it is difficult to generalize what will be reacted to negatively, since different judgments of "normal" or "acceptable" are made.

Consultation with a psychologist, psychiatrist, or counselor may also be considered in other situations where reticent behavior is found in the classroom, for more serious emotional-relationship problems may be present. Psychologists often identify certain communication behaviors as associated with deeper psychological problems of depression, alienation, and such. If a teacher has considered other referral courses and changes in technique of dealing with the child that have not been fruitful, the school psychologist might be consulted.

Despite additional referrals of some students noted as "reticent" by the teacher, it is the teacher himself who can be the greatest help in changing reticent behavior in the classroom. The reticent student must be helped to learn how to handle the situations new to him, or situations with unclear expectations. He must be shown that he can change his behavior in small steps that are successful, and thus be helped to feel better about himself.

Virtually everyone who appears reticent seems to be both aware and concerned about it. Reticents feel their relationships with others are impaired because of their difficulty; they feel they could produce more, be more effective people, if only they were more skillful in conversation. They would like to talk more and have a greater effect on others around them. However, even when they succeed in having a successful experience, it doesn't seem to do much to change the image they have of themselves as ineffective communicators. Sometimes it seems to heighten their distress and makes subsequent encounters even more difficult because they feel they could never do it again. It is as though they believed they only had a few successful encounters in their system and each time they have one it reduces the possibility of having another one.

Reticent behavior may serve well in certain contexts. Certainly in classrooms where silence is defined as learning, the reticent student appears to be the wisest of all. If he can learn how to respond to teachers on papers and examinations he is rewarded. This, in turn, reinforces his silence. The tendency is for the reticent to decide that his survival depends on how little he can transact with others. When he experiences a different situation which requires him to contribute orally, he is unable to do so. He cannot adapt to changing circumstances. Because he cannot defend himself orally, he takes the chance of earning no evaluation at all, rather than risk creating a poor impression.

If reticent patterns are allowed to root into personality, the quiet person can become the prisoner of his own silence. He is likely to base vocational choices more on the criteria of their lack of contact with others, than on his own interests or capabilities. His relationships with his spouse and children are impaired by his inability to talk things out. He has no capacity for leadership even when he is qualified to lead. This is most unfortunate, for the evidence seems to indicate that reticent people are somewhat more intelligent and sensitive than the norm. They are particularly sensitive to the injury that can be done to others through communication. This, in itself, may represent a reason why they withdraw from communication.

Sometimes teachers have a hard time separating reticent behavior from stage fright, a factor discussed in speech communication literature. The reticent person is generally concerned about his communication adequacy. He is likely to feel inadequate and to act minimally or withdraw in many kinds of situations, including conversation with family and friends, talk in classes and with teachers, in social situations when meeting new people, and in formal situations, including the giving of reports or the explanation of anything. The reticent is concerned that what he has to say in these situations may sound "dumb" or not worth listening to by others; he is concerned about his conversation in many different contexts.

The student who experiences stage fright does so in single, specific situations only. Most often, these involve public or formal performance in some way. Stage fright is related to the clinical phenomenon of phobic behavior, in which a person fears certain objects or situations, such as snakes or riding in airplanes. Stage fright is a situation-specific reaction which has many meanings. When it is a severe phobia it cannot be treated in the classroom. When it refers to apprehension about speaking, there are a number of possible approaches. Although past treatment of stage fright included forced experience to help overcome the feared situation and attempts to "will" the student to tackle it, a more recent treatment involves a process called "systematic desensitization," which is carried out in therapy. This treatment is based on the premise that if a person can learn new stimulus-response pairings through conditioning, these will replace this reaction of fear.

Recently, a good deal of work has been done by speech specialists and psychologists on the problem of speech apprehension. Through systematic desensitization, people with deep fears about performance in public have been helped to achieve the ability to participate. Systematic desensitization, originally, was a psychotherapeutic method designed to treat deep phobias. Experimentation has demonstrated that it can be administered simply in groups. In some cases it has been administered in automated fashion, that is, students were permitted to go at leisure and take a treatment on their own. The basis of the treatment is to learn to relax in the presence of frightening stimulation or thoughts of such stimulation. Through a systematic procedure of tension building and relaxation, the patient learns to remain at ease in the presence of his symptoms. Recent investigations indicate that there is some promise that systematic desensitization can be administered in the classroom by teachers. Care should be taken, however, at these early stages, about embarking on this kind of treatment program without adequate training. Furthermore, it is not clear whether relaxation results in mastery of the situation. To be unafraid is different from being skilled.

Thus, we can assume that even if desensitization is administered, and the subject relaxes when confronted with a public-speaking situation, the teacher still has the obligation of teaching the student how to cope effectively with the situation.

The most current effective dealings with reticent behavior, however, are focused on skills acquired in the classroom. We have talked about the importance of people recognizing their needs and goals which communication can help fulfill. If the reticent student can be helped in defining what it is that he (1) needs to do differently and (2) wants to do differently, so that he can be seen as more effective in communication by himself and others, he can achieve these needs in conjunction with others in the classroom.

A first step in setting goals for behavior is recognizing that these goals must be understood and stated in actual behaviors that can be seen and evaluated. It is difficult to improve a student's "confidence," for example, without pointing to certain actions which lead to the evaluation "confident"; to pursue "confidence" as a goal without recognizing that it is a behavior or set of behaviors which people react to, is likely to lead to failure. Robert Mager in his book *Goal Analysis* explains in detail the process needed to spell out accomplishable goals. We offer some specific communication goals appropriate to students at different grade levels in Chapter 9.

Furthermore, communication goals must be realistic and within the student's ability to accomplish in a certain time period. We would not expect a person with a broken leg to be able to walk unaided within a few days; neither should we expect a student to be able to learn different communication behaviors in a short period of time or to feel differently about himself right away. Some assessment needs to be made of how likely it is that the student can achieve a goal in a given period of time, and care needs to be taken that goals are simple, focusing on specific aspects of communication competency.

Finally, in accomplishment of communication goals, steps need to be spelled out that can be taken in some order to achieve goals, and alternative strategies of achievement need to be clarified in case there are problems along the way.

Aiding a child in learning how to ask and answer questions in class or how to explain what his hobby consists of are simple communication tasks which the teacher can perform with students in his class as a whole or with particular students who act reticent. The teacher can talk about the importance to the child of learning certain communication activities, demonstrating that communication is needed to get along with friends and family as well as in class. He can then proceed to spell out certain accomplishable steps. Students can learn to take these steps one at a time in mastering situations which they have neither learned nor understood before. Support of the student's efforts in mastering goals is important, as he needs continued affirmation that change of behavior is important and rewarding to him.

Thus, the teacher should consider that nonparticipation in the classroom has a number of possible explanations which can be checked out. Immediate evaluation of a student who is reticent as "stupid" or "bored" does him a great disservice.

SUMMARY

Hopefully, this chapter has helped you to think in more specific terms about rhetorical alternatives the teacher needs to develop and have on hand to meet the needs of his students. Because our society as a whole appears to be developing more rather than less communication-emotional problems, there is no reason to believe that our students will demonstrate an opposite trend of behavior. Thus, the teacher needs to be armed with the most useful responses available. We have presented some rationale for why people develop ineffective communication relationships with others through idealistic and nonanalytical goal setting, and we have noted specific communication signals that people often show when their worlds are not so rosy and they need help. The specific behaviors that characterize "healthy" communication behavior serve to guide in the development of an oral communication program in the classroom, thus meeting the needs of some ineffective communicators. We have focused on a particular cue to distress, reticence or withdrawal in the classroom, and have compared it with the problem of stage fright, which is different, but also found in student reactions to instruction (usually public performance). The authors feel, from their experiences in the classroom over the years, that the reticent student deserves particular attention from the teacher, since reticent behavior easily permeates all contacts with other people and blocks the development of effective communication and a positive identity.

WORKS CITED:

Johnson, Wendell. *People in Quandaries.* New York: Harper & Row, 1946.

Mager, Robert. *Goal Analysis.* Belmont, Calif.: Fearon, 1972.

Szasz, Thomas. *The Myth of Mental Illness.* New York: Harper & Row, 1961.

WORKS RECOMMENDED:

A thorough exposition of communication in psychiatry is found in Jurgen Ruesch, *Therapeutic Communication.* New York: W. W. Norton, 1961.

An explanation of brief forms of therapy can be found in Chapter 3 of Jay Haley. *Strategies of Psychotherapy.* New York: Grune and Stratton, 1963 and in William Glasser, *Reality Therapy,* New York: Harper & Row, 1965.

The problem of the retient student is detailed along with a classroom teaching plan in Nancy J. Metzger and Gerald Phillips, *The Reticent Student,* New York: ERIC-SCA 1973.

Objectives Chapter 8

• To explain how the teacher can utilize small classroom groups to introduce the processes of inference-making, cooperation, and competition which are found in all communication situations.

• To note that people usually engage in cooperative meeting of goals when they "trust" the other persons involved, when the others have established a set of consistent, fairly predictable behaviors that are not threatening.

• To recognize that we need to develop communication responses that offer the other person in a relationship the chance to protect his self-esteem by "saving face."

• To outline three propositions that determine success in a communication situation, and to discuss which reactions people generally prefer and which they react to with hostility.

• To present examples of classroom activities that might be used to direct student observation of communication behavior.

• To explain the need for teachers to withhold verbal evaluations of student behavior unless that behavior clearly obstructs the general goals of the teacher and other students.

• To discuss the role of nonverbal communication in our decision making that involves the people we choose to relate to, and to explain that physical appearance and movements are often unreliable criteria on which to assess relationship potential.

8.

Building the Communication Atmosphere in the Classroom

Overview

This chapter tackles the difficult problem of explaining the process of observing behavior of others and drawing inferences and generalizations about it before we respond to it. Most people appear to approach others in a rather haphazard manner. Often, because of physical appearance which attracts them, they assume that an "attractive" personality will follow. This approach explains one reason why there seems to be so much interpersonal hurt going on around us. Teaching students that the behavior of others needs to be observed and assessed, in line with one's own goals, is a difficult, yet necessary, task. Approaching this kind of instruction is even more challenging. We propose small group settings and sample activities which help clarify options for this sort of instruction. Additional and more specific plans will be presented in the following chapter.

Students need to be taught that verbal evaluation, either positive or negative, is usually reacted to negatively by the receiver of the evaluation. In fact, verbal evaluation often cuts off our contact with other people before we have given them a chance to demonstrate their behavior and we have compared it with our own needs. Some alternatives to verbal evaluation are discussed in this chapter. Our focus is on teacher behavior with students, as well as strategies for presenting this type of information to students in oral communication instruction.

THIS CHAPTER is about the teacher as a communicator and how he can build his own rhetorical skills in order to persuade students to participate in productive classroom activities. The chapter deals mainly with interpersonal business, how people treat one another in the normal and ordinary encounters of the day. The assumption is that at least part of what students learn about communication, they learn from models. It has been pointed out earlier that children learn their original communication style in the home by modeling after parents. There is no reason to believe that this process changes very much when the child enters school. Even adults seem to learn a good deal of their behavior by specifying someone they see as a model and by trying to emulate his behavior.

To summarize what we have presented thus far in the book:

1. We have described the process and relationship known as communication.

2. We have demonstrated that communication is purposive, that is, it is rhetoric directed at the accomplishment of some goal.

3. We have shown that our identities develop through the responses to our rhetoric and that failure of rhetoric often means failure of the self.

4. We have discussed the urgency to teach rhetorical skill systematically in the school by instruction in goal setting, analysis, strategy, and evaluation.

5. Throughout, we have stressed the importance of providing alternatives for the student, of finding ways where he can make his goals harmonious with the goals of the school.

We now turn to the secret of communication teaching—how the teacher behaves. In the following chapter we will discuss alternatives for his curriculum. Our first step is an understanding of the interpersonal process and its implications for the communication behavior of the teacher.

When we interact with others, we like to feel that it is an honest meeting. We seek relationships in which we receive enough information from the other for us to draw reasonable inferences about what he is feeling and what he seeks from us. We interpret the actions of the other so that we can modify our own behavior in relation to him. We attempt to predict outcomes so that we can control our own output and heighten the chances of achieving our rhetorical goals.

Normally, we prefer that the "honesty" of the other person not be displayed in destructive form. We favor suggestions of disapproval rather than outright disapproval. Subtle indications permit us to

It is hard to treat a student with unconditional positive regard

modify our behavior graciously. When someone seeks to have us modify behavior, we need a chance to decide whether or not we want to comply with his expectations. If he attacks us directly, we really do not have this choice. Our first reaction is to resist, to fight back, and at that point the tone is set for a hostile relationship. In the classroom this signals warfare between teacher and students.

Interpretation of responses is not easy. Often we are treated paradoxically by others. Their words may mean one thing to us; their actions may mean something entirely different. We need to adjudicate between them. We do the same things as we deal with our students. Often we cannot conceal our anger, displeasure, or contempt. The student receiving negative cues has the same choices we have when we receive negative cues. He may withdraw from us or he may retaliate. It is easy to declare that every teacher should treat students with unconditional positive regard, but for most of us this would require severe masking of our real feelings, and we may not be good enough actors to do it.

What we must remember is that we all seek to accomplish goals when we interact. Chief among these goals is the maintenance of self-esteem. The ability to understand the position of the other is the crucial element in successful communication. Without this understanding it is hard to avoid injuring the other. This means that every interaction is much more complicated than it appears, for whatever is going on outside is complicated by what is going on in the minds of the participants. It takes considerable struggle to discover common goals or topics without someone getting hurt in the process. Furthermore, each interaction with an individual depends on developing a set of actions exclusive to that individual, as well as complying with the public norms of conversation. When we talk with a person whose behaviors we cannot predict well, or whose cues we cannot understand, we feel ill at ease, and our ability to cope with the requirements of the situation is materially reduced. Since we are not able to predict what the other person is likely to do next, we find it difficult to select our own rhetorical strategies. If we persist in our normal modes of talk, we may evoke more hostility than we can handle. This difficulty is characteristic of most white-black interactions these days. Middle-class teachers who persist in adhering to middle-class styles of talk with black students often find themselves the targets of great hostility.

Most communication breakdowns result from inability of people to find a common ground on which to meet. Parents have difficulty speaking with their children, for example, because the children tend to resist the parent's ideas as outmoded, while the parents are not familiar with the jargon the children are using. Furthermore, their inner worlds are miles apart. The experiences they have had in common are limited. Their goals are different, and each must cling to his goals tenaciously since they are usually rooted in basic human needs. Thus, the parent who opposes long hair and lets it interfere with communication cannot see that the boy who wears it may define it as a symbol of his manhood, his identity, a projection of his personality. The long-haired boy cannot see that his hair symbolizes to his parents a total rejection of family values. When they talk about hair, both take recourse to anger and wounded feelings. Thus, neither can accomplish his goal. The parents do not get the boy to cut his hair. The boy does not win respect for his value system. In addition, each unsuccessful contact subverts the next communication, for the memory of failure looms large in the life of most people. The question is, when people conflict in this way, is it "honest," or "authentic," or would it make more sense to be a little more oblique and perhaps bypass those topics that might exacerbate tensions in the relationship.

If everyone simply declared what was on his mind about and to other people, what could be wrong? The problem, of course, lies in the variable in perception of the other person's goals. We started with the premise that the optimum relationship is one where both parties are cognizant of the fact that the other person has goals, and each displays some care in seeing to it that the other has a fair chance to accomplish them.

A good example of how this might work in the classroom is the experience of teachers in disadvantaged areas when they come into contact with the scatalogical language characteristic of most students. A teacher's first reaction is to show dismay and consternation; the language is like a bullfighter's cape to the bull. The teacher cannot see beyond the language to the emotion it represents. The students, perhaps, did not intend to disrupt the teacher; the language is part of their natural vocabulary. But they discover that the four-letter word gives them power over the teacher, who reacts negatively; and the teacher finds in the four-letter word an excuse for permitting his natural bigotry to operate.

A common method of teaching children, even very young ones, about what is needed in satisfactory relationships is to encourage working together in groups to solve problems. This can take many forms. Students may be asked to make choices about what the entire class should do, or they can be offered alternative project assignments and asked to group according to their choices. They might be divided at random into groups and told that their task is to be evaluated competitively, that they will be competing against the other groups, and that all of the members of their group will receive the evaluation the group will receive. This use of groups provides a realistic flavor to the act of learning and also provides some impetus for the development of group cohesiveness. Instruction is even more effective when the students are then asked to share their group experiences, while, at the same time, the teacher offers information about how group work may be improved, how people interacted, what kinds of interferences with processes took place, and how inferences were made by the various group members.

Our process of drawing inferences about others is based on our experience. For most of us, we learn to draw inferences as a trial and error process. As children we experiment with communication strategies, but we may not have enough information to determine what is effective and ineffective. Often we consider immediate gratification as effective and ignore possible long-term gain as a goal. Regardless of age, there is much that children can learn about the drawing of inferences and the building of judgments, about what to expect from others and how to evaluate it. Using the small-group format, the teacher can develop a system of discussion and critique directed at learning the inference process.

There are some excellent resources available for teachers to implement some of these ideas. The first chapter of *Speech: Science-Art* (listed in readings at the end of the chapter) contains a program format for a communications-centered classroom in which students are responsible for the major decisions as well as for the consequences of carrying these decisions out. The Irving Lee, "Talking Sense" series of motion pictures is an excellent resource for teaching

Bridging the gap with rhetoric

students on the secondary and early college level about the problems they may encounter in dealing with one another. The final section of Bess Sondel's *Humanity of Words* is invaluable as a methodology for understanding possibilities in communication strategy. An excellent discussion of the basic requirements in interpersonal communication is contained in the second edition of *Communication and the Small Group.* These sources and others listed provide materials from which the teacher can select options. The emphasis needs to be on choice and responsibility, the basics of the rhetorical process. Thus, the opportunity must be provided for the student to read about ideas, talk about them informally, hear the teacher talk about them, ask questions about them, and implement them in the form of oral and written communications. Throughout the process, it is necessary that students set individual goals and move to competence through small steps, accomplishment of each of which constitutes a reward. The teacher's rhetoric is devoted toward generating commitment and involvement in the process.

The question of inter-racial communication poses a significant problem to teachers of communication. The assumption has long been that there is some basic difference between blacks and whites which needs to be compromised in some way. Our understanding of human needs, however, does not make this distinction. What the teacher needs to know is that any student, regardless of race or sex, has some personal goals and a style of communication that he has learned and which probably serves him well in his own environment. The reconciliation that needs to be made is between those individual goals and strategies and goals and strategies that implement the work of the classroom. This cannot come about unless the rhetoric of the teacher is employed to help the student see how the classroom and its activities can help him to greater competence *outside* of the classroom. The notion that every teacher needs to become some sort of anthropologist in dealing with students from other cultures has seriously interfered with productive growth of in-class methodologies. The teacher does need to maintain a rhetorical posture. This may call for information and understanding, but not for sacrifice of legitimate school goals. The bridge between goals represents the essential element of a successful rhetorical exchange between teacher and his students *in any case.*

Most of us seek a condition of interpersonal trust in our relationships with others. Trust is an evaluation of a condition that exists when we think a person's actions are consistent with his words. When we can predict the responses of another with reasonable accuracy, we trust him. Trust is the result of analysis. Students can be helped to discover what actions they look for in the other person that lead them to the conclusions they draw. A recent series of interviews conducted with third- and sixth-graders produced the conclusion that children make friends with other children largely because of shared activities and because the children are "nice." Few of these children were able to pin down the behaviors carried on by their friends that led them to the conclusion "nice," but "nice" also is not a state of being; the judgment is based on some observation. By helping children to make systematic observations before drawing conclusions, they may also be helped to make more viable judgments about what to expect from others.

SAVING FACE

Another area that needs attention in the classroom is the problem of "face." Territoriality keeps us directed toward conscious awarness of our position in a group and our rank in that group. Once we have achieved a rank, we resist attacks on our position. For that reason, in dealing with others, we need opportunities to save our status and consequently our self-esteem. It doesn't help very much to win an argument with another person if the result of the victory is a feeling of reduction of self-esteem on the part of the loser. The blow to self-esteem will often produce resentment and even a desire for vengeance. Teachers and children alike need to learn how to control their language so that others are offered an "out" from unpleasant situations. A teacher can usually force a student to apologize for some objectionable act, but the forcible act often leaves bitterness in the student that may manifest itself in an even more detrimental act at some later date. Children learn early that "I'm sorry" is a magical formula for forgiveness. They need to be convinced that restitution is even more important.

Because of our natural suspicion of potential dishonesty, our communication behavior in most situations is likely to be characterized by the use of offensive and defensive verbal ploys. For example, we must assume that every person with whom we deal is working toward satisfaction of one of the four basic animal needs, and the reason he is interacting with us is because he sees us as instrumental in helping him. We also need to be aware of our goals in dealing with the other person. The teacher, for example, enhances his homeostasis and improves his territorial position by being successful with children. It is not sufficient, however, for the teacher to use the student to "fatten his batting average"; he must offer exchange to the child so that he, too, gets something out of the relationship. One possibility is information about the relationship itself, which will help in building an understanding of the communication process in general. The teacher can take care to explain his actions to the students. He need not conceal his goals. When an altercation becomes an object of analysis, it becomes less threatening. It is easier to exchange with people who know what their goals are, than with the confused and bewildered. Once both parties to an interaction have their goals on the table, it is possible to make some sort of a satisfactory deal on which future trust can be built.

The goals we seek, at any given time, may be major or trivial. When both parties have trivial goals, the conversation usually takes place on a trivial level; there is little emotional involvement. Usually all that is at stake is structuring a small unit of time so that it is not unpleasant for either party. The threat level is very low. At times like this it is easy to find things to talk about. We do not know, however, at what point threat may set in, unless we know what is really valuable to the other person. In any conversation, it is possible to disturb the other in a way that threatens his sense of self-esteem. When this happens, we are not aware of it until we evoke a hostile or aggressive response. Usually, it is not even possible to discover what we said that evoked the unexpected response, but if we are skilled and concerned we may recognize that it has been our behavior that did it, and we can take steps either to find out what stimulated the hostility, change the subject to something less threatening, or break off the encounter before it gets too unpleasant. In the classroom, groups of students can work through social conversation to the point where they are skilled in group problem solving. As in life, social talk provides an opportunity for rhetorical analysis to be applied to subsequent engagements.

Casual conversations carried on in every facet of life are preludes to deeper relationships. We all seek deep relationships, though often we do not know their implications, and we cannot cope with very many of them. The skilled communicator is able to make decisions about the value of specific individuals to him. These decisions have serious ramifications. In unmarried males and females, the conversational excursions can be preludes to marriage. And there is, perhaps, no deeper relationship in our society than marriage. However, if both parties are not skilled at communication, decisions about the appropriate mate may be erroneous and the relationship itself may be fraught with pain. It is not irrelevant to teach students some of the varied decision criteria that they might use in making decisions about the value of other people.

The goals each person brings into relationships come from perceptions of the world, including other persons. The needs (survival, stimulation, security, status) that he seeks to meet are determined by his perception of the nature of the situation. Since no two people can have the same perceptions, it is reasonable to assume that their goals will be dissimilar. Since neither can actually see the self-image of the other, it is possible for each to make inaccurate decisions. If you perceive yourself as competent and strong, while the other person perceives you as weak and inept, he may aggress unduly and receive a stronger response than expected. If you perceive him as dishonest when he is acting honestly, you may stir his anger.

Differences in perception of the situation mean that every relationship needs time to develop some common history. Even very small children tend to trust peers they have known longer than those they have just met. Regrettably, in the school situation, there is really not enough time to build a firm bond, and consequently, the possibility for error in any teacher-student interaction is very great. But students need to be set for the society of today, which Alvin Toffler characterizes as a society in which friends are "disposable." Students need to learn methods of assessing others so that bonds can be built early in a relationship. Using realistic assignments in the classroom, the teacher can help his students to understanding.

Whatever the behavior in relationship, however, it must be assumed that each person is acting rationally. There is, somewhere in the conscious or unconscious mind, a reason for the things said and done. No matter how mystifying the behavior of another person may be, assumption of rationality at the time of behavior must be made, even though hindsight may lead either party to evaluate the behavior as nonproductive, and one may be impelled to modify or make amends for what he said. To the best of his ability, the person who talks with you is doing exactly what you are doing in interaction. He is attempting to maximize his personal safety and pleasure and minimize his risk and pain. He seeks some goal, as do you, and he will assist you only so long as you are assisting (or at least not impeding) him. It does not help interaction for you to label him "fool" or anything else, since to himself, he is not. Such labeling and the responses that come from it do not help the other person to adjust his behavior to meet your expectations. Therefore, it is wise to avoid acting on inferences and judgments unless there is a high probability that they are accurate.

What is needed is a relationship based on information about the goals of the other person in relation to his perception of himself. This information is necessary before a decision can be made about compatability of goals and a determination of how close each person can be to the other in working things out. To discover what common goals exist demands some exposition of private goals. If the parties to the relationship do not feel safe and secure, they will not reveal private information. And private information cannot be pried out through the use of formalized routines like sensitivity training. Personal goals are generally only revealed to people who are trusted over a period of time. If common aims cannot be found, then differences must be made explicit so that they can be negotiated. In life-experience, differences occur more frequently than concurrences. One real service the teacher can render to his students is to help them through the small-group format to learn how to negotiate differences, make deals, engage in barter, so that the group, as a collectivity, can achieve its goals. If trust cannot be achieved, at least people can be trained to work together for the common good. The thrust of rhetoric is to this end.

Most people, teachers included, assume that the rules of interaction are understood by everyone. This is an intriguing notion since teachers seem to have about the same amount of interpersonal difficulty in their lives as anyone else, and if we consider that there is interpersonal interaction with all of the students, teachers may have considerably more. It does not seem reasonable for adults who cannot cope with their relationships to expect their less mature students to be able to cope at all times. Furthermore, since there are no explicit rules for relationships, both students and teachers need rhetorical skill so that they can work for effective exchange.

DETERMINING SUCCESS

There are three propositions that determine whether or not you are successful in any talk situation, public or private:

1. You are successful when you have sufficient credibility in the eyes of the other to make what you say believable to him.

2. You are successful when what you have to say is sufficiently clear so that it is understood, and sufficiently documented to that it is credible.

3. You are successful when you speak to the needs of the other individual in order to meet your own needs.

Training in public performance is useful to illustrate these three propositions. The methods and procedures used in making a successful public speech, such as audience analysis and outlining, can be adapted to instruction in interpersonal communication by showing how even in private relationships, people must set goals and plan strategies.

The imperative need seems to be an understanding of the receiver of the communication. Students need to be helped to gain this understanding. The process can be taught even to the very young, but sociocultural immaturity, particularly in the realm of understanding the other, sometimes impedes understanding of the nature of the communicative relationship. By helping the student to understand something about how people in general respond to talk, we help him to select from among his own options.

Communication proceeds based on generalizations. The same scientific propositions we discussed earlier in this book as they related to communication research are also important in interpersonal communication. It is hard to develop generalizations about people. With all of the complicated studies that have been done about human behavior we still discover that most generalizations about people leave something to be desired, particularly when we try to adapt them to specific cases. Teachers make generalizations about students all the time, and are often dismayed when an individual child does not seem to conform.

Usually, the generalization process does not help us cope with the unexpected. When one has a deep relationship with another person, much of his behavior is predictable. However, even the prediction about a single individual is a generalization; actually a mean of data accumulated from previous experience. The combination of a new mood, a new situation, or a new perspective may alter behavior at any time; consequently, the old theory from which generalizations are drawn may no longer be valid. Each new behavior provides data which alters expectations in subsequent encounters, anyway. The concept of "audience analysis" associated with the act of platform speaking is helpful in explaining to the student how data is gathered and how generalizations emerge from the data. Most important of all, however, is inculcating the understanding that in any communication experience, it is necessary to be set to deal with the unexpected. The teacher can point this out, too, when he observes responses to the unexpected in his small task groups.

Despite the proposition that when you know someone well, most of his behavior is predictable, most relationships carry threat in that small proportion of behavior that can never be predictable. Furthermore, the threat level is proportional to the amount of affection you have invested in the other. The person you truly care for may not be very likely to hurt you, but if he hurts you it will hurt deeply. It is also not safe to assume that another person has had no reason to change since the last meeting. For example, a child who requests to go to the playground (a request that had previously been granted without question) does not know that his father has just finished reading a grisly newspaper story about child molesting. The child will not be able to understand why, on this occasion, his father bellows, "no!" A teacher asking for information from a usually tractable child may not know that the child has just lived through a terrible quarrel between his parents and may not want to tell anything to anyone.

Man seeks homeostasis (predictability). His capacity to manufacture symbols gives him the capacity to manufacture images as well, and some of his image-making is about the future. He plans his moves and attempts to influence events so that they will come out the way he wants them to. Even when he is not consciously planning ahead, if he has cognitive maturity, he has a sense of outcome, and his hopes and fears of what lies ahead affect his behavior a great deal. Consciously or unconsciously, every action is preplanned and based on a principle or some image he has of the world and the way he wants it to be. Conscious planning, of course, is more effective, since it is possible to select strategies to accomplish a conscious goal, but it is not possible to do so when under the control of the unconscious mind.

Even though a mature person understands some of the possibilities, it must be assumed that he is more concerned about his own homeostasis than about the needs of the other person. Normal human egocentrism leads each person to inquire constantly about the limits of his own powers. He may ascribe initial failures at talk to defective symbols, and he may make another attempt. Next, he may attribute failure to willful resistance by another. Finally, he may understand that the problem may lie in his inability to make symbols that speak to the needs of the other person. His alternatives are to proceed rhetorically and attempt to achieve his own goals by phrasing his talk in terms of the goals of the other; or, he may attack and suffer the attendant rupture of the relationship.

Despite the complex nature of the interaction process, it is possible to generalize some attitudes and behaviors that will be helpful in understanding and accommodating the responses of others. This provides a fertile field for application by the teacher to his own behavior and for teaching to students as they interact with one another. The authoritarian teacher may control his class at the sacrifice of opportunity to guide students through live situations to help them discover their own abilities. Some of the propositions that might be considered as bases of data about interactions in the classroom are:

1. *The nature of unpredictability in interaction.* Teacher and class can make a series of predictions about the mood of the principal, attendance records, and so on, and keep track of how cogent the predictions were. The class should be able to point to the information on which they based their predictions.

2. *An "interference" chart can be kept.* A public log can be kept of the times that interferences disrupted communication. The class might predict which kind of interference would predominate, while the teacher keeps a record and count to confirm or deny the class hypothesis.

3. *Exercises in self-image can be tried.* Having students write the answers to two questions: (1) "How would you like to be seen?" and (2) "How do you think others see you?" provides some raw data for the discussion of self-image and how it can be enhanced. The written information should, of course, be anonymous.

4. *The nature of social norms can be examined.* By having the students work in task groups and monitoring their behavior, periodic comparisons can be made of the problem-solving and conversational styles of the various groups to prove to the class that everyone has a hand in the formation of communication norms.

These and other ideas can be generated out of the taxonomy of objectives offered in the final chapter. Because there is so little already prepared on the teaching of interpersonal communication in the classroom, every teacher is his own experimenter.

NONVERBAL COMMUNICATION

Most teachers of communication tend to overlook one of the most influential forces in communication, the nonverbal. What people may not say with words, they may tell you with their eyes, hands, and bodies. There is more to communication than oral manipulation of symbols. Both conscious and unconscious communication are transmitted nonverbally. Often, this can have a more definitive impact on the receiver than the words that are actually said. Those whose task it is to work with people need considerable training in perceiving and interpreting nonverbal communication.

Much of nonverbal communication is unconsciously controlled. A person can send messages about his mood without even being aware that he is doing it. We have all encountered the person who appears to be listening to us, but who signals with his eyes that he is totally bored. Sometimes we can delude ourselves about what we are seeing. As stated earlier, teachers often believe that lack of movement and silence in the classroom means that children are listening carefully. Recent experiments, however, indicate that this is not so. The data seem to indicate that each person has his own listening demeanor which can only be interpreted by understanding the person. The generalizations we make about the meaning of nonverbal cues do not seem to be applicable enough to be regarded as useful.

The actor is able to control many of his face and body movements at least some of the time. All of us, in part, are actors as we try on occasion to conceal our true feelings from others lest we hurt them. Yet, every director knows that no matter how good the actor or how stylized the role, the actor will always put some of his own personality into a part. There is no way that people can escape their own uniqueness except in the generalizations of the people who judge them.

We are often misunderstood because people cannot interpret our cues. One of the authors, for example, can only listen well to his students when he is doodling intently. As long as his pen moves, he is listening carefully. When he stops doodling, he falls asleep. Students who do not know this, however, interpret his doodling as inattention. The professor discovered that it was necessary for him to warn students in advance about what his behavior meant. "Leveling" with students about your idiosyncrasies of behavior is a wise idea. It may also open the channel for some talk about their own unique behaviors as well. An insight into the wide range of meanings associated with nonverbal cues is very useful for the person who seeks effectiveness in speech.

To maintain optimum communication, it is necessary to get beyond words and into the emotional state of the person with whom we talk. On some levels this is not so important. The public speaker in front of a large audience can afford to draw the inference that he will capture the attention of some and not others, and he can try, through application of technique, to raise the number of people who listen to him. Though, in some respects, the teacher resembles the public speaker, his responsibility is much more personal. The teacher must maintain a dyadic relationship with every student. If a student displays agitation or ennui, the teacher cannot afford to ignore it and hope for success with someone else. Thus, the teacher may feel greater tension in front of the class than he would on the public platform. His concern must be with the response pattern of the individual student.

We make judgments about people partly on the nonverbal information they emit. The process is subliminal for the most part. We may not even know we are even perceiving the cues, let alone analyzing them. When we enter a room full of strangers, however, we make immediate judgments. There is something about this person we like, about that one we mistrust. The "somethings" are the nonverbal cues that are being given off. We move toward someone and interact with him; hopefully, it will be someone who is compatible. We make a decision about who will be worthwhile spending time with before we have a chance to exchange a word. The substance of our judgment is our past experience with people. The theoretical basis is the notion that people who look alike act alike (a particularly untenable assumption). It is no wonder that we make so many errors in our initial choices. Yet, so intent are we on preserving our record as predictors, that we will tolerate maltreatment from another person rather than admit we were wrong in our initial opinions.

When a teacher meets a class for the first time, he cannot avoid making judgments about the students. It is unfortunate that our first decisions are so important to us that we tend to defend them. When an interaction works out, it tends to confirm our wisdom. If it does not work out, either we blame it on the other person, or we twist what happens to make it appear that it did work out. Sometimes we even succeed in adjusting the impression that we have of the physical appearance of the person who disappointed us. We make ugly into beautiful and beautiful into ugly in our minds. For the students, this kind of behavior on the part of the teacher can be disastrous. It may mean that he will display rejecting behavior toward students he has initially classified as unpleasant looking, and hostility to those who do not confirm his initial judgments. It is helpful if the teacher is aware of the bases of his judgments, and if he takes time to help students to understand what their bases of judgments are.

All of us have accustomed ourselves to interpret certain kinds of movements, body positions, contours of face, expressions of mouth and eyes. We classify some as "pleasant," others as "threatening," and so on. We tend to seek contact with people who appear pleasant to us, and we select data from the cues they emit to confirm our initial judgments. Perhaps this is why it is so difficult for people of different races to comfortably accommodate each other. What we seek are appearances, movements, and behaviors that we can count on. Something as simple as an unfamiliar contour of face may interfere with our decision making. When we discover someone who seems to enjoy having us around, we accept his behavior as a reward, and we do not question very deeply whether his behaviors actually meant what we interpreted them to mean. The investigation of college students mentioned earlier seemed to indicate that many people struggle so hard to confirm their initial judgments that they open themselves to egregious maltreatment by others, simply because to reject someone that has been voluntarily selected is a serious admission of error and consequently a blow to self-esteem. This also means that teachers are often "conned" by behaviors that seem to indicate attention and commitment to learning. Some students have learned the rhetoric of persuading teacher to believe they are good students, when frankly, they couldn't care less. Translated into its simplest terms, what the teacher must remember is that *the good student won't always look like a "good student."*

Failure to understand nonverbal communication disrupts relationship. We have all resented the speaker who sees us yawning in the audience and yet continues to speak at length. We regard him as insensitive to our needs. Yet, we all have the capacity to be insensitive when we do not make a conscious effort to perceive and interpret what the other person is indicating to us about our impact on him. We normally do not voluntarily choose to see the negative information that people give us and often we twist it to mean positive things so we can be justified in continuing to behave in ways that are comfortable to us. It is possible for anyone to be an annoying bore in the eyes of the person to whom he is speaking.

The task of interpersonal accommodation is exceedingly difficult. For most interactors, there are a number of choices available, for it is not essential that they interact with everyone they meet. The teacher, however, must interact with everyone in his classroom. The tendency of students to talk with a teacher will depend to a large extent on the teacher's willingness to adjust to the data he receives from every child. If he can reach through the nonverbal screen, then the student may reach back. It is in this sense that the teacher offers a model for students to emulate. If they cannot copy the skill of the teacher, they can perhaps duplicate the effort.

CHOOSING VERBAL STRATEGIES

As speakers we watch and listen. As listeners, we wait for our chance to talk. We acquire information about the other that serves to help us adjust our own behavior to make it more effective. We are constantly concerned with response. We try to train ourselves to look for reaction and to do a rational job of interpreting and replying to it. In order to do this, we need a set of criteria which we can use to choose our verbal behavior. There are some simple strategic categories which can be used for this purpose. Some behaviors are consistently appreciated by people, some result in hostility and rejection. By choosing behaviors in the former category, we are able to improve our relationships with all of our students. By avoiding behaviors in the second category, we are able to increase the probability of peace and harmony.

PEOPLE PREFER:

1. Acceptance of themselves and their actions. Acceptance is not approval. Acceptance means willingness on the part of one party to permit the behavior of the other party to go on.

2. Understanding of their actions and motives. This means that the other party not only regards the action as legitimate but also has some awareness of why it is employed.

3. Support for themselves, their actions, and their motives. This means willingness to help them achieve whatever goal they are seeking—that you regard their behavior as effective and productive.

It is, of course, impossible to support every behavior of every student. There are people whose behaviors offend or interfere with your important goals. It is not difficult, however, to accept a person along with his behaviors, so long as he is not directly threatening you. Even if his appearance is grubby, his voice too loud, his gestures too gross, since none of these things gets in the way of your goals, it is not necessary to evaluate them verbally or interfere with them. Awareness of the fact that the other person is behaving as he must is the first step toward acceptance. Once you have accepted a behavior, it is then possible to indicate to the other person that it might not be the most effective thing he could be doing. He may then help you try to understand it. You may discover that there is an irreconcilable conflict between you because of that behavior. But, even when this discovery is made, it may be possible for both of you to adapt so that the conflict does not impair the relationship. Throughout all of the accommodation process, it is not necessary for either party to interfere with the behavior of the other.

Most of the behaviors we reject are really not threatening at all. They may offend sensibilities, but they do not really get in the way of our behavior. We must take care in determining what it is we oppose, for if we are opposing something because we have some arbitrary standard of the way things are "supposed to be," we have violated the integrity of the other person. For years, for example, the dialect of black people was regarded as substandard, a judgment made against norms of language set in 1927. It was not until someone decided that black dialect, while different from white dialect, was perfectly viable, that some teachers stopped threatening black children by attempting to compel them to change the way they spoke.

It is not appropriate for a teacher to demand that the student cast off everything he has learned from his family and his friends. The student brings to class with him a life history, a self-image, a set of learned behaviors, any of which could offend his teacher. The teacher can do something about improving skills and suggesting alternatives, but he has no right to demand change in behaviors that are important to the student's survival in the world in which he spends most of his time. If a behavior is alien or offensive to the teacher, it is much more productive for him to expand his limits of tolerance than it is to attempt to enforce change. He can make the child feel comfortable in the classroom, he can set models of behavior before him, and work cooperatively with him in generating accommodations. He must interfere when a student's behavior really threatens him or other students, but he cannot be a moralist about that student's behavior. Depredations on the social and psychological values of the student tend to reduce his capacity to be productive, and often force him to react strongly against school. The rules of encounter in the classroom are essentially the same as in life: acceptance comes first, understanding next, and then approval or disapproval as demanded by the situation, not according to some arbitrary set of standards. In life, we can break off encounters when they do not work out. In school and at work, an encounter must continue with whatever pain it carries. For this reason, to work toward the elimination of interpersonal pain should be the goal of the mature communicator.

PEOPLE GET HOSTILE WHEN:

1. We attempt to analyse their behavior and personality and the analysis does not come out the way they want it, or they did not invite us to analyse them in the first place.

2. We verbally evaluate them and their actions negatively. They may even suspect our affirmative evaluations, if they do not like us or suspect that we are "phony" and are trying to "con" them with approval.

3. We get in the way of actions they regard as important. The policeman can arrest a criminal but neither policeman nor judge can make the criminal like him.

One important premise about interpersonal interaction is that it is sometimes necessary to modify behavior. When a behavior threatens the safety or tranquility of others; when it is defeating and nonproductive for the person himself; when a person asks for help, it is necessary that teachers (and parents, employers, clinicians, and good friends) take a hand and make a rhetorical foray into the social and psychological world of the other in order to generate more productive behavior. When this is necessary, it ought to be done with a minimum of pain and a maximum of reason, and the person who finds it necessary to interefere has no right to expect that the person he interferes with will particularly like it.

Many students resist instruction because they are not convinced that it is useful or smart. People usually persist in nonproductive behaviors because they care very little about what the goal is supposed to achieve or they don't have very much respect for the person who is trying to change them.

Most people (children and adults) try to avoid the painful. A student may be perfectly willing to fit into the classroom so long as he does not have to make a huge effort to do so. Asking him to cast off everything he values in his society is too great a price. If the playground peer group demands that he *verbalize* contempt for school, there is no reason why he should be interfered with, provided he also works. In fact, he can be encouraged to do his verbalizing of hostility openly, making it a matter for discussion. He can justify doing what the school expects so long as he can also satisfy the expectations of those who are important to him on the outside. If the teacher polarizes him by demanding that he choose between school and peers, he will of course choose the latter, and the teacher will have lost his chance of effectiveness.

What must prevail in order to bring about interpersonal accommodation is a sense of respect. If you do not respect the person with whom you deal, very little that is productive can go on. Much in teaching represents an intervention into the life of the student, anyway. The teacher may have goals for his teaching, but getting the student to see them as goals for himself means that the teacher must employ rhetoric to convince the student that they make sense. The demands of school mean that a student must change his value system from focus on play to work. Students cannot be expected, automatically, to share the teacher's goals, nor can they be expected to accept interference with their life style without rebellion unless they have reason to respect both the teacher and his goals. Respect is often based on power; power, on competency. Focus on skills rather than on values enhances personal power and makes later discussion of values possible.

This need for respect is not unique to the classroom. It is also true in life. We take a lot from people we like and respect. In fact, we often seek them out to solicit criticism and advice. But we resent it bitterly when a stranger or a person to whom we are hostile attempts to interfere verbally with our lives. (We don't like to be talked about when we are not around. The tendency of teachers to discuss their students among themselves is very defeating if news of it reaches students.) When we need help we find a friend or pay a professional. The teacher's analysis of a student's behavior is pointless to the student unless it is solicited or the student is given a very good reason for it. That is why, perhaps, oral composition courses are often so unsatisfying to teacher and student alike. The student seeks acceptance of his ideas when he presents them. The teacher seeks conformity in performance with some standards. Consequently, he tends to focus his criticism on performance mannerisms rather than on ideas. A student who really wants to learn performance will submit himself to criticism hungrily, but a student who does not have this goal will ignore the best of advice. He will give absolute minimum compliance to teacher demands, and will get out of the business with a minimum of threat to his self-esteem. When a student merely complies with the system for the purpose of getting the teacher "off his back" or to earn a grade, the teacher is often deluded into believing that learning has happened. This, in turn, reinforces unproductive teaching behavior. It is almost more useful for the teacher when the student openly rebels or "cops out," for then, at least, he knows what he is dealing with and can consider alternative rhetoric.

Evaluation is more frightening than analysis. When someone makes pronouncements of "good" or "bad" about a person's behavior, it is disruptive. It is a frontal assault, unless he is prepared to receive it. Even a positive evaluation is hard to take when it comes from someone he does not know well or trust. Most people would prefer to figure out where they stand from observation of responses.

Interference, of course, always evokes hostility—sometimes blatant, sometimes overt. It may be necessary to interfere with someone else's behavior, but when it is necessary to demand that someone "cease and desist," it should not be expected that he will be particularly happy about it. Mandates to "stop" are normally effective only when the behavior is so bad that others in the classroom will support the mandate. Many teachers have experienced a situation when they ordered one person's activity to be stopped and received the hostility of the entire class. Directives issued by schools against the use of alcohol, drugs, (or necking in the hallways) are generally ineffective because there is so much support for the activity that the students regard getting caught as the fault rather than doing what they are doing. While no one could assert that students should develop their own curriculum or activities, getting them to participate in planning is a very useful idea. They are less likely to oppose what they have planned, than what is imposed upon them.

Many teachers believe that "ought to" and "is" are synonyms.

Teachers are trained to know what productive behavior is, but merely pointing out to a student that his behavior is unproductive and "ought to be" altered is not sufficent to bring about change. It is at this point that rhetoric is most important to the teacher, for the student must be persuaded that change is necessary before he can commit himself to it. Once the student has committed to change, it cannot be assumed that he will change unless the teacher is prepared to show him how to go about it, and even lead him through the steps. Change in behavior demands the strong hand of a guide and firm support during the process of change. Understanding that change is necessary is not so difficult to come by. Most people who are doing things that are dangerous to themselves are aware that they need to change, but they are unable to do so without someone guiding them along the way.

The foregoing should not be interpreted as a plea for permissiveness. Rather, it is a sense of realism that we seek; a realistic understanding of what is possible rather than merely desirable. Obviously rules must be made and enforced so that society can go on about its business; but if the rules seem senseless or capricious to the student, or if they are obviously contrived to suit the convenience of the authorities without any benefit to the student, he will resist them or evade them. Even rule making demands a rhetorical approach.

Generally, in relationships with others, we must remember that communication is an intrinsic part of their personality. It is impossible to separate communication behavior from the person as a whole. The way we respond to his communication is the way we respond to him as a total person. The only part of himself that he submits to us for examination is his communication; it is impossible for him to give anything else. This is why effective communication is so vital to satisfactory human relations.

SUMMARY

Trying to decide what people to "trust" these days is a difficult task: often we do not allow another person to build much of a history or record of relationship on which to base our decision of whether or not we can trust him, or count on his behaviors. We are prone to quick evaluation of others, often based on spurious criteria of facial and body contour or movement. Sometimes, we verbally evaluate the behavior of a person without really knowing why it bothers us or without considering the effect of our verbalization on any possible future relationship with that person.

In this chapter, we have considered how some of these difficult interpersonal issues may be handled more effectively and how they may be presented to students through small-group experiences. The goal of these group projects should not be to entice students into a sensitivity-training format where personal feelings about specific others are solicited, but to discover how generalizations are made about relationship potentials from behaviors that can be seen. Throughout, the goal should be to impart to students ways of setting their own communication goals and developing rhetorical strategies that will help them meet their goals in exchanges with others. When students are persuaded that oral-communication-instruction experiences can benefit them in their lives outside the classroom, they will adapt their behavior to the teacher's constructive perspective.

WORKS CITED:

Murray, Elwood, et al.,*Speech: Science-Art.* New York: Bobbs-Merrill, 1970.

Phillips, Gerald. *Communication and the Small Group*, 2d ed. New York: Bobbs-Merrill, 1973.

Sondel, Bess. *The Humanity of Words.* New York: World Publishing Co., 1958.

Toffler, Alvin. *Future Shock.* New York: Random House, 1970.

WORKS RECOMMENDED:

A thorough explanation of the operation of self-esteem is found in Stanley Coopersmith, *Antecedents of Self-Esteem.* San Francisco: W.H. Freeman, 1967.

The most recent and decisive discussion of T-Groups, Encounter groups, and sensitivity training in general is found in Morton Lieberman, et al., *Encounter Groups: First Facts.* New York: Basic Books, 1973.

For more discussion of face behavior see Irving Goffman, *Relations in Public.* New York: Basic Books, 1971.

Another source for studying the behavior of Americans is Vance Packard, *Nation of Strangers.* New York: David McKay, 1972.

The most recent discussion of nonverbal communication can be found in Mark Knapp, *Non-Verbal Communication.* New York: Holt, Rinehart and Winston, 1973.

- To offer cognitive, affective, and behavioral goals that can be selected from and combined for classroom implementation.

- To point out limitations in using objectives to build an oral communication curriculum.

- To note specific illustrations of inductive, deductive, and utilitarian approaches to oral-communication instruction.

- To offer a model plan for a ten-week course in oral communication for secondary and early college-level students.

- To offer a model plan for a five-session course in oral-communication skills for early elementary-level students.

COGNITIVE

AFFECTIVE

BEHAVORIAL

POOL OF OBJECTIVES

9

A Taxonomy of Possible Contents for an Instructional Program in Oral Communication

Overview

In this chapter, we offer the resources for you to begin your work as a teacher, of speech, of oral communication, or as a teacher who simply uses oral techniques in the classroom.

The objectives are listed. A syllabus is provided for secondary application. Model lessons for elementary school are provided. We even offer some cautions about the use of this material.

Read the chapter! Go out and teach! Win one for Aristotle!

THE OBJECTIVES offered in this chapter, although not exhaustive, represent more than can be provided by any school system even if oral communication were taught from kindergarden through twelfth grade. They represent a pool from which teachers and students can select learning goals.

Objectives must be adapted to the capabilities of students. In the early grades, teachers must take biological and cognitive maturity into account before selecting a pool of options, for the effective teaching of oral communication depends on the availability of options for commitment. A student should not be threatened by objectives beyond his grasp.

Diagnosis of the capability of students to handle the

various objectives is not a simple matter. Secondary students should be capable of handling most of them provided that alternative activities are permissable. Care should be taken, however, to select objectives that concord with real speaking opportunities. The teacher's rhetoric is enhanced when he has the ability to guide students into commitments that meet their needs outside the classroom rather than attempt to gain commitment to an arbitrary syllabus. Social objectives are usually easy to connect to life experience. Public performance can be related to reporting in other classes. Group activities and interviews are somewhat more difficult if not all students function on committees or are seeking jobs. Where outside applications are unavailable, the teacher will need to generate optional in-class activities that are sufficiently realistic in order to preserve the possibility of carryover.

Younger children cannot be expected to have the maturity required to achieve analytic objectives. Concentration in the lower grades must be on performance, with main emphasis on activities that are normally part of the curriculum such as sharing in groups, asking and answering questions in class, and giving brief, informative reports. Each teacher has the obligation of determining how far beyond this the students can go. In the lower grades, many alternatives must be available so that students can adapt to activities on their own level.

Some of the goals presented are simple and some complex. It is presumed that methods can be devised to implement all of them. The simple goals should not be regarded as less important than the complicated ones. The needs of students determine the importance of the goals. It is not wise to assume that children will carry over learnings into life experience unless a direct effort is made to help them do so. Consequently, several of the goals are phrased directly for carryover.

Following Bloom's *Taxonomy of Educational Objectives,* the goals here are divided into *cognitive, affective,* and *psychomotor* (called *behavioral)* goals. There are more cognitive than any other goals. Once again, we are caught in the educational trap that declares that children need to know something. Actually in teaching communication, we have discovered that children can learn how to communicate without ever learning the vocabulary of communication, or the theory. Often, cognitive learning can come after techniques have been mastered. Many of the cognitive goals can be interpreted in teacher terms, i.e., *they are what the teacher ought to know about communication before trying to teach it to his students.* Cognitive mastery is more important to critique than lesson planning.

We advocate that facts be learned only when knowing them will help the student improve his behavior. We do not believe that any of the facts about communication are worth knowing in their own right (except for scholarly specialists). Our concern is with improving communication behavior, and this should provide the central thrust in selection of goals. It would be a mistake if a teacher were to use this taxonomy to build an information-packed course about communication. The only excuse for paying attention to it is to determine how learning what is stipulated might result in constructive attitude change and more effective behavior. *Learning about effective communication is not the same as learning to communicate effectively.* It is the latter that represents the main goal of all instruction in communication.

COGNITIVE GOALS

    I. The student should understand the basic elements of the communication process.

       A. He should understand that it takes more than one person to carry on communication.

         1. He must understand the nature, obligations, and possible purposes of the sender of communication.

           a. Communicators can seek to convey information.

           b. Communicators can seek to bring about an emotional response.

           c. Communicators can seek a behavioral change in others.

           d. Communicators can seek to reinforce behaviors in others.

           e. Communicators can seek to release their own emotions on others.

           f. Communicators can seek merely to relate to others.

           g. Communicators can seek to amuse and entertain others.

         2. He must understand the nature, obligations, and possible purposes of the receivers of communication.

           a. The receiver may be seeking to acquire information.

           b. The receiver may be seeking an emotional experience.

           c. The receiver may be seeking assistance with choices of behavior.

           d. The receiver may be seeking personal pleasure.

           e. The receiver may be seeking merely to survive the experience.

         3. The sender must make a conscious effort to achieve his purpose.

           a. The effort must take the receiver into account throughout.

b. The effort must be adapted to the receiver.
4. The receiver must make an effort to understand.
   a. He is not obligated to do what the speaker requires.
   b. Courtesy requires that he hear the speaker through.
   c. Practice in methods of outlining will help the receiver.
5. Speaker and listener are related through responses.
   a. Response consists of information transmitted from one person to another which both use to determine how effective they are.
   b. Decisions about content and style of communication are based, in part, on response cues.
   c. Communication does not exist unless response is present.
   d. Response is the substance of relationship.
6. The act of communication is a process and a relationship.
   a. The process is that of sending and receiving symbolic data.
   b. The relationship is provided through response.
   c. Effectiveness is measured in both process and relationship.
B. There are a variety of channels and media for communication.
  1. There are written channels.
    a. There are public efforts such as books, magazines, newspapers.
    b. There are private efforts such as letters, diaries, notes.
  2. There are oral channels.
    a. There is one-to-one communication in friendship, marriage, family, therapy, etc.
    b. There is one-to-several communication in public speaking.
    c. There is many-to-many communication in group discussion.
    d. There is group-to-group communication in cultural communication.
  3. There are channels through media.
    a. There are personal media such as telephone and telegraph.
    b. There are public media such as radio, television, film.
  4. There are nonverbal channels.
    a. There are facial, gestural, and kinetic cues.

     b. There are artistic and musical productions.

     c. There are mathematics, computer programs, etc.

C. There are impediments to the communication process —interferences.

  1. Some impediments result from mechanical interference with the process.

  2. Some impediments result from defective production of symbols.

  3. Some impediments result from the physiological conditions of the sender, receiver, or both.

  4. Some impediments result from unwillingness or lack of interest of sender, receiver, or both.

  5. Some impediments result from inadequate selection of words in the message.

  6. Some impediments result from inappropriate construction of the message.

  7. Some impediments result from inapposite social positions of sender and receiver.

  8. Some impediments result from psychological problems in sender, receiver, or both.

D. The code selected for communication is an important factor.

  1. Language develops in the child based on physiological growth, concept formation, social growth, formal teaching and perceived need.

  2. To be understood, language must conform to accepted modes of usage.

  3. Language is arbitrary in nature.

     a. Symbols do not have meaning; people impose meaning on symbols.

     b. Language develops as a reflection of a culture.

  4. The rules of usage in nonverbal communication are difficult to apprehend.

E. Communication is purposive in nature.

  1. Communication assists in meeting the needs of the human animal.

     a. Communication is used for purposes of survival.

     b. Communication is used to maintain homeostasis.

     c. Communication is used to achieve territorial goals.

     d. Communication is used for stimulation and pleasure.

     e. Communication is used to form identity.

     f. Communication is used for time-binding.

  2. A communicator has at the base of his purpose a residual message.

     a. This is the content of communication that remains when all else is forgotten.

     b. The residual message represents the criterion for achievement of the speaker's goal.

3. In generating a purpose, the speaker must distinguish between the desirable and the possible.

     a. The speaker's capabilities must be taken into account.

     b. The nature and requirements of the message must be taken into account.

     c. The restrictions of the medium must be considered.

     d. The capacity and beliefs of the receiver must be considered.

     e. The norms of the situation must be considered.

     f. A speaker should have some means of assessing his success against criteria.

     g. Communication must utilize ornamentation and style to be successful.

          1) Stylized redundancy is employed to reinforce the residual message.

               a) Communication content is built to support the residual message.

               b) The residual message must be repeated in various forms to appeal to a maximum number of minds and to suit a maximum number of conditions.

          2) Metaphoric and literary language is often used to make a communication palatable or enjoyable to receivers.

          3) Digressions and attention-getting devices are employed to sustain attention for the speaker and his message.

     h. Both speakers and listeners have a stake in the communication process.

          1) Each can gain or lose through the process.

          2) Self-esteem can be expanded or deflated through communication.

     i. Communicators have an ethical responsibility in the process.

          1) They must seek to accomplish their goals without deceit.

          2) They must not distort their subject, ideas, or both in order to obtain a better hearing for them.

        3) They must maintain the burden of truth.

        4) They must take care to interest their listeners.

     j. Listeners also have an ethical responsibility in the communication process.

        1) They are obligated to give a fair listening and to accept what appears reasonable to accept.

        2) They have the responsibility to evaluate critically what they hear.

        3) They have the obligation to make some deference to the purposes of the speaker.

        4) They are obligated to integrate what they hear with what they know.

    k. The potential for diverse behavior of participants in a communication situation should be understood.

        1) Speakers respond to inferences, not realities.

        2) Communication disruption occurs when the unexpected happens.

        3) Generalizations about human communication are often unreliable.

        4) People respond based on their unique values.

II. The nature of the group process should be understood.

  A. There are many purposes for groups.

    1. Groups come together because people feel a mutual problem.

    2. Groups come together because an emergency exists.

    3. Groups come together because they are paid or assigned to do so.

    4. Groups come together to share information.

    5. Groups come together to seek help for various members.

    6. Groups come together to socialize or seek pleasure.

  B. Groups center their activities around definition of task.

  C. Groups develop norms of interaction, ranks, and roles.

  D. Leadership in groups derives from group needs and norm development.

  E. There are many kinds of leaders for groups.

    1. Democratic leaders guide groups to consensus.

    2. Autocratic leaders direct the group to consensus.

    3. Anarchic leaders permit the group to find its own consensus.

  F. Consensus is the legitimate group goal.

  G. Group problem solving proceeds through a series of rational steps.

    1. The problem is defined and specified.

2. The facts bearing on the problem are discovered and analyzed.
3. The major causes of the problem are discovered and analyzed.
4. Criteria for evaluating solutions are generated.
5. Goals for group action are specified.
6. Restrictions on group action are identified.
7. Alternative solutions are examined and tested.
8. The optimum solution is selected.
9. The solution is put into operation.
10. The effect of the solution is analyzed and evaluated.
    H. Learning groups provide a format for sharing information.
    I. Therapy groups provide a vehicle for self-improvement.
    J. There are many variations in the use of groups.
    K. Groups can be utilized for administration as well as planning.
III. The elements of oral composition should be understood.
    A. Success of communication depends on three variables.
        1. The reputation of the speaker and his credibility are important.
        2. The logic and organization of the speech are important.
        3. The emotional content and impact of the speech are important.
    B. Speech preparation proceeds through a series of logical steps.
        1. An idea is conceived and related to an audience and situation.
        2. The idea is elaborated, organized, and documented.
        3. The idea is put into words, phrases, and paragraphs.
        4. The mode of presentation is selected.
        5. The speech is delivered and evaluated.
    C. The elements of oral presentation should be understood.
        1. Delivery of a speech is usually accompanied by some tension.
        2. The act of delivery should resolve the tension.
        3. Some people are impeded in delivery because of tension.
        4. Some people have excessive communication tension which pervades all communication experiences.
    D. The relationship between speech and personality should be understood.

1. Identity is established through the communication process.
2. Feedback from the social milieu shapes the personality.
3. Communication plays a role in mental illness.
    a. People signal mental distress through communication.
    b. People can be communicated into mental illness.
    c. Communication is essential to bring people back to health.
4. The school milieu presents communications that play a major role in shaping personality.
5. There are demands imposed by society for participation in communication.
    a. The individual should be able to work with others to solve mutual problems.
    b. The individual should be able to derive pleasure from socialization.
    c. The individual should be able to communicate about his problems and his needs.
    d. The individual should be able to exert his influence on the behavior of others.

IV. Communication plays a major role in life which should be understood.
    A. Communication is the vehicle for human affiliation.
    B. Communication is a major source of recreation and pleasure.
    C. Communication is the substance of persuasion.
        1. Communication in politics determines winners and losers.
        2. Communication holds complex organizations together.
        3. Communication in the pulpit meets religious needs.
        4. Communication tends to shape the national character.
        5. Communication reflects the national mood.
        6. Examination of the communications of a society gives insight into the nature of that society.
    D. Communication is the agent by which education is carried.
        1. The capacity to communicate enables us to connect past, present, and future.
        2. Communication enables the teacher to motivate interest on the part of the student.

3. Communication enables the student to display his learning.
4. Most of what goes on in school is communicative in nature.

E. The mass media play a prominent role in the life of the individual.
1. The media provide a link between facets of society.
2. The media provide a vehicle for the dissemination of popular culture.
3. The media are a source of information and learning.
4. The media offer a channel for artistic expression.

F. Communication is a prime entertainment vehicle.
1. Comedy, vaudeville, and burlesque provide intimate entertainment.
2. Legitimate theater, film, television present the results of artistic writing.
3. Various kinds of writing also provide entertainment.

G. Communication in various forms is important to science and technology.
1. Scientists and mathematicians work with precise language.
2. Computer technology uses linguistic techniques.
3. There is a degree of universality in scientific language.

V. Communication improves through performance and application of criticism.

A. Criticism is worthless to the person who is not committed to improvement.
B. Criticism should distinguish between the possible and the desirable.
C. Criticism should offer methods by which improvement can take place.
D. Criticism should allow options in goals for improvement.
E. Prognosis for improvement under criticism is variable.

AFFECTIVE GOALS

I. The student should feel committed to participating in oral communication.

A. He should feel a need to speak.
B. He should feel affiliation with the fulfillment of communication needs in his society.
C. He should feel that oral communication assists his growth as a person.

II. The student should be willing to accept responsibility for his communication.
   A. He should feel empathy for the effects of communication on others.
   B. He should be able to deal with his own emotions generated by speaking.
   C. He should be able to expand and defend his remarks when requested.
III. The student should feel an ethical responsibility to others in his speaking.
   A. He should feel committed to the truth of his message.
   B. He should feel responsible for making an effort to reach his listener.
   C. He should feel that communication can help him reach his own goals.
IV. The student should desire to make an oral contribution to society.
   A. He should feel that he is a person of worth who can contribute.
   B. He should feel that society needs his communication.
V. The student should feel a sense of personal competency.
   A. He should feel that he is able to cope with normal communication demands.
   B. He should feel that he is capable of coping with some extraordinary demands.
VI. The student should feel empathy with the communication needs and problems of others.
   A. He must feel that others need to accomplish their goals as he does.
   B. He should feel empathy with the kinds of tensions others might feel as they try to communicate with him.
VII. The student should feel challenged by the complexity and excitement of the communication process.
   A. He should regard the act of speaking as a complicated process that requires careful preparation.
   B. He should feel a desire to achieve relationship with others that comes from effective speaking.
   C. He should feel the impulsion to work as hard at speaking to one person as he feels speaking to many.
VIII. The student should feel it is necessary to have a set of critical standards against which to check his speaking.
IX. The student should feel a need to be aware of and sensitive to nonverbal communication from others.
   A. He should feel the subtlety of the nonverbal process.

B. He should feel appropriately suspicious of his own inference process when he interprets cues from others.
X. The student should be aware of and sensitive to differences in communication patterns in various societies.
   A. He should understand the differences in communication styles of various races.
   B. He should feel the difference between communication styles of various age groups.
   C. He should feel the difference between communication styles of various educational levels.
   D. He should feel the difference in communication styles with people of different educational abilities.
   E. He should understand the influence of physical and mental health on communication.
XI. He should feel committed to the avoidance of perpetrating deleterious acts when speaking to others.
XII. He should be able to derive a personal feeling of pleasure and satisfaction from the act of speaking with others in many different situations.

BEHAVIORAL GOALS

I. He should be able to participate in classroom discussions and recitations.
   A. He should be able to contribute when directed to do so by a teacher.
   B. He should be able to contribute when directed to do so by himself.
   C. He should be able to stay with a point of discussion without digression.
   D. He should be able to avoid excessive personalization of his contributions to discussion.
   E. He should be able to speak succinctly and with limited digression when he has something to say.
   F. He should be able to share communication time with others.
II. He should be able to ask and answer questions in the classroom.
   A. He should be able to say so when he does not know the answer.
   B. He should be able to state an answer when he is asked and when he knows the answer.
   C. He should be able to phrase questions to obtain information he desires.
   D. He should be able to provide information when asked by his peers.

E. He should be able to provide information when asked by school authorities.

F. He should be able to obtain information from other people.

III. He should be able to present information and opinion in formal fashion to an audience of classmates and teachers.

A. He should be able to report on books as assigned by the teacher.

B. He should be able to prepare and present reports on scientific questions and issues when assigned by a teacher.

C. He should be able to present reports expressing his own attitudes.

D. He should be able to present reports sharing information with others.

IV. The student should have the ability to converse intelligently with others.

A. He should be able to carry on normal interaction with peers.

B. He should be able to speak with teachers about matters related to the classroom and other matters as well.

C. He should be able to maintain communication links with parents and other adults.

V. He should be able to read literature aloud, coherently, and with expression.

VI. He should be able to communicate his emotions in socially acceptable ways.

VII. He should be able to phrase ideas informally when motivated to do so.

VIII. He should be able to organize and support his ideas when he presents them so that they appear coherent to his listeners.

A. He should be able to follow the steps of organization for oral presentation.

B. He should be able to assume the burden of proof.

C. He should be able to prepare formal organization documents, outlines, etc.

IX. The student should be able to construct oral sentences using generally understood English words that convey the meaning he wishes to communicate.

X. He should be able to connect English words so that they comply with the rules of grammar generally accepted in this culture.

XI. He should be able to perceive and interpret the impact his speaking has on others.

XII. The student should be able to perceive and interpret the impact that the speaking of others has on him.

XIII. The student should be able to make sets of working notes, outlines of presentation, or manuscripts for oral presentations.

XIV. The student should have the ability to speak to an audience without being distracted by notes, visual aids, and other impediments.

XV. The student should be able to speak without interference from defects in his vocal mechanism.

XVI. The student should be able to speak without distraction by awkward mannerisms.

XVII. The student should be able to deploy forms of support for ideas appropriately.

XVIII. The student should be able to present information about personal matters when necessary to relevant people.

A. He should be able to inform someone when he is ill.

B. He should be able to inform someone when he is emotionally disturbed.

C. He should be able to inform someone when personal problems are interfering with his normal competencies.

D. He should be able to discuss intelligently and answer questions about his personal problems.

E. He should be able to listen intelligently and sympathetically when personal problems of others are discussed with him.

XIX. The student should be able to listen intelligently to oral presentations from others.

A. He should be able to see the point when there is one to see.

B. He should be able to store and retain a reasonable portion of the information presented.

C. He should be able to understand the emotional content of messages from others.

D. He should be able to suspend reaction until the message from the other is completed.

E. He should be able to maintain a demeanor of courtesy to encourage the continued efforts of others.

F. He should be able to suspend his capacity to criticize others.

G. He should be able to offer assistance in the form of recommendations for improvement in the messages of others, when solicited.

XX. He should be able to distinguish between the requirements of oral and written communication.

A. He should be able to utilize oral and written styles.

B. He should be able to determine in which situations oral or written communications are most appropriate.

XXI. He should be able to make satisfying interpersonal connections with peers.

XXII. He should be able to maintain a satisfactory level of phatic communion with others.

XXIII. He should be able to support and defend controversial ideas.

XXIV. He should be able to transmit information accurately.

XXV. He should be able to give and accept legitimate criticism.

XXVI. He should be able to generate and accomplish reasonable goals for the improvement of his own communication.

XXVII. He should be able to function effectively in informal group processes.

A. He should be able to share experience in learning groups.

B. He should be able to contribute in problem-solving groups.

C. He should be able to participate in therapeutic groups when needed.

D. He should be able to participate in formal, parliamentary meetings.

E. He should be able to derive pleasure and satisfaction from group participation.

Cognitive goals are relevant only when applied to behavior change. While much instruction in higher education is devoted to cognitive mastery and research, in the grades and early college experience, focus is on performance. Rather than attempting to teach performance through cognitive mastery, the teacher must focus on performance instruction in its own right, teaching cognitions as ancillary to performance. Live performances can be used as laboratories in which cognitions can be taught. Teachers of oral communication must remember that there are only a few specialists in theory of oral communication, and that it is not necessary to know formal theory in order to perform effectively. There is no evidence to indicate that understanding cognitive propositions influences performance, any more than that the reading of history makes a man a historian.

Cognitive goals are easy to measure, but criteria of measurement should not enter into selection of goals. Teachers are invariably confronted with the task of evaluating and grading. This is singularly difficult for the teacher whose task it is to train students in performance skills. The question of whether to award high grades to skilled performers, or to award grades on the basis of improvement, is not an easy one to answer. Our recommendation is that oral-communication training should be "tracked," and that improvement of skill be the criterion for grading. This would mean that exceptionally skilled speakers could be permitted to function on a still higher level, while deficient speakers could be trained in fundamental skills. It is for this reason that we have stressed the necessity of providing alternative goals and assignments for students. What needs to be accomplished by the teacher is to persuade students to commit themselves to behavior change, so that they can improve communication behavior regardless of their starting point.

Behavioral goals cannot be accomplished by talking about them; they can only be achieved through performance. Extreme care must be taken, however, in the stipulation of goals. To accept as a goal a statement like, "I want to be more poised when I speak," is senseless, unless the student can specify what "poised" looks like. Behavioral goals mean behavior. How does the student sound, move; how long can he speak; how does he respond to others? Checklists of performance behavior can be used to map changes in skill. How many vocalized pauses does he have? How many undocumented assertions? How many incomplete proofs? How many awkward pauses? Behaviors are quantifiable, and during initial steps in training, quantity is more important than quality. The first question is, can a student do a task at all? Then it is possible to inquire about how well he does it.

When teachers choose to evaluate quality, they are confronted with the task of making their criteria clear to the students. No student should be evaluated negatively on quality unless he has had an opportunity to understand what the bases of the teacher's judgments are and unless he has been trained to meet them.

Goal achievement can be measured both by observation and student report. Care needs to be taken, however, so that the teacher is not "conned." Many students will say what they think the teacher wants to hear; it is part of their rhetoric. In seeking personal reports teachers should stress information about what the student could not do before instruction that he can do after instruction. Once the statements are made, the teacher can seek confirmation in his own experience. Did he classify the student as unable to perform at the outset? Can the student now perform?

It is virtually impossible to measure accomplishment of affective goals with any certainty. While feelings are important in the communication process, it is difficult to discover whether reports of feeling changes are accurate, and whether or not they are fleeting changes if, indeed, they are accurate. The recent testimonial from sensitivity groups, for example, indicates that while many people feel they have changed their emotions and evaluations immediately after the experience, a short time later, they not only do not feel that they have changed, but there is no behavioral evidence of the change. It is safer to make the assumption that if behavior has changed, there has also been an attendant change in feelings. Affective goals are provided for guidance, therefore, not as valid teaching objectives. One hopes that affect changes, but beyond that, there is little than can be done.

The student is the prime agent in measuring goal accomplishment. High scores on objective tests do not necessarily measure accomplishment of behavioral goals. There is no paper and pencil measurement yet validated that assesses whether or not a student has met his objectives. Thus, the communication teacher is confronted with the problem of careful performance contracting. The student must commit himself to the accomplishment of a goal even before he is amenable to real training. This is another reason why communication teachers need to be equipped with many options for activities and exercises. It is also why it is necessary to gear instruction to carryover. When the student finds meaning in application to his life experience, he is more likely to commit himself to goal accomplishment. The simple specification of a performance goal in a teacher's syllabus has little to do with whether or not the student will want to accomplish it. The teacher's rhetoric is improved when alternatives are available. He might be able to persuade the student that the objectives in the syllabus are worth achieving. He is more likely to be able to get the student to convince himself that a given objective is worth attaining.

Limits must be set on what can be reasonably expected in a given time period. It is not necessary to cover the whole list of objectives provided. Even when a year is devoted to the teaching of the subject, there will be only a few goals that can be reasonably accomplished. This is the reason that such heavy stress was laid on developmental information and on reality-based objectives. The teacher must select objectives that are possible for the student to attain, and those objectives must be related to actual experiences in the student's life, both in and out of school.

The foregoing has some serious implications for the style of instruction needed to accomplish communication goals. In the first place, communication is a method through which all other instruction is accomplished. However, the same methods used for the acquisition of cognitions about subject matter cannot be utilized in teaching communication. It is not necessarily important that a student know the names of communication elements and processes. What is important is that he be able to meet the communication demands that the rest of the curriculum puts on him.

The teacher of oral communication must avoid the lecture-recitation-drill syndrome and utilize laboratory experiences in his teaching of communication. Traditional methods of imparting skill at communication feature assigned performances followed by criticism. The act of criticism is threatening, so it needs to be handled with care. An opportunistic method seems much more productive; the teacher can use virtually any interaction in the classroom as substance for instruction in oral communication. Using learning groups, oral reports, role plays and creative dramatics, oral interpretation of literature, outside projects, independent study with individual time with the teacher are all productive of data that can be used for instruction in communication skills. This kind of approach helps the student learn communication in "real" settings, at least real enough so that something more is at stake than simple performance. The model syllabus that follows suggests several possibilities.

It appears that any oral-communication curriculum must provide considerable leeway so that goals can be generated by and for students. The compromise between class goals and individual goals can be made by the teacher based on his clinical understanding of the communication process as it relates to the needs of his students. The easy way out should be avoided. While it might appear more convenient to offer a general curriculum with the same skills prescribed for everyone, stress on carryover increases the likelihood of carryover.

A number of teaching approaches can be devised to facilitate the systematic development of oral communication skills and attitudes. One approach emerges *inductively* as communication problems and irregularities encountered during the regular school routine become the substance of discussion and practice for students. In this kind of format communication is treated as a consequence and element of life experience, and the students are more likely to get involved when they discover that something else (like their evaluations in social studies or science) is "riding" on it. They are not learning skill for its own sake but because it is useful to them.

Students can be encouraged to recognize the symptoms of communication breakdown in their exchanges with the teacher and others, and to anticipate difficulties that might arise in executing curricular assignments. Even the instructions the teacher gives accompanying an assigned project are legitimate meat for critique as a form of oral presentation. By permitting the students to inquire into his own skills the teacher accomplishes two goals. First, the students are given a live exercise in communication. Second, it is entirely possible that as a result of the discussion, the students will have a better idea of what it is that they must do to complete the assignment.

Teacher and students can compile communication logs or diaries which reflect their experiences at communication in and out of the classroom. Discussion of these documents can provide a kind of anonymous sharing of real problems that can be discussed by the class, functioning either as a whole or in small groups. The teacher can clip anonymous excerpts from various diaries and duplicate them as agendas for class discussion. Furthermore, the diaries or logs provide a source of data for the teacher about what his students are experiencing. Often he can get into a frank exchange in writing which might not have happened if the student had had to expose his experiences in front of the class.

Another, more formal approach requires that communication be approached *deductively*. Students are introduced to definitions and concepts pertaining to communication and are encouraged to use these in understanding their own behavior and the behavior of others. For example, students might be taught a theory of arrangement, then steps of preparation, from which they would have to extract advice for their own preparation of a given speech experience. Additional concepts pertaining to how we communicate, why we communicate, and when and where we communicate can be added. These can be built as curricular packages and used as a kind of ancillary subject matter supporting instruction in the formal academic realm.

A third approach emphasizes the *utilitarian* function of communication and requires the teacher to take time out to offer communication instruction prior to asking students to participate in some assignment that requires the use of communication. Before requiring a book report, for example, the teacher can give students formal training in book reporting. Before using task groups, the students can be offered instruction in group discussion. This is particularly suitable to teachers of other subjects who employ communication exercises in their instruction.

The utilitarian approach is largely helpful to teachers of subjects other than speech. The student is introduced to communication concepts as necessary to help him cope with problems and activities in the regular curriculum. For example, a social studies teacher may discover that some students need to learn how to prepare a report and others how to deliver it, before they can do an adequate job of reporting on social studies topics. Communication skills are dealt with as students display needs and as they undertake projects, exercises, and assignments. This approach demands that priorities be reordered and that teachers think in terms of teaching students rather than subjects. It means that the myth of the neat, orderly classroom must be dispelled, and opportunities provided for the student to select the way he wants to present material, and to request and receive necessary aid in acquiring sufficient skill to do it well. The approach also requires that the teacher serve as a guide to the student so that he will choose assignments that he can fulfill, for part of communication involves the expansion of self-image, inculcating the student with the idea that he is a capable learner and communicator.

Workshop training in some states instructs teachers to use communication approaches with their students regardless of subject matter. Because of the skills basis of communication training, it is relatively simple to show teachers of science how to utilize small groups in the production of projects, or social studies teachers how to employ debate to delineate political and social issues. Those teachers who have tried these activities note that their students respond well to various options given them to present material orally. Particularly in the case of students whose writing skills may be minimal, allowing an oral option provides a way for the teacher to determine whether a student's problem lies with the subject matter or with implementation of reporting.

Beginning teachers sometimes fail when they attempt oral methods for the first time. Students, recognizing the comparative freedom of the oral approach, often take advantage of it. Group projects are sometimes bizarre and overwhelming, reports are excessively long, debates too loud and boisterous. Careful restriction at the outset prevents this difficulty. In establishing oral options in the curriculum, care should be taken to *rule out* what is unacceptable, specify limitations on each option, and show students what their choices are and the consequences of their choices.

Chances to communicate orally are welcomed by students. Teachers are frequently surprised at the capacity for decision making that develops in their students when confronted by options. They have found that students come to understand subject material more efficiently, that they are able to apply it, and that they enjoy displaying their knowledge to teacher and classmates.

What is most important, however, is that no student should be assigned to *perform activities for which he has not been trained.* Hopefully, if there is an oral-communication course in the school, a reality based program will prepare students for the options provided in other classes. If there is no such program, then teachers must take care to give both training and an opportunity to practice with no risk before offering students the chance to participate in oral activities. This may mean time out from the regular curriculum, but the time devoted to training is well warranted by the quality of production that can result.

Following are two examples of how oral-communication training can be applied. The first is a plan for a ten-week course in oral performance, based on options and setting goals. It is applicable to secondary schools and early college. Following that is a five-session plan for introducing oral communication concepts and performance skills on the early elementary level. Both have been implemented with considerable success.

AN OUTLINE FOR A SYLLABUS IN RHETORICAL COMMUNICATION

(Based on 10 weeks of instruction, approximately 4½ hours per week)

OBJECTIVES

1. The student will demonstrate ability to phrase a rhetorical goal by specifying the precise behavior changes he wishes to see in the person to whom he speaks and in himself.

2. The student will be able to analyze self, audience, and situation by responding coherently to a set of heuristic questions provided for that purpose.

3. The student will demonstrate ability to structure interpersonal and public communication into one of seven basic formats: time, space, classification, comparison, contrast, relationship, problem solution.

4. The student will demonstrate ability to support contentions with supports: citations, statistics, examples, literary allusions, metaphors, visual aids, demonstrations, narrations, and expositions.

5. The student will demonstrate ability in social conversation by sustaining a thirty-minute conversation with three other people in which he speaks at least five minutes.

6. The student will demonstrate ability in group problem solving by participating in a group activity in a way that his colleagues deem productive.

7. The student will demonstrate ability to respond quickly and accurately to questions asked in a mock job interview.

8. The student will demonstrate ability at public speaking by presenting five minutes of connected oral discourse on an informative and persuasive topic.

PROCEDURES

1. The student will define an experience which he will have outside of class in each of four categories: 1. a social experience, 2. a formal group experience, 3. an interview experience, 4. a public presentation experience.

2. In conjunction with the teacher, the student will set accomplish-

able goals for each of those experiences. He will then define steps he must move through in order to prepare himself for the experiences.

3. The student will then prepare himself according to his own plan and will rehearse experiences in the speech classroom. Instructor and classmates will respond with suggestions directed at improving the potential for success in experiences outside of the classroom, if the student desires.

4. The student will perform outside the classroom as specified in the first step.

5. The student will report back to the speech class on the results of his experience.

(Note that the speech classroom functions as a rehearsal arena for a live experience. Students are to be encouraged to integrate what they learn in the speech class with performances and experiences required of them in other classes or in other phases of their life. Usually the student will have no difficulty specifying a social situation. A common one is "initiating conversation with strangers." Most classes require some sort of oral reporting. Many students are involved in committee work. There may only be a few who will face real interview situations. In the latter two cases, the teacher may help the students devise a project to be implemented for a grade in the speech classroom, and to subject the student to an interview in which teacher and student attempt to ascertain a "fair grade" for the course so far. The process works best when each of the experiences can be applied outside the classroom. To this end, students can be encouraged in their group experience to undertake some real project that might benefit the class or the school, like planning a resource file, gathering data on some controversial school issue, or planning an assembly.)

MATERIALS NEEDED

1. Textbook: Virtually any contemporary speech text that contains information on goal setting, forms of support, group experience, and interpersonal communication, as well as information on public speaking.

2. Materials Kit for Structured Communication. (Available from the Pennsylvania State University Department of Speech at minimal cost.)

3. Excerpts from Robert Mager, *Goal Analysis* (Fearon Publishing, 1972).

Procedure in the classroom. (Time allotted to each of these items will vary depending on the length of time devoted to the communication experience, and the amount of time allotted to individual classes. The topics below represent main heads that need to be covered.)

1. Introduction to goal setting.
2. Practice in goal setting.
3. Generating the four goals for outside experience.
4. Developing plans and procedures for goal accomplishment.
5. Introduction to structuring communication.
6. Practice in structuring communication.
7. Introduction to forms of support.
8. Practice in deploying forms of support.
9. Modes of analysis of situations: social, group, and public.
10. Exercises in analysis of self, topic, situation, and audience.
11. Orientation to social conversation. Use of structuring in preparing for and responding to social conversation.
12. Experiences in social conversation.
13. Introduction to group problem solving.
14. Exercises in group problem solving.
15. Introduction to interviewing.
16. Exercises in interviewing.
17. Introduction to public speaking.
18. Experience in public speaking.
*19. Time should be allotted for rehearsals of outside performances and for reports on outside performances.
*20. Time should be allotted for private conferences with students as needed. During private conferences, the teacher may function to assist students in utilizing their experiences in outside performances in preparation for subsequent performances.

*These are not formal class periods. Provision can be made during study hall and teacher conference hours.

Heuristics Applicable to All Situations

Heuristics should not be introduced formally as such, but serve as a model for teacher critique and evaluation. When presented as a list, they often look like a workbook. Teachers may suggest improvement based on the heuristics about where students have failed to meet the requirements of the system. This is done experimentally. Students will learn to emulate teacher behavior and will learn to use heuristics on their own terms.

Heuristics about Situations

1. What is the nature of the situation: social, group, interview, public? Who will be present? How many? Why are they there? Why are you there?

2. What is the physical nature of the situation? What does the room look like? Where will you be? How will you be related physically to others in the room?

3. Who are you in relation to this situation? Are you a featured speaker? One of the many people engaged in conversation? A formal member of the group? An interviewer or interviewee? What are the other people required to do by the nature of the situation? What are you required to do by the nature of the situation?

4. How will others see you? Are you one of them? Are you an outsider? A friend or an enemy? What experience have you had with them? How do they normally behave toward each other? Toward you? What are their expectations of your behavior? What can you expect from them?

Heuristics about Goals

1. What do I want to accomplish? (This should be phrased in behavior terms: "I want to hold a conversation with Tom for ten minutes; I want to present my plan to the group and answer questions about it; I want to ask three questions in class today.")

2. "How will I know I did it? What must others see me do in order for them to agree that I did it?"

3. "What do I expect my listeners to do?" (Again, list specific behaviors so someone else can confirm them: "The students must sit quietly while I talk; Tom must agree to go to the movies with me; the group should ask me at least three questions following my presentation," etc.)

4. "Are there some people in the situation that are more important than others whose needs must be taken into account?" (In giving a report in science class, for example, who is the student trying to please, the teacher for a grade or his classmates or both?)

5. "What are the conditions that will specifically influence the

selection of things to say? What do I know about the needs, behaviors, of the others? What do I know about the norms of the situation?"

Heuristics about Finding Something to Say

1. "In social conversation, what do I have to offer? What topics am I knowledgeable about? What questions can I ask? Where can I get more information to introduce?"

2. "What are the possible ways I can say it? What order should the ideas be in?"

3. "In a topic-directed situation, what do I know about the topic? What do I need to know? Where can I get the information?"

4. "How do people commonly talk about the topics under consideration? How do they expect me to talk? What would I have to say to get their attention? What would I have to say to hold their attention? Are there any original twists I can give to my subject?"

Heuristics about Putting Ideas in Order

1. "What is the main structure I will use? What are the possible structures I can apply (in social conversation)?"

2. "What substructures will best accommodate the subunits of discourse?"

3. "What supports do I need? Where should they fit?"

4. "What do I need to do to meet the needs of my audience (one or many)?"

5. "Are there holes or weak points? Where can I get more information?"

Heuristics about Performance

1. "Do I need some notes, some main heads in my mind? What form should they be in?"

2. "With whom should I rehearse? What should I tell them to do during the rehearsal?"

3. "What kind of criticism do I want following the rehearsal? How can my rehearsal mates best help me?"

4. "What modifications must I make as a result of rehearsal?"

5. "How do I get myself ready just before the experience?"

Heuristics about Examining the Results

1. "Did I meet my goals? Did I do what I set out to do? How close did I come? Where did I miss? Where did I accomplish more than I had planned?"

2. "What did I see my audience do? What did I interpret it to mean? How did these behaviors compare to what I expected?"

3. "What do I need to do next time as a result of this experience?"

This skeleton plan should equip junior and senior high school teachers of oral communication to develop a curriculum and lesson plans to implement instruction. Specific headings can be selected from the taxonomy. Modifications can be made as necessary. There is no reason to believe that this format will not work in late elementary or early college. The specialized materials can be replaced with any good book on outlining and organization.

The problems of teaching communication to the early elementary child are somewhat more complicated since the social maturity of the child may interfere with conceptualization necessary to accomplish formal communication goals as specified in this plan. We offer a five-session plan for introduction of communication concepts into an early elementary classroom. The goals for elementary instruction are less performance oriented than in the previous syllabus. The teacher's main goal is to help the students understand what is going on when they communicate. Implementation of instruction in the elementary grades is materially helpful to expansion of instruction in oral communication within the following grades.

SELF AS COMMUNICATOR (TEACHING PLAN)

(A five-session teaching plan)

SESSION 1—Verbal and Nonverbal Approaches to Understanding Self.

For the teacher: Notions concerning the learning climate in which concepts and skills are to be developed:

Education has done very well in these gathering and imparting functions. It has done far less well in helping its students discover the personal meaning of such information for their own lives and behavior.

(Combs and Snygg, INDIVIDUAL BEHAVIOR)

Talking is not teaching, listening is not learning. The teaching-learning experience is an organic whole characterized by communication.

(Cantor, THE TEACHING LEARNING PROCESS)

The organism reacts to the field as it is experienced and perceived. This perceptual field is, for the individual, "reality."

(Rogers, CLIENT-CENTERED THERAPY)

For effective teaching, the point of departure is where the pupil is; not where the teacher thinks he is.

(Cantor, THE TEACHING LEARNING PROCESS)

The essential problem, then, is to alter the traditional approach to learning from a negative to a positive one, to help students to learn how to learn, rather than support their pattern of learning how to avoid exposing themselves for fear of being hurt and disapproved.

(Cantor, THE DYNAMICS OF LEARNING)

Goals

1. The student will be able to distinguish verbal and nonverbal communication.

2. The student will express his feelings verbally and nonverbally to another student.

3. The student will recognize a symbol.

4. The student will identify influences of his symbols on the behavior of another person.

Concepts to Be Developed

1. Communication is a process that allows satisfaction of emotional needs.

2. Communication is a process of sending and receiving messages.

3. Communication is structured by our beliefs, expectations, and feelings about ourselves and those with whom we communicate.

Activities

1. Interpersonal-contact experiences to provide insight into feelings about self and others (children organized into small groups, about five).
   a. Construction of badges (nonverbal to show how we feel about ourselves in a group).
   b. Showing and explaining the badge to someone we'd like to know better.
   c. Showing badges to the group and talking about how individuals are similar and different from each other.
   d. Feedback for whole class, teacher-led discussion of the following topics:

What did we discover about ourselves? About others?

How did the shapes, colors, and so on, help us show how we felt?

How did the badges assist others in understanding how we felt?

What happens inside us as we talk about ourselves?

2. Introduction to the communication process.

   a. Making a message; each student to define communication, message, language, interference, response, in his own terms.

   b. Each student to draw a picture of communication: as he likes it; as he dislikes it.

   c. Students practice sending and receiving messages in small groups: games such as Hangman, Password, Pantomine and Whisper a Story.

   d. Response demonstration: students in pairs (one blindfolded) attempt to guess objects, shapes, and so forth as described by sighted partner.

   e. Students in dyads to pantomime ideas, or events from story read by teacher; pantomime to be guessed by rest of class.

   g. Whole class to play "Can you guess what I'm holding?" Teacher and students to use scarves to suggest feelings, animals, etc.

Critique of Session: One or a combination of the following may be used to generate student reactions to the session. Reactions may be used privately by the teacher in planning future sessions or they may be discussed with students individually, in small groups, or as a class.

Approach 1: Draw a picture showing what you liked best in today's session. Tell me (write) about how you felt.

Approach 2: Using a tape recorder (which even very young children can learn to operate quickly), tell me what we learned, what you liked, what you're confused about. . . .

Approach 3: Suggestion box, or suggestion bag. Indicate on 3 × 5 cards what you liked best and what you liked least; suggest one way to improve the next session.

Approach 4: Have students fill in questionnaire anonymously.

   1. What you liked best in today's session.

   2. What you learned about yourself.

   3. What you didn't like.

   4. What you learned about others in the class.

   5. What you would like to do in communication next time.

   6. One thing you're really afraid of when you communicate.

7. What you'll tell your friends about today's session.
8. What you'll tell your parents about today's session.

SESSION 2—Words: Their effect on how I feel, how I think, and what I do.

For the teacher: Notions concerning the climate in which concepts and skills are to be developed:

But as a teacher also, I have found that I am enriched when I can open channels through which others can share themselves with me.

(Rogers, ON BECOMING A PERSON)

I have emphasized the value of understanding, discipline, and hard work in the more creative process. High and sustained achievement demands even more—the concentration of a life. And even this is not all. In the absence of fresh insight, devotion is powerless and the best technique is meaningless.

(Gishlin, THE CREATIVE PROCESS)

Goals

1. To provide experiences in which the student can inspect his language behavior.
2. To enable the student to go beyond language in sensing, thinking, feeling, and behaving.
3. To encourage the student to recognize helpful and potentially limiting functions of language.

Concepts to Be Developed

1. Words are important and useful as tools for thinking and communicating.
2. Words enable us to stabilize experience.
3. Words help us act appropriately when we're uncertain about what to do.
4. Words sometimes dominate our thoughts and make us see what is not really in experience.
5. Words enable us to attack, defend, and support others.
6. Words create an illusion of permanence, and consequently encourage us to depend on them.
7. It takes courage to use words and not be used by them.

Activities

1. Creating verbal and nonverbal messages:
   a. Student dyads construct representations of various sensory and conceptual images (sounds, touches, tastes), emphasis is placed on role language plays in distorting as well as clarifying experience.
   b. Students create verbal and nonverbal responses (movement, drawing, writing) to imagery presented through music, dance, slides, film.
2. Using language to create appropriate responses:
   a. Individually or in dyads, students to role play various uses of language (to help, hurt, inform, comfort, etc.)
   b. Students to participate in the game, "What am I touching?" Bag full of objects is passed around circle; each student reaches in and, without looking, must describe what he felt; next student to feel around in a second bag filled with similar objects until he picks one he thinks is being described. Objects should be familiar and unfamiliar, easily labeled as well as nondefinable.
   c. "Messages about me and the way I feel about myself": Using current magazines, students individually or in pairs make collages pertaining to the theme, "How we see ourselves." Students should be encouraged to use verbal and nonverbal symbols.

Critique of Session: See Session 1.

SESSION 3: Listening as Communication

For the Teacher: Notions underlying climate:

I have come to feel that the only learning which significantly influences behavior is self-discovered, self-appropriated learning.

(Rogers, ON BECOMING A PERSON)

Both researchers and pedagogues have much to learn from psychotherapists. For one thing, therapists must know how to listen. For another, they deal with the knottiest problems of creativity or lack of it. And they specialize in that self-awareness which is a prerequisite to control in the process of learning how to learn and in learning how to teach.

(Elton Carter, PERSONAL COMMUNICATION)

Goals

1. To introduce the student to the various phases of the listening process.
2. To provide opportunities for examination of listening behavior.

Concepts

1. Listening is a complex process involving sensing, perceiving, conceptualizing, and interpreting.
2. Listening involves a restructuring of the messages.
3. Listening is selective.
4. Listening is frequently limited and distorted.
5. Listening helps us discover who we are.

Activities

1. Students individually or in pairs to create models (pictures, sculptures, three-dimension schematics) to illustrate various phases of listening.
   a. Students to discuss how language controls listening.
   b. Students to discuss how feelings about self and others distort listening.
2. Students sitting back to back to carry on a conversation, then face-to-face to discuss the importance of feedback.
3. Students to listen to randomly selected bits of conversation (tape recorded) and to identify situation, to suggest who's communicating, why, and to tell how they were able to guess.
4. Students divided into four groups to listen to music and describe (pictures and sentences) what the music is about. Each group is told something different about the music prior to listening (unknown to other groups), all groups listen and respond together. Teacher to encourage students to discover why each group heard the music differently.
5. Various locations in and around the school are listed on slips of paper and put into a paper bag. Students draw one slip and have to describe how to get to the place (without revealing where it is). Rest of class to guess where it is, and to recognize how identification was possible.

Critique of Session: see Session 1.

SESSION 4: Working with Others in Groups

For the teacher: Notions concerning climate:

> We learn also about our own strengths and limits and extend them by overcoming difficulties, by straining ourselves to the utmost, by meeting challenge and hardship, even by failing.
>
> (Maslow, TOWARD A PSYCHOLOGY OF BEING)

There are two aims which the teacher should have in view when addressing his students . . . first, to help the student to solve the problem at hand. Second, to develop the student's ability so that he may solve future problems by himself.

(Polya, HOW TO SOLVE IT)

By and large, the things taught children are useless and quite alien to their personal reality. It is a tragedy that our society puts so much value on data rather than insight, behavior rather than personal integrity. So much youthful beauty gone to waste.

(Fromm, LOOK MAGAZINE, May, 1964)

Goals

1. To encourage students to identify sources of inter- and intra-group conflict.
2. To encourage students to experiment with ways of resolving conflict.
3. To encourage students to discriminate between the various functions and purposes served by groups.
4. To encourage students to become aware of task and interpersonal roles.
5. To encourage an awareness of problem-centeredness and problem-solving approaches appropriate for task-oriented groups.

Concepts

1. Groups help in getting jobs done.
2. Groups provide an opportunity for self-development.
3. Groups present a variety of opportunities for becoming involved.
4. Roles, rules, and interpersonal relationships underlie behavior in groups.
5. Communication within the group serves task as well as interpersonal functions.

Activities

1. Students to discuss the various groups to which they belong, how they are similar, how they differ.
2. Students to decide why their behavior changes from group to group.
3. Groups to be assigned to complete "quickie group projects": projects involving no more than fifteen minutes, to reflect on their

behavior and on why the group either succeeded or failed to accomplish the task.

4. Dramatization of roles:
   a. Students to be encouraged to recognize roles and rules operating in contexts familiar to them (home, playground, club, ball team, etc.); to be assigned various situations and required to role-play situations.
   b. Students in groups to be assigned roles which provide attack, support, protection, assistance for individuals in the group situation (friend in trouble, someone has fallen, John is lost, etc.).

5. Group problem solving:
   a. Projects out of a Junk Box: students divided into groups, each group presented with a shopping bag or box full of craft materials. Each group required to plan or build something that tells the rest of the class about a communication idea.
   b. Groups assigned responsibility of planning and leading class through some activities the next day.
   c. Groups to discuss "problems in our school," to decide on one problem, and to organize the class in solving the problem. (Teacher to act as resource.)

Critique of Session: See Session 1.

SESSION 5: Understanding Behavior in Groups

For the Teacher: Notions concerning climate:

Learning must be translated by the student. He must determine what data means to him.

Learning is personal and must result from self-motivation and eventuate in self-discipline.

(Cantor, *The Teaching Learning Process*)

Goals

1. To encourage understanding in greater depth of the origin and function of roles students take in groups.
2. To provide for the opportunity for development of alternative roles.

Concepts

1. Behavior in groups is related to the situation and task in which the group is involved.

2. Opportunities exist for taking constructive as well as destructive group roles.

3. Awareness of role possibilities makes it easier to change behavior in groups.

4. Roles are frequently organized into games or strategies for limiting the behavior of others in the group.

Activities

1. Students to discuss conflict situations familiar to them and to label the games played by individuals involved:
   a. What teachers do when they're mad.
   b. How students get out of trouble.
2. Students to role-play situations in which games operate: Playground, homework, principal's office, etc.
3. Students to switch roles with others as they play conflict situations, to discuss alternatives for dealing with conflict.
4. Students to complete and discuss the following questionnaire and to understand why they responded as they did.

"What I Usually Do and Say"

1. "When my friends ignore me"
2. "When someone older than I picks on me"
3. "When I get yelled at for no reason"
4. "When I'm confused"
5. "When I'm punished at school"
6. "When I'm punished at home"
7. "When I see someone who needs help"

Situations can be role-played once discussed.

Critique of Session: See Session 1.

SUMMARY

We have introduced you to communication, but we have only scratched the surface. The readings at the end of each chapter might be helpful to you, and some of them are enjoyable reading on their own. What is important now is that you try. You are as much an expert as any other teacher. Try to understand communication; try to apply it in your classroom; integrate it with your other subject matter. Be a scientist doing your own experiments with communication exercises and games. Be a rhetor by helping your students do a better job of learning by making it possible for them to show what they have learned and what they can do.

And share what you find out with others. Communication is for everyone. Communicate with your fellow teachers, teachers in other schools; find out what they do and how they inspire and involve their students. Forget, for a while anyway, about professors who tell you about learning theory and maturation. Think about yourself and what you have to do in the classroom, and involve yourself in the practice of rhetoric. Communicate with your students and encourage them to communicate with you. Show them that learning is important, exciting.

Communicate!

WORKS RECOMMENDED:

For purposes of comparison and contrast with more traditional approaches to teaching speech and communication see Allen and S. Clay, Willmington, *Speech Communication to the Secondary School.* Boston: Allyn & Bacon, 1972. Also, Alan Huckleberry and Edward Strother, *Speech Education for the Elementary Teacher.* Boston: Allyn & Bacon, 1966.

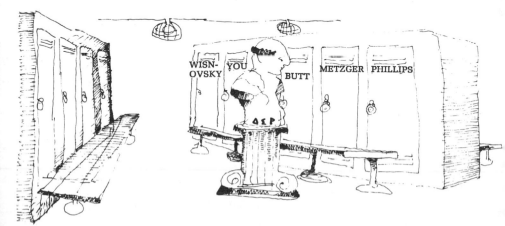

Win one for Aristotle!!!

Index

Index

A

Abstract communication perspective, 64 ff.
Abstract dual perspective, 51 ff.
Actor, 200
Affection, exchange of, 130
Affective goals, in communication, 200 ff.
Aggression, 135
  through controlling social rule, 149
  symbolically, 119
Alternative-filled classroom, 105
Anxiety, 171
Appeal system, 76
Ardrey, Robert, 72, 127, 134
Aristotle, 5, 6
Articulation problems, 179
Ashton-Warner, Sylvia, 20
Audience, 7
Audience analysis, 198
Authentic self, 164

B

Basic language patterns, 40
Becker, Ernest, 4, 65, 145
Behavior alternatives, 34
Behavioral goals in communication, 222 ff.
Behavioristic approach to communication, 14
Berelson and Steiner, 5
Berko, Roy, 26
Bilingual children, 178
Biological models, 37
Bitzer, Lloyd, 140
"Black boxes," 13
Black children, 74
Blanda, George, 126
Bloom's Taxonomy, 212
Boredom, communication skills as defense against, 129

C

Capacity to relate, 104
Casual conversation, 195
Characteristic communication patterns, 167
Charming, Prince, 126
Chicago Riots of 1968, 125
Child, as communicator, 29
Church, Joseph, 65
Cicero, 5, 6
Cognitive-developmental theory, 39
Cognitive development, deficiencies in, 93
Cognitive goals in communication, 213 ff.
Cognitive maturity, 147
Communication, behavior evaluating, 33
  breakdown in, 228
  change in, 31
  definition of, 12
  effects of failure in, 174 ff.
  holistic study of, 15
  model of, 89 ff.
  needs, 5
  opportunity restricted, 107
  process and relationship, 12, passim.
  rhetorical view of, 141
  studies of performance in, 69
  studies of process in, 14
  style of, 42
  teaching in, 8
  utilitarian function of, 229
Communication skills, developed indirectly, 32
  mastery of, 47
  teaching of, 34
Communicative development, naive perspective on, 29
  scientific perspective on, 30
  pedagogical perspective on, 30
Compliant behavior, 102

Computer analogy, 16
Conversational ability, development
    of, 78 ff.
Conceptual development, stages of,
    40
Creativity, 17, 94
Criticism, 7, 205
Cybernetic analogies, 11

D

Daydreams, 96, 132
Decision making, 48
Dictionary, 13
Differential performance, 81
Dombrowski, Mike, 83
Dunham, Robert, 26
Dyadic relationship, 201

E

"Educational revolutions," 27
Emotional illness, 169
Empirical investigation, 4
Encounter, 159
Erikson, Erik, 65, 68
Ethologist, 118
Ethological goals, 122

F

Fantasy, 45, 71, 78
    as weapon, 79
Flavell, John, 70, 71
Fluency problems, 179
Four-letter word, 191
Friendship, 156

G

Games, 72
    defined, 127
    development of, 126
    socialization in, 158

Geocultural units, 121
Goal achievement, 227
Goal accomplishment, measuring,
    227
Goal seeking, 143, 145
Goal setting, 171
Goals, compatibility of, 196
Goodman, Paul, 148
Greece, academies of, 4
Group, 42
Group activities, 212
Group discussion, 5
Group goals, 44
Group process, 43
Group structure, 42

H

Hard sciences, techniques used by, 27
Healthy transaction, 173
Herndon, James, 20
Heros, 148
Heuristics, application to all
        situations, 233 ff.
    about examining results, 236
    about finding something to say, 235
    about goals, 234
    about performance, 235
    about putting ideas in order, 235
    about situation, 234
Homeostatic skills, 130
Horizontal behavior, 152
Human communication, theory
        building in, 21
Human interaction, 157
Human relations, idealism about, 147
Human speech, 13
Humpty Dumpty, 77
Hutchins, Robert M., 8
Hymes, Dell, 60

I

IFD Syndrome, 170
Identity, 105, 118, 135, 165

Identity building device, 164
Indoctrination, 105
Initial encounter, 154
Inner-city education, hazards of, 95
Inner-city schools, 125
Inner-city students, 33
Intellectual development of the child, 19
Interactive combat, 150
Interactions, data about, 199
   rules of, 197
Interpersonal accommodation 203, 205
Interpersonal communication, 172
Interpersonal interaction, 204
Interpersonal process, 188
Interpersonal relations, goals of, 152
Interpersonal rhetoric, 152
Inter-racial communication, 193
Isocrates, 4

J

Jencks, Christopher, 15
Johnson, Wendell, 170

K

Katz and Sanford Studies, 122
Khulyages, 12
Kohl, Herbert, 20
Korzybski, Alfred, 119

L

Language acquisition device, 38
Language code, restricted, 48
Language, conceptual use of, 84
   critical period of development 37
   readiness, 40
   propositions about development, 60 ff.
   stages of cevelopment, 61 ff.
Language skills, interrelationship of, 80

Laws, 120
Learning behavior, 102 ff.
Learning, process of in communication terms, 103
Lecture-recitation-drill syndrome, 227 ff.
Lee, Irving, 191
Linguistic identity, 47
Linguistic performance, 37
Linguistic theory, 36 ff.

M

Mager, Robert, 182
May, Rollo, 104, 126
Mead, George Herbert, 105
Measurement, criteria of, 225
Mental illness, 17
Mental images, 97
Message flexibility, 58
Message strategy, 67 ff.
Mitty, Walter, 126
Montessori approach, 37

N

Naive perspective, 20
New Orleans Conference of the Speech Association of America, 60
Nonverbal communication, 199 ff.
Nonverbal visual presentation, 78
Norms, 43

O

Oral communication, teaching of, 139
Oral communication skills,
   development of, 228
   goals for instruction in, 28
   improvement of, 4
   instruction in, 9
   systematic instruction in, 28
Oral interpretation, 5
Oral-language skills, 80

P

Pedagogical perspective, 20
Pedagogy, rhetorical view of, 34
"People game," 75
Performance, criticism of, 108
Personal goal seeking through
     communication, 26
Persuader, questions about teacher as,
     101 ff.
Perception apparatus, 153
Performance contracting, 227
Phonetic skill, 59
Physiology, role of in
     communication, 14
Piaget, Jean, 19
Plato, 5
Pleasure Principle, 140, 145
Power, 152
Pragmatics of communication, 60
Private images, 85
Public performance, 212
     training in, 197
Public speaking, 5, 6
     instruction in, 8
Pure researcher, 28

Q

Quintilian, 5

R

Reinforcement, 160
Relationship, goals in, 151
Research activity, 18 ff.
     influence of myth in, 19
     rhetorical approach to, 21
     tools of, 4
Response, sensitivity to, 59
Resources, symbolic, conceptual, and
     linguistic, 59
Reticent speaker, 175 ff.
Rhetoric, 15, 18, 27, 52, 69, 82, 101,
     106, 107, 110, 119, 126, 141, 171

Aristotle's definition of, 5
exchange of, 121
norms for, 143
as resolution of uncertainty, 123
responses to, 148
of schooling, 108
as tool of competition, 124 ff.
Rhetorical analysis, 195
Rhetorical approach to the classroom,
     18
Rhetorical capability, development
     of, 42 ff.
Rhetorical communication, kinds of,
     110
Rhetorical competition, 112
Rhetorical control, 73
Rhetorical development of the child,
     60
Rhetorical impact, 108
Rhetorical model, 172
Rhetorical perspective, 32, 51
Rhetorical process, basics of, 192
Rhetorical purpose, 111
Rhetorical readiness, 73
Rhetorical relationship, 142
Rhetorical situation, 140 ff.
Rhetorical skills, development of, 130
Rhetorical view of teaching, 16
Role, 42, 44, 46, 69
     choice of, 48
     performance of, 45, 46
     repertoire of, 45
     system of, 46
     taking of, 58, 71
Routine dialogues, 156

S

Saving face, 193 ff.
Scatological language, 191
Scher, Jordan, 72, 104
School, as microcosm of society, 121
     as survival agent, 121
Scientific perspective, 20
Security, maintaining of, 129
Self-esteem, 49, 189
     reduction of, 193

Self-image, 157, 168, 195
Sense of time, 119
  of mortality, 119
Sensitivity training, 173, 175
Shannon-Weaver Model, 10, 11
Silberman, Charles, 20
Situational awareness, 58
Skinner, B. F. 104
Small-group format, 196
Small-group sociology, 133
Social control, 51
Socializing agents, 49
Social marginality, 178
Sociocultural model, 44
Social myths, 123
Social role, barrier of, 156
Social system, 42
Sondel, Bess, 192
Speech communication, as cognitive
  subject, 5
Speech education, rhetorical view of,
  17, 27
Speech readiness, 36
Symbolic activity, daydream as, 126
Symbolic interaction, 49
Systematic desensitization, 182
Stage fright, 176, 181
Szasz, Thomas, 169

T

Taxonomy, 211 ff.
Teacher as communicator, 188
  goals of, 194 ff.

Teaching-learning process, 99 ff.
Territoriality, 135, 193
Territorial position, in classroom, 134
Territory, communication for, 132 ff.
Therapeutic relationship, 154
Theory, value of, 34
Time-binding, 119
Tinbergen, Niko, 134
Toffler, Alvin, 195

V

Values, 108
  as expressed in symbolic behavior,
  109
Van Riper, Charles, 177
Verbal behavior, of young children,
  70
Verbal strategies, 203 ff.
Vertical behavior, 152
Voice problems, 179

W

Walwick, Paul, 26, 28
White-black interactions, 190
Winning and losing, symbols of, 148

Z

Zero-sum game, 146